GSA

CONSUMER ACTION HANDBOOK

USA.gov

CONTRIBUTORS

 GSA

Office of Citizen Services and Innovative Technologies/18F

January 2015

I'm excited to have the opportunity to welcome you to a new edition of USA.gov's *Consumer Action Handbook*, your guide to being an informed consumer.

Over the last year, you emailed and tweeted your consumer questions and concerns to me. I've read and responded to hundreds of your questions about credit cards, refinancing, defective cars, and more. I truly appreciated you sharing your issues; you helped me know what American consumers are really facing. In fact, we actually addressed some of the most popular questions in this edition of the *Handbook*.

The *Consumer Action Handbook* strikes a balance between providing answers to common consumer questions, as well as giving you a first peek into the latest scams and trends that can affect your wallet. For instance, in this edition you can find out what factors affect your credit score as well as learn about synthetic identity theft and farcing frauds. As always, I want to empower you with practical tools to help you resolve your consumer disputes. This *Handbook* includes it's crown jewel, the sample complaint letter and the consumer assistance directory, both of which can help make it easier to protect your consumer rights.

This resource isn't the only reliable source for consumer information. Visit USA.gov and GobiernoUSA.gov (in Spanish) to get answers to other questions. If you'd prefer to speak to someone, call 1-844-USA-GOV1. You can also visit Publications.USA.gov to download or order other government publications on topics that matter to you, like money management, healthcare, travel, and more.

I hope that this *Handbook* provides you with information that is both informative and practical for your daily life. If you have questions or ideas for additional topics, please share them. Email me at askmarietta@gsa.gov or tweet using #AskMarietta.

Sincerely,

Marietta Jelks

Marietta Jelks
Editor-in-Chief, Consumer Action Handbook

The Federal Citizen Information Center would like to express its gratitude to the partners listed below who helped make possible the publication of the *Consumer Action Handbook*.

American Financial Services Association Education Foundation

The Colgate-Palmolive Company

Department of Veterans Affairs

Direct Selling Education Foundation

Federal Deposit Insurance Corporation

Federal Trade Commission

Financial Industry Regulatory Authority

Kellogg Company

LeadingAge

National Futures Association

The Procter & Gamble Company

Securities and Exchange Commission

Society of Consumer Affairs Professionals International

Unilever

WASHINGTON

January 2015

Welcome to the Consumer Action Handbook.

Every day, Americans navigate tough choices about the products and services that affect us over the course of our lives. That is why everyone needs access to clear information about financial decisions and a marketplace with a basic sense of fairness.

The Consumer Action Handbook is a vital resource for American consumers. By clarifying rights and protections, the Handbook helps prevent consumers from being taken advantage of. With topics ranging from buying a home to shopping online, the Handbook offers advice to guard against deceptive practices and weigh potential risks and benefits in the open market.

I encourage all Americans to use this valuable resource, as well as other helpful information and tools available on www.USA.gov.

GSA

GSA Administrator

January 2015

Welcome to the Consumer Action Handbook.

This publication, updated regularly by the U.S. General Services Administration's (GSA) Office of Citizen Services and Innovative Technologies, gives the American public the information and resources they need to be informed consumers. Every day, GSA helps agencies throughout the federal government maximize their buying power with limited budgets—a challenge many Americans can relate to as well. The Consumer Action Handbook will help you get the most out of your budget.

This Handbook provides consumers with the options they need to make informed decisions. With explanations of rules that are in place to protect American consumers as well as alerts to potential frauds and scams, the Handbook provides a practical, easy to use guide to the ever-changing consumer landscape. This publication is also available on USA.gov, along with other useful financial information. I encourage everyone to take full advantage of all the valuable information this Handbook offers, and to share it with friends and family.

Sincerely,

Dan Tangherlini
Administrator

USING THIS HANDBOOK

This everyday guide to being a smart shopper is full of helpful tips about preventing identity theft, understanding credit, filing a consumer complaint, and more. The information and resources you will need are arranged as follows:

PART I—BE A SAVVY CONSUMER

Read this section for advice before you make a purchase. Look in the Table of Contents (p. 1) and Index (p. 134) to quickly locate specific topics and information.

PART II—FILE A COMPLAINT

Turn to this section for suggestions on resolving consumer problems. The sample complaint letter on page 54 will help you present your case.

PART III—KEY INFORMATION RESOURCES

Look here for a list of public resources for teachers, disabled consumers, and military families.

PART IV—CONSUMER ASSISTANCE DIRECTORY

Find contact information for corporate offices, consumer organizations, trade groups, government agencies, and more.

VISIT US ONLINE

Visit www.USA.gov and in Spanish at www.GobiernoUSA. gov for more consumer information, resources, and tools. You can also order or download an electronic version of the *Handbook* and hundreds of other consumer publications at Publications.USA.gov.

QUICK CONSUMER TIPS

As a savvy consumer, you should always be on the alert for shady deals and scams. Keep these things in mind to avoid becoming a victim:

- Be wary of promises to fix your credit problems, low-interest credit card offers, deals that let you skip credit card payments, work-at-home job opportunities, risk-free investments, and free travel. A deal that sounds too good to be true usually is!

- Don't share personal information with someone you don't trust. Learn how to recognize fraud.

- Beware of payday and tax refund loans. Interest rates on these loans are usually excessive. A cash advance on a credit card may be a better option.

- Read and understand any contract, legal document, or terms of service before you sign or click "I Agree". Do not sign a contract with blank spaces or where the terms are incomplete. Some contracts include a clause that prohibits you from taking legal action and requires you to engage in mandatory arbitration with a company in the case of a dispute.

- Get estimates from several contractors for home or car repairs. Make sure the estimates are for the exact same repairs for a fair comparison.

- Before you buy, make sure you understand and accept the store's refund, return and early termination or cancellation policies, especially for services and facilities that charge monthly fees.

- Double-check the final price when you pay for your purchases. Speak up if you think the price that has been charged is incorrect. Remember, when shopping online, your purchase may include additional fees, such as shipping, handling, and convenience fees that are not calculated until you check out.

- When shopping online, look for the padlock icon in the bottom right-hand corner of your screen or a URL that begins with "https" to ensure that your payment information is transmitted securely.

- Don't buy under stress. Avoid making big-ticket purchases during times of duress (e.g., coping with a death or debt).

- Notify your lender immediately if you are having difficulty making payments on loans, so that you can work out a payment plan.

To contact an organization, use the directory beginning on page 60.

TABLE OF CONTENTS

BUYER BEWARE

BEFORE YOU BUY

Use this checklist BEFORE you make a purchase to avoid problems and make better decisions:

- Decide in advance exactly what you want and what you can afford.
- Do your research. Ask family, friends, and others you trust for advice based on their experience. Gather information about the seller and the item or service you are purchasing.
- Review product test results from consumer experts and comments from past customers. See Key Information Resources (p. 56).
- Get price quotes from several sellers.
- Make sure the seller has all appropriate licenses. Doctors, lawyers, contractors, and other service providers must register with a state or local licensing agency.
- Check out a company's complaint record with your local consumer affairs office (p. 102) and Better Business Bureau (p. 63).
- Get a written copy of guarantees and warranties.
- Get the seller's refund, return, and cancellation policies.
- Ask whom to contact if you have a question or problem.
- Read and understand any contract or legal document you are asked to sign or give agreement to online (by clicking "I Agree"). Make sure there are no blank spaces or incomplete terms. Insist that any extras you are promised be put in writing.
- Consider paying by credit card. If you have a problem, you can dispute a charge made on your credit card (p. 14).
- Don't buy on impulse or under pressure; this includes donating to charity.
- Check your browser settings when shopping online if you don't want your shopping history shared with data brokers.

WARRANTIES

A warranty is the promise that a manufacturer or seller makes to stand behind a product's quality. Federal law requires that warranties be available for you to read before you buy, even when you are shopping by catalog or on the

QUICK TIPS FOR AVOIDING FRAUD

There are many varieties of consumer fraud, but the most common ones are variations of fake check scams, credit repair, free trip offers, and sweepstakes. Here are some tips to help you avoid being a victim:

- **Don't give out personal information.** Be suspicious of anyone you don't know who asks for your Social Security number, birthdate, credit card number, bank account number, password, or other personal data.
- **Don't be intimidated.** Be suspicious of calls or emails that want you to provide or verify personal information immediately. Answer that you are not interested and hang up or don't reply to the email.
- **Monitor your accounts.** Review bank and credit card statements carefully, and report unauthorized transactions to your financial institution immediately.
- **Use a shredder.** Tear or shred credit offers, bank statements, insurance forms, and other papers with personal information.
- **Ignore unsolicited offers.** Don't respond if someone you do not know asks you to send money or money orders to claim a prize, lottery, credit card, loan or other valuable offer.

To learn more about avoiding identity theft and fraud, go to page 37.

Internet, so that you can comparison shop. A standard warranty is part of the item you purchased, and there is no additional cost for this protection from the company. There are three main types of warranties:

- Written warranties are printed and come along with the item you purchased. In order for a written warranty to take effect, or to make a claim against it, the seller or manufacturer may require you to perform specific maintenance or that you use the item as instructed.
- Spoken warranties are verbally communicated to you by a salesperson, or other staff at a retailer or service provider, for services like free repairs. If you receive this kind of warranty, have the person who gave it, and their manager, put it in writing. Otherwise, you may not be able to get the service that was promised to you.
- Implied warranties promise that the item you purchased will do what it is supposed to do and that it can work under the circumstances that it was designed for. These warranties are created by state laws, and are not specifically stated or written.

If you purchase an item and it doesn't have a written warranty, it is still covered under the implicit warranty laws in your state, unless it was marked "as is" when you purchased it.

CHECK HERE FOR RECALLS

Before you buy a product, especially a used or second-hand item, check that it has not been recalled for safety or health reasons. Some recalls ban the sale of an item, while others ask consumers to return the item for replacement or repair.

- www.recalls.gov lists government-initiated recalls from federal agencies.
- www.nhtsa.gov publishes safety information on vehicles and equipment such as children's car seats.
- www.fsis.usda.gov lists recalls that involve meat, poultry, or processed egg products.
- www.fda.gov lists recalls that involve food, medicines, medical devices, cosmetics, biologics, radiation emitting products, veterinary drugs, and pet food.

Service Contracts and Extended Warranties

Service contracts or "extended warranties" extend the guarantee or promise that a product will work, and are purchased for an additional cost. Sellers offer these service contracts at the time of purchase, and sometimes months or years after your purchase. They are commonly offered when you buy a car, major electronics, or household appliances. Third party firms (not the manufacturer or the seller) may also try to sell you a extended warranty; some even make cold calls to you with high pressure sales tactics. Some extended warranties duplicate the warranty coverage that you get automatically from a manufacturer or seller. These add-ons may not be worth the cost. Ask these questions before you agree to one of these contracts:

- Does the dealer, the manufacturer, or an independent company back the service contract?
- How are claims handled? Who will do the work, and where will it be done?
- What happens to your coverage if the dealer or administrator goes out of business?
- Do you need prior authorization for repair work?
- Are there any situations when coverage can be denied? You may not have protection from common wear and tear, or if you fail to follow recommendations for routine maintenance.

Problems with Warranties

If you have problems receiving the services that were promised in your warranty, you can report your dispute. First read your warranty to make sure you know your rights. Then you can file a complaint with the retailer; if the retailer cannot help, contact the manufacturer. If neither the retailer or manufacturer can help, file a complaint with your local consumer protection agency (p. 102).

Visit www.consumer.ftc.gov/articles/0252-warranties for more information about warranties.

SHOPPING FROM HOME

Late delivery, shipment of wrong or damaged items, and hidden costs are common complaints when consumers shop from home. To avoid problems and resolve them more easily, follow the advice in the Before You Buy checklist (p. 2). In addition, here are some general tips:

- **Be wary of post office boxes and sellers in other countries**. It may be difficult to find the seller to resolve a problem later.
- **Know the total price.** Make sure it includes all charges, shipping, handling, insurance, and taxes. Coupons and other discounts should be deducted properly.
- **Be clear on what you are buying.** Watch for words such as "refurbished," "reconditioned," "closeout," or "discontinued."
- **Prepare to provide the security code** on the back of your credit card. The merchant may ask for that number to ensure that the card is in your possession.
- **Keep a record of your purchase.** Save any information the seller gives you, such as order confirmation number, product description, delivery date, cancellation policy, privacy policy, and warranties.
- **Keep track of your order.** If it's late, you have the right to cancel and demand a refund.

WHEN PRICES AREN'T FINAL

Retailers, both online and physical stores, sometimes use aggressive strategies to change the price of an item.

Drip pricing is a pricing strategy where a seller adds fees,, some of them mandatory, to the advertised price for the product or service. This practice makes it difficult for you to determine the full cost and compare similar options, when all the fees are not disclosed up front. You can protect yourself by asking questions of sales personnel about fees before you buy, or asking for a complete price list.

Another strategy is dynamic pricing, when a retailer adjusts an item's price multiple times over a few days, or even within hours. The changes may be based on inventory, changes in demand, your browsing history, and even your personal information. Dynamic pricing is common with online retailers and airlines. Make dynamic pricing work to your advantage by taking these actions:

- Use price tracker websites to compare the prices at different retailers.
- Use price predictor websites to track if the price is expected to go up or down.
- Clear your Internet cookies so online retailers cannot use your browsing history to adjust prices.

GREY CHARGES

"What's this charge?" may be your first thought when you see a small charge on your credit card statement that you cannot figure out. These are known as "grey charges" and there are several common types:

- **Unintended subscriptions**. You thought you made a one time purchase, but it was really a subscription.
- **Zombie fees**. Membership fees that you had cancelled, but the fees will not stop.
- **Free trial to paid**. When a free trial is over the seller converts it to a paid subscription.
- **Negative option**. You bought one product, but did not realize that you were buying others at the same time.

Take these steps to protect yourself from grey charges:

- Read the terms of service before you buy. Disclosures about fees may be hidden or near the end, so read the entire document.
- Mark your calendar as a reminder to cancel free trials by a set date.
- Read your credit card statements closely. Pay attention to the names of companies and charges for small amounts.
- Contact the seller to have the grey charges removed.
- Dispute the charges with your credit card company.

Your Rights

When you order something by mail, phone, or online, the Federal Trade Commission (FTC) requires the company to:

- Ship the merchandise within the time promised, or if no specific delivery time was stated, within 30 days of receiving your order.
- Notify you if the shipment cannot be made on time and give you the option of waiting longer or getting a refund.
- Cancel your order and return your payment if the new shipping date cannot be met, unless you agree to another delay.

If you cancel your order, your money must be refunded within seven days; if you charged the order on a credit card, your account must be credited within one billing cycle. The company cannot substitute a store credit. If you applied for a charge account with the merchant at the same time that you placed your order, the company has an extra 20 days to ship the merchandise to allow time for processing your credit application.

These FTC rules only apply to the first shipment of magazine subscriptions or other merchandise you receive repeatedly. Your state may also have rules that apply. Report suspected violations to your state or local consumer protection agency (p. 102) and to the FTC (p. 98).

3-Day Cooling-Off Rule

This federal law protects consumers in their homes during door-to-door sales pitches, or at sales in temporary business locations. The 3-Day Cooling-Off Rule does NOT apply to the purchase of new automobiles or items sold online. It only applies when a company is selling something that costs $25 or more at your home or more than $130 at other temporary business locations.

To comply with the 3-Day Cooling-Off Rule, a seller must inform buyers of their right to cancel the sale and receive a full refund within three business days.

Be aware that there are situations in which the Cooling-Off Rule does not apply:

- You made the purchase entirely by mail, online, or telephone.
- The sale was the result of prior contact you had at the seller's permanent business location.
- You signed a document waiving your right to cancel.
- Your purchase is not primarily for personal, family, or household use.
- You were buying real estate, insurance, securities, or a motor vehicle.
- You cannot return the item in a condition similar to how you received it.

Remember, if you paid by credit card and are having difficulty getting your refund, you may also be able to dispute the charge with your credit card company under the Fair Credit Billing Act. See Credit Card Billing Disputes (p. 14).

Online Shopping

Online shopping websites often offer great deals, variety, and convenience. However, consumers need to be careful and make informed decisions about their purchases. Some tips for shopping safely online:

- Stick to websites that are known or recommended.
- Compare prices and deals, including free shipping, extended service contracts, or other offers.
- Search for online coupons, known as promo codes, which may offer discounts or free shipping.
- Get a complete description of the item and parts included, and the price, including shipping. Also find out the delivery time, warranty information, return policy, and complaint procedure.
- Read reviews from other consumers and independent experts.
- Pay with a credit card. Federal law protects you if you need to dispute charges, but it does not apply to debit cards, checks, cash, money orders, and some mobile payment apps, or other forms of payment.
- Use a secure browser. Look for a URL that starts with "https" rather than "http." Also look for a closed padlock icon, usually in the lower right-hand corner of the screen.

- Avoid making online purchases on public Wi-Fi hotspots; these may not be secure, and your payment information could be stolen over the network.
- Print or save your purchase order with details of the product and your confirmation number.

Visit www.onguardonline.gov for more information.

Online Auctions and Sellers

Many people sell items on the Internet through auctions and classified ads. Review the general tips on shopping from home (p. 3) to prevent being a victim of online fraud. When participating in an online auction, remember to:

- Check how the auction works. Can you cancel a bid? Don't assume that the rules one auction site uses apply to another. Some sites offer step-by-step instructions that will take you through the bidding process.
- Find out what protections you have. Does the site provide free insurance or guarantees for items that are not delivered or are not what the seller claimed?
- Follow the strategies used in any auction. Learn the value of the item before you begin bidding, then establish your top price and stick to it.
- Read past customers' ratings and comments to determine if the seller is reputable and delivers quality products, as promised.
- Only bid on an item if you intend to buy. If you are the highest bidder, you have bought it.
- Use an escrow service if the seller cannot accept payment by credit card. A third party holds your money until you get your purchase and approve release of your payment to the seller.

AFTER YOU BUY

Even careful buyers can run into unforeseen problems later on. To minimize them, follow these steps after you buy:

- Save all papers that come with your purchase. Keep all contracts, sales receipts, canceled checks, owner's manuals, and warranty documents.
- Read and follow product and service instructions. The way you use or take care of a product might affect your warranty rights.
- You may be able to get a refund for the difference if the price of the item you bought has decreased within a certain number of days.
- Find out how to dispute a purchase, based on if you paid with cash, credit, or a mobile app, or payment device.

If you made a purchase using a mobile phone or an app, your dispute options depend on how the payment was processed. If the payment is passed through to a credit or debit card, then you can dispute any purchase you made with that card. If the app payment requires that you move money into a separate account, then the app provider determines how you can dispute the purchase.

If you have a problem with the item you purchased, file a complaint (p. 53).

Your bank accounts are primary ways to store your money, pay your bills, and build a savings. When you shop for a bank, consider the actual products and services, location of branches, and online and mobile banking features.

SAVINGS AND CHECKING

When it comes to finding a safe place to put your money, there are a lot of options. Savings accounts, checking accounts, certificates of deposit (CD), and money market accounts are popular choices. Each has different rules and benefits that fit different needs. The bank or credit union must provide you with the account terms and conditions when you open your account. When choosing the one that is right for you, consider:

Minimum deposit requirements. Do you have to keep a minimum dollar amount in your account to earn interest or avoid account maintenance fees?

Limits on withdrawals. Can you take money out whenever you want? Are there any penalties for doing so?

Interest. Can you earn interest on your accounts? How frequently is it paid (monthly, quarterly)? Check with banks or credit unions to see and compare their current published rates.

Online bill pay. Can you pay your bills directly from your bank or credit union's website?

Deposit insurance. Make sure the bank is a member of the Federal Deposit Insurance Corporation (FDIC) or that a credit union is insured by the National Credit Union Share Insurance Fund.

Mobile banking. Can you access your accounts and make deposits from your mobile phone or tablet? Does the bank charge fees for this access?

Convenience. Are there branches or ATMs close to where you work and live? Can you bank by phone or Internet?

Money transfer. Does the bank have a system that lets you transfer money to your accounts at other banks or to other people?

If you are considering a checking account or another type of account with check-writing privileges, add these items to your list of things to think about:

Number of checks. Is there a maximum number of checks you can write per month without incurring a charge?

Check fees. Is there a monthly fee for the account or a charge for each check you write?

Holds on checks. Is there a waiting period for checks to clear before you can withdraw the money from your account?

Debit card fees. Are there fees for using your debit card?

Account fees. Does the bank charge fees on your checking or savings account to cover things like maintenance, withdrawals, or minimum balance rules?

Overdrafts and Bounced Checks

What happens if you try to cash a check, withdraw money, or use your debit card for an amount greater than the amount of money in your account? It depends on whether or not you opted in for overdraft protection:

- If you did not opt in, your bank will reject the payment and not pay on your behalf, and no fee is charged.
- If you opted in for overdraft transfer protection, your bank will transfer money from your savings account or a line of credit, for a fee.
- If you opted in for overdraft protection, your bank will pay for transactions and charge you a fee for each payment it covers for you.

Go to www.fdic.gov/consumers/overdraft for more information.

Transaction Reordering

Some banks reorder the processing of your daily transactions. Instead of processing your payments and deposits in the order that you made them, the bank can choose to reorganize them based on type of debit (check, electronic payment) or size of the debit (larger amounts processed first). Transaction reordering can cause your account to have insufficient funds to cover your purchases, even if you made a deposit on the same day. If you have opted in for overdraft protection, your bank could cover the purchases, but would charge you a fee for each instance.

MOBILE BANKING

Many banks have made it convenient to do your banking from your phone or tablet. Your bank may have a mobile app to make it easy to keep a close track on your finances, pay bills, or transfer funds right from your smart phone. To get the best of these benefits and protect yourself:

- Make sure that your mobile device and your banking app are password protected.
- Sign up for text message alerts to know when transactions hit your account, or if your account balance goes below a minimum threshold.
- Access your accounts on secured connections.
- Use the fraud protection features, so you will know when someone, other than you, tries to change your password or account information.

Mobile Deposits

You can take a picture of a check with your smart phone's camera, and then use your bank's mobile app to upload and deposit it in your account. Remember, just because you make a deposit through your mobile app doesn't mean that the funds are immediately available. Some banks hold the funds on mobile deposits for more than a week, before the funds are available to you. This wait time is longer than the standard one or two day funds hold for a deposit made at a local branch or ATM. This extended hold can cause you to overdraw your account. Before you snap that picture of your check:

- Find out your bank's rules on the timing of funds availability for mobile deposits.
- Hold on to the physical check, just in case there was a problem. After it has cleared, you should shred it.
- Find out if there are fees to use this feature. If so, is it monthly, or per transaction?
- Upload the check over a secured network, to protect your account and that of the person who wrote the check to you.

Contact the Federal Deposit Insurance Corporation (p. 98) for more information on mobile banking.

ATM/DEBIT CARDS

With a debit card and personal identification number (PIN), you can use an Automated Teller Machine (ATM) to withdraw cash, make deposits, or transfer funds between accounts. Some ATMs charge a fee if you are not a member of the ATM network, or are making a transaction at a remote location.

Retail purchases can also be made with a debit card. You enter your PIN or sign for the purchase. Although a debit card looks like a credit card, the money for the purchase is transferred immediately from your bank account to the store's account. When you use a debit card, federal law does not give you the right to stop payment; you must resolve problems directly with the seller.

BEWARE: STOP PAYMENTS

Banks offer, for a fee, the ability to stop payment on a check you have written. However, a stop payment is not a guarantee that your bank will not cash the check. This could mean you have spent the amount of the check you did not want cashed, plus the fee to use the service.

Before you submit a stop payment request, check your transaction history and call your bank's customer service department to find out if that check is pending, but just not included in your online statement. Also, if you submitted your stop payment orally, you need to send your bank written confirmation of the request within four days so it does not expire.

MOBILE PAYMENTS

You can now pay for purchases through digital wallets stored in your smart phone, apps, a keyring fob, or even a watch. These items store your credit or debit card numbers. When you  get to the checkout counter, you just touch or swipe your device at the store's mobile payment terminal.

Before you decide to use a digital wallet provider, make certain that your phone has the chip that allows you to make mobile payments. You also need to know if your card issuer participates in that mobile payment service. Some questions to ask:

- Can you change the default card that is used for purchases?
- Does the device transmit your credit card numbers or send a device specific account number to the retailer?
- How does the mobile payment provider protect your privacy?
- Is there a PIN or fingerprint needed to access or use your mobile payment service?
- Do the retailers you buy from accept these payment methods?
- Who is responsible for fraudulent or unauthorized purchases? What is your liability?
- Is it possible to freeze your wallet if your phone is lost or stolen? Can this be done remotely?
- How do you dispute a purchase? See After You Buy (p. 5).

Review Consumer Action's article at www.consumer-action.org/modules/articles/your_digital_dollars-mobile_banking_and_mobile_payments for more tips.

If you suspect your debit card has been lost or stolen, call the card issuer immediately. While federal law limits your liability for a lost or stolen credit card to $50, your liability for unauthorized use of your ATM or debit card can be much greater, depending on how quickly you report the loss.

- If you report a debit card missing before it is used, you are not responsible for any unauthorized withdrawals.
- Your liability is limited to $50 if you report the loss within two business days after you realize your debit card is missing, and increases to $500 if you report the loss between two and 60 days.
- If you have not reported an unauthorized use of a debit or ATM card within 60 days after your bank mails the statement documenting the unauthorized use, you could lose all of the money in your bank account as well as

PROTECT YOUR PIN

Beware of "shoulder surfers." Be suspicious of anyone lurking around an ATM or watching over your shoulder while you use your debit or ATM card. Some thieves even put a device over the card slot of an ATM to read the magnetic strip and record your PIN; this is known as "skimming." If you suspect criminal activity, walk away and use a different ATM.

the unused portion of your line of credit established for overdrafts.

- Sign up for text message or email alerts each time your debit card is used, so that you can know immediately if it has been used fraudulently.

Check the policies of your card issuer; some offer more generous limits on a voluntary basis.

UNSOLICITED CHECKS AND CREDIT OFFERS

If you cash an unsolicited check, you could be agreeing to pay for products or services you do not want or need. In addition, those "guarantees" for credit cards or loans, without consideration of credit history, are probably a scam. Legitimate lenders never guarantee credit.

Legitimate offers of credit often come in the form of "convenience checks," which credit card companies enclose with your monthly statement. However, convenience checks may carry higher fees, a higher interest rate, and other restrictions. If you do not want the checks, be sure to shred them to protect yourself from "dumpster divers" and identity thieves.

Watch out for checks from someone in a foreign country who claims that you have won a foreign lottery. Also beware of accepting foreign checks for investment opportunities or to pay for an item you sold online. These could be scams. Even if you deposit the check, the check may not be legal. Don't rely on money from a check, especially foreign or unsolicited, until your bank says the check has cleared or if you know and trust the person who sent it to you.

PREPAID CARDS

Prepaid cards, also known as prepaid debit, stored value, or gift cards, are convenient ways to pay for your purchases. Banks and retailers issue them to offer consumers a way to make payments and conduct other financial transactions. You do not need to have a bank account or a credit history to use a prepaid card. Be sure you understand the card's terms and conditions BEFORE you buy.

Many cards carry protections similar to credit and debit cards. To obtain these benefits, you must follow the instructions for registering and activating your card. Be sure to record your card information, including the customer service telephone number listed on the back of the card in a separate place, so you can get a replacement if your card is lost or stolen. Some prepaid card issuers may charge fees for card activation, maintenance, and cash withdrawals.

If you have a problem with a prepaid card, first contact the customer service number. Some cards are issued by state or national banks. If the problem still is not resolved with the bank or issuer, file a complaint with the proper authorities listed in the chart:

Visit the Network Branded Prepaid Card Association at www.nbpca.com for more information.

Contact the proper regulatory agency below:

TYPE OF INSTITUTION	REGULATORY AGENCY
State-chartered banks and trust companies	Federal Deposit Insurance Corporation (p. 98) and state banking authorities (p. 115)
Banks with National in their name or N.A. after their name	Office of the Comptroller of the Currency, U.S. Department of the Treasury (p. 96)
Federal savings and loans and federal savings banks	Office of the Comptroller of the Currency, U.S. Department of the Treasury (p. 96)
Federally chartered credit unions	National Credit Union Administration (p. 99)
State-chartered banks that are members of the Federal Reserve System	Federal Reserve System (p. 98)

CARS

BUYING A CAR

Whether you are buying or leasing a vehicle, these tips will help you get the best deal and avoid problems:

- Decide what kind of vehicle best suits your needs and budget.
- Check out the seller. Research car dealers with your state or local consumer protection agency (p. 102) and Better Business Bureau (p. 63). If you are buying from an individual, check the title to make sure you are dealing with the vehicle's owner.
- Take a test drive. Drive at different speeds and check for smooth right and left turns. On a straight stretch, make sure the vehicle does not pull to one side.
- Handle trade-ins and financing separately from your purchase to get the best deal on each. Get a written price quote before you talk about a trade-in or dealer financing.
- Shop in advance and compare financing options at your credit union, bank, or finance company. Look at the total finance charges and the Annual Percentage Rate (APR), not just the monthly payment.
- Read and understand every document you are asked to sign.
- Don't take possession of the car until all paperwork is final.
- Choose an auto insurance policy that is right for you (p. 30).

Buying a New Car

Do your research first and compare vehicles.

- Research the dealer's price for the car and options available. It is easier to get the best price when you know what the dealer paid for a vehicle. The dealer invoice price is available on a number of websites and in printed pricing guides. Try to locate the wholesale price; this figure factors in dealer incentives from a manufacturer and is a more accurate estimate of what a dealer is paying for a vehicle.
- Find out whether the manufacturer is offering rebates that will lower the cost.

- Get price quotes from several dealers. Find out if the amounts quoted are the prices before or after rebates are deducted.

- Avoid low-value extras such as credit insurance, extended warranties, auto club memberships, rustproofing, and upholstery finishes. You do not have to purchase credit insurance to get a loan. See Service Contracts and Extended Warranties (p. 3).

- Hybrid cars are popular among consumers interested in fuel economy and reducing their negative impact on the environment. These cars combine the benefits of gasoline engines and electric motors and can be configured to achieve different objectives, such as improved fuel economy, increased power, or additional auxiliary power. Also look for the SmartWay logo to identify cleaner, more fuel-efficient cars and trucks. Visit www.epa.gov/greenvehicles/find/index.htm and www.fueleconomy.gov for more information about hybrids, electric vehicles, and alternative fuels.

Buying a Used Car

- To learn what rights you have when buying a used car, contact your state or local consumer protection office (p. 102).

- Contact your state's motor vehicle department to find out what paperwork you will need to register a vehicle.

CHOOSE A SAFE VEHICLE

Crash tests can help you determine how well a vehicle will protect you in a crash. These organizations perform crash tests and rate vehicles:

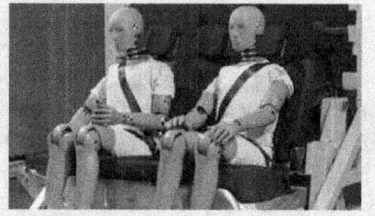

- **The National Highway Traffic Safety Administration.** Each year, NHTSA (www.nhtsa.gov) crashes vehicles head-on into a wall and bashes them broadside to test their ability to protect their occupants. NHTSA focuses on evaluating vehicle restraints such as air bags and safety belts.

- **The Insurance Institute for Highway Safety.** A different test by the IIHS (www.hwysafety.org) uses offset-frontal car crashes to assess the protection a vehicle's structure provides.

- **Consumer Reports.** The annual auto issue of *Consumer Reports* (www.consumerreports.org) rates vehicles in terms of overall safety. Its safety score combines crash test results with a vehicle's accident-avoidance factors — emergency handling, braking, acceleration, and even driver comfort.

- Check prices of similar models using the *NADA Official Used Car Guide* (www.nadaguides.com), published by the National Automobile Dealers Association, or the *Kelley Blue Book* (www.kbb.com). These guides are usually available at local libraries.

- Research the vehicle's history. Ask the seller for details concerning past owners, use, and maintenance. Find out whether the car has been damaged in a flood, crash, or labeled a "lemon." Also visit www.vehiclehistory.gov to buy vehicle history reports gathered from state motor vehicle departments and other sources. These reports are helpful but do not guarantee that a vehicle is accident-free.

- Research the car's title history with your state motor vehicle department.

- The Center for Auto Safety (www.autosafety.org) provides information on safety defect recalls, complaints, and technical service bulletins.

- Make sure any mileage disclosures match the odometer reading on the car.

- Check the warranty. If a manufacturer's warranty is still in effect, contact the manufacturer to make sure you can use the coverage.

- Ask about the dealer's return policy. Get it in writing and read it carefully.

- Have your mechanic inspect the car. Talk to the seller and agree in advance that you will pay for the examination if the car passes inspection, but the seller will pay if significant problems are discovered. A qualified mechanic should check the vehicle's frame, tires, air bags, and undercarriage as well as the engine.

- Examine dealer documents carefully. Make sure you are buying—not leasing—the vehicle. Leases use terms such as "balloon payment" and "base mileage" disclosures.

DEALER VERSUS PRIVATE-PARTY PURCHASES

The Federal Trade Commission requires dealers to post a Buyer's Guide in the window of each used car or truck on their lot. This guide specifies whether the vehicle is being sold "as is" (in the vehicle's current condition, without a warranty) or with a warranty, and what percentage of repair costs a dealer will pay under the warranty. Keep in mind

GOVERNMENT FUEL ECONOMY WEB PAGES

- www.epa.gov/greenvehicles The Green Vehicle Guide tool helps you find the cleanest and most fuel-efficient vehicles to meet your needs.

- www.fueleconomy.gov compares the miles-per-gallon ratings of different vehicle models manufactured since the mid-1980s and calculates annual fuel estimates.

- www.epa.gov/carlabel allows you to compare the fuel economy of different types of vehicles (diesel, hybrid, electric, gasoline).

that private sellers generally have less responsibility than dealers do for defects or other problems. FTC rules do not apply to private-party sales.

Expect to pay higher prices at a dealer than if you buy from an individual. Many dealers inspect their cars and provide an inspection report with each one. However, this is no substitute for your own inspection. Some dealers provide limited warranties, and most sell extended warranties. Watch out for dealer warranties that are "power train" warranties only, and not "bumper-to-bumper," full-coverage warranties. It is best to compare warranties that are available from other sources.

Some dealers sell "certified" cars. This generally means that the cars have had a more thorough inspection and come with a limited warranty. Prices for certified cars are generally higher. Be sure to get a list of what was inspected and what is covered under the warranty.

In general, buying a used car from a dealer is a safer option because you are dealing with an institution, which means you are better protected by law. Purchasing a car from a private seller may save you money, but there are risks. The car could be stolen, damaged, or still under a finance agreement. If a private seller lies to you about the condition of the vehicle, you may sue the individual if you have evidence and you can find him or her. An individual is very unlikely to provide a written warranty.

FINANCING

Most car buyers today need some form of financing to purchase a new vehicle. Many use direct lending, that is, a loan from a finance company, bank, or credit union. In direct lending, a buyer agrees to pay the amount financed, plus an agreed-upon finance charge, over a specified time period. Once a buyer and a vehicle dealership enter into a contract to purchase a vehicle, the buyer uses the loan proceeds from the direct lender to pay the dealership for the vehicle.

Another common form is dealership financing, which offers convenience, financing options, and sometimes special, manufacturer-sponsored, low-rate deals. Before you make a financing decision, it is important to do your research:

- Decide in advance how much you can afford to spend and stick to your limit.
- Get a copy of your credit report and correct any errors before applying for a loan.
- Check car buying guides to identify price ranges and best available deals.
- Request a loan that does not include a prepayment penalty if you pay off your loan before the loan is due.

More information about vehicle financing, deciding what you can afford, and consumer protections is available at www.consumer.ftc.gov/articles/0056-understanding-vehicle-financing. Visit www.consumerfinance.gov if you need to file a complaint about your auto loan.

DRIVING HOME WITH PRIVACY

There are many types of computer systems at work in your car. Some of which are needed so that the car can operate and communicate to the car manufacturer about how the car is running. Others are optional to improve comfort and convenience, such as internal GPS and infotainment systems that allow you to sync to your mobile phone or digital music, toll collection transmitters, and Wi-Fi.

These are great benefits, however these conveniences come at the price of your privacy. The terms of service for in-car computer systems may let companies record data about how and where you drive, radio stations you listen to, and may record entire phone conversations and text messages you dictate over the communication systems. Even if you cancel your subscription, the service provider can sell data about you to marketers and advertisers. Before you subscribe to these services:

- Read the terms of service and privacy policies.
- Disconnect Bluetooth or in-car Wi-Fi networks when you aren't using them.
- If you resell your car be sure to erase all the navigation data, phone contact lists, and stored locations from the in-car computer and communication systems.

LEASING

When you lease, you pay to drive someone else's vehicle. Monthly payments for a lease may be lower than loan payments, but at the end of the lease, you do not own or have any equity in the car. To get the best deal, follow this advice in addition to the general suggestions for buying a car (p. 8):

- Compare leasing versus owning. The Consumer Leasing Act requires leasing companies to give you information on monthly payments and other charges.
- Shop around to compare lease offers from multiple dealers.
- Find out what the down payment, or capitalized cost reduction, is for the lease. Consumers with better credit scores qualify for the low down payments and rates that are advertised in commercials.
- Calculate the total cost over the life of the lease, and include the down payment. A lease with a higher down payment and low monthly payments may be a better deal for you.
- Consider using an independent agent rather than the dealer; you might find a better deal. Most financial institutions that offer auto financing also offer leasing options.
- Ask for details on wear and tear standards. Dings that you regard as normal wear and tear could be billed as significant damage at the end of your lease.

- Find out how many miles you can drive in a year. Most leases allow 12,000 to 15,000 miles a year. Expect a charge of 10 to 25 cents for each additional mile.
- Check the manufacturer's warranty; it should cover the entire lease term and the number of miles you are likely to drive.
- Ask the dealer what happens if you give up the car before the end of your lease. There may be extra fees for doing so.
- Ask what happens if the car is involved in an accident.
- Get all of the terms in writing. Everything included with the car should be listed on the lease to avoid your being charged for "missing" equipment later.

Get more information about auto leases from www. consumerfinance.gov/askcfpb /815/should-i-buy-or-lease-whats-difference.html.

RECALLS, "LEMON" LAWS, AND SECRET WARRANTIES

Sometimes a manufacturer makes a design or production mistake on a motor vehicle. A technical service bulletin notifies the dealer of the problem and how to resolve it. Because these free repairs are not publicized, they are called "secret warranties."

If you have a problem with a vehicle that is a safety hazard, check whether the manufacturer has recalled your vehicle. Find information about recalls, and other safety defects in NHTSA's database at www-odi.nhtsa.dot.gov/recalls/recallsearch.cfm or call the DOT's Vehicle Safety Hotline at 1-800-424-9393. You should report hazards that are not listed to your dealer, the manufacturer of the vehicle (p. 61), and NHTSA at www-odi.nhtsa.dot.gov/ivoq. If a safety-related defect exists, the maker must fix it at no cost to you—even if your warranty has expired.

"Lemon" Laws

If you have a vehicle with a unique problem that just never seems to get fixed, you may have a "lemon". If your car is declared a "lemon" you will have the right to return the car for a refund. The "lemon" law requirements vary from state to state, but the criteria to qualify as a lemon often depends on things like:

- The defects must occur early within the car's first year or within the first 12,000 to 15,000 miles.
- The car must have a substantial defect on parts like the engine, transmission, or steering controls.
- You have to have given repair shops a reasonable number of attempts to fix the problem.
- Your car was in a repair shop and you were unable to use it for a certain number of days within the year.

Contact your state or local consumer protection office (p. 102) to learn whether you have such protections and what steps you must take to get your problem solved. If you believe your car is a "lemon":

- Give the dealer a list of the problems every time you bring it in for repairs.

- Get and keep copies of the repair orders listing the problems, the work done, and the dates the car was in the shop.
- Contact the manufacturer, as well as the dealer, to report the problem. Check your owner's manual or the directory of automotive manufacturers (p. 61).

The Center for Auto Safety (p. 100) gathers information and complaints concerning safety defects, recalls, technical service bulletins, and state "lemon" laws.

REPAIRS

Whenever you take a car to the repair shop:

- Choose a reliable repair shop. Family, friends, or an independent consumer-rating organization should be able to help you. Look for shops that display various certifications that are current. You should also check out the shop's record with your state or local consumer protection office (p. 102), or the Better Business Bureau (p. 63).
- Describe the symptoms. Don't try to diagnose the problem.
- Make it clear that work cannot begin until you have an estimate (in writing, preferably) and you give your okay. Never sign a blank repair order. If the problem cannot be diagnosed on the spot, insist that the shop contact you for authorization once it has found the problem.
- Ask the shop to return the old parts to you.
- Follow the warranty instructions if a repair is covered under warranty.
- Get all repair warranties in writing.
- Keep copies of all paperwork.

Some states, cities, and counties have special laws that deal with auto repairs. For information on the laws in your state, contact your state or local consumer protection office (p. 102). View the FTC's consumer guide to auto repair at www.consumer.ftc.gov/articles/0211-auto-repair-basics for more information.

CAR REPOSSESSIONS

When you borrow money to buy a car or truck, the lender can take your vehicle back if you miss a payment or in some

other way violate the contract. You should also be aware that the lender:

- Can repossess with cause without advance notice.
- Can insist you pay off the entire loan balance to get the repossessed vehicle back.
- Can sell the vehicle at auction.
- Might be able to sue you for the difference between the vehicle's auction price and what you owe.
- Cannot break into your home or physically threaten someone while taking the vehicle.

If you know you are going to be late with a payment, talk to the lender. If you and the lender reach an agreement, be sure to get the agreement in writing. Contact your state or local consumer protection office (p. 102) to find out whether your state gives you any additional rights.

RENTING

Before renting a car:

- Ask what the total cost will be after all fees are included. There may be an airport surcharge or fees for drop-off, insurance, fuel, mileage, taxes, additional-drivers, and equipment rental (for items such as GPS and car seats).
- Check in advance to be sure you are not duplicating insurance coverage. If you decline coverage, make sure to get it in writing to prevent surprise charges. You might also have coverage through your personal auto insurance (p. 30), a motor club membership, or the credit card you use to reserve the rental. See credit card perks (p. 14).
- Review your rental receipt to make sure that you were not charged for services you did not request.
- Carefully inspect the vehicle and its tires before renting, and when you return it. Try to return the car during regular hours so you and the rental staff can look at the car together to verify that you did not damage it.
- Check refueling policies and charges. Some rental companies, particularly at airports, may require you to refuel within a 10 mile radius of the airport or show a fuel receipt when you return the car.
- Pay with a credit card rather than a debit card, to avoid holds on the funds in your checking account.

Visit www.insureuonline.org/consumer_auto_car_rental_insurance.htm for more information about renting a car and the insurance options. Some states have laws to address your rights with short-term car and truck rentals. Contact your state or local consumer protection office (p. 102) for information or to file a complaint.

CAR SHARING SERVICES

Even if you do not own a car, there are times when you may need access to one. In addition to car rental companies, you can now subscribe to services offered by car sharing companies. These companies allow you to borrow a vehicle for short-term use. These car sharing services charge members on an hourly basis, as opposed to a daily or weekly rate. These services allow you to have the convenience of a car when you need one, without the costs of car ownership. Do some research. Talk to or read online reviews from subscribers about their experiences. Ask about:

- **Fees**. What fees does the company charge (annual fees, application fee)? Are they refundable, even if you cancel or are denied membership?
- **Availability of cars**. Are there cars available at times that you need one? How far in advance do you need to reserve it?
- **Attendants**. Are there on-site staff present when you check out your car and return it? This can be very helpful when you need to verify that the car is returned in the same condition as when you borrowed it.
- **Fuel**. Do you have to pay for gas out of your own pocket or does the company pay for it?
- **Extension of time**. How easy is it to extend the length of your rental? Is it done through an app or is there a dedicated customer service hotline?
- **Cancellation**. How far in advance must you give notice in order to cancel a reservation or your membership? Can the company cancel your membership without notification?
- **Damages**. Are you responsible for damages, even if they were not your fault or happened after you returned the car? This is especially important if you return the car to a lot that does not have on-site staff.
- **Insurance**. Do your fees include insurance? Remember, you may be insured by a personal policy or the credit card that you use to pay for this service.

CREDIT

Like everything else you buy, it pays to comparison shop for credit. Shop online personal finance websites for up-to-date interest rate reports on mortgages, auto loans, credit cards, home equity loans, and other banking products.

The Equal Credit Opportunity Act protects you when dealing with anyone who regularly offers credit, including banks, finance companies, stores, credit card companies, and credit unions.

When you apply for credit, a creditor may not:

- Ask about or consider your sex, race, national origin, or religion.
- Ask about your marital status or your spouse—unless you are applying for a joint account or relying on your spouse's income, or you live in a community property state (Arizona, California, Idaho, Louisiana, Nevada, New Mexico, Texas, Washington, or Wisconsin).
- Ask about your plans to have, or raise, children.
- Refuse to consider public assistance income, regularly received alimony, or child support.
- Refuse to consider income because of your sex or marital status, or because it is from part-time work or retirement benefits.

You have the right to:

- Have credit in your birth name, your first name and your spouse/partner's last name, or your first name and a combined last name.
- Have a co-signer other than your spouse if one is necessary.
- Keep your own accounts after you change your name or marital status or if you retire, unless the creditor has evidence that you are unable or unwilling to pay.
- Know why a credit application is rejected—the creditor must give you the specific reasons, or tell you where and how you can get a copy of the credit report, it used to determine its rejection, if you ask within 60 days.
- Have accounts shared with your spouse reported in both of your names.
- Know how much it will cost to borrow money.

For more on your credit rights, visit www.consumer.ftc.gov/articles/0347-your-equal-credit-opportunity-rights or www.consumerfinance.gov/fair-lending.

CREDIT CARDS

There are many types of credit cards with various features, but there is no one best credit card. The card you choose depends entirely on how you plan to use it. Are you going to use it for everyday purchases or larger purchases? Do you plan to pay off your balance each month?

When you apply for a credit card, consider:

- **Annual Percentage Rate (APR)**. If the interest rate is variable, how is it determined, and when can it change?
- **Periodic rate**. This is the interest rate used to determine the finance charge on your balance each billing period.
- **Annual fee**. While some cards have no annual fee, others expect you to pay an amount each year for being a cardholder.
- **Rewards programs.** Can you earn points for flights, hotel stays, and gift certificates to your favorite retailers? Use online tools to find the card that offers the best rewards for you.
- **Grace period.** This is the number of days you have to pay your bill before finance charges start. Without this period,

LOST AND STOLEN CREDIT CARDS

Immediately call the card issuer when you suspect a credit or charge card has been lost or stolen. Once you report the loss or theft of a card, you have no further responsibility for unauthorized charges. In any event, your maximum liability under federal law is $50 per card.

you may have to pay interest from the date you use your card or the date the purchase is posted to your account.

- **Finance charges.** Most lenders calculate finance charges using an average daily account balance, which is the average of what you owed each day in the billing cycle. Look for offers that use an adjusted balance, which subtracts your payment from your beginning balance. This method usually has the lowest finance charges. Check whether there is a minimum finance charge.
- **Other fees.** Ask about fees when you get a cash advance, make a late payment, or go over your credit limit. Some credit card companies also charge a monthly fee. Be careful: sometimes companies may also try to upsell by offering other services such as credit protection, insurance, or debt coverage.
- **Terms and conditions.** Read the agreement before you apply for the card to make sure that you agree with the requirements, such as mandatory arbitration or repossession clauses.
- **Security features.** Does the card allow you to receive fraud alerts or text messages immediately after purchases, or let you turn your card on and off?
- **Chip and PIN.** Does the card issuer offer chip and PIN security features, that rely on an embedded chip instead of the magnetic strip? You may need this type of card if you travel internationally.

BEWARE: CREDIT CARD SURCHARGES

Retailers are permitted to place a charge or surcharge on your credit card purchases, up to 3%, of your total purchase. If a retailer charges a surcharge, it must be clearly disclosed in the store and on your receipt.

These checkout fees may also come in the form of a discount to consumers that pay with cash. Retailers in CA, CO, CT, FL, KS, MA, ME, NY, OK, TX, and UT are not permitted to charge credit card surcharges.

Retailers are also allowed to set a $10 minimum purchase amount for credit card purchases. However, they cannot charge fees or set minimum purchase amounts on debit card purchases. Visit www.knowyourcard.org for more information on credit card surcharges.

CREDIT CARD PERKS

Did you know that your credit card may offer you some other protections that are not typically advertised? For instance, if you rent a car, your credit card issuer may offer you auto insurance coverage for the rental. You may also have travel insurance available if your trip was delayed, you had to cancel your trip because you or an immediate family member became ill, or your luggage was lost during the trip. Some credit card networks even offer return assistance programs that extend the window for returning unused merchandise. The rules vary between cards and the issuers. Check out the Consumer Financial Protection Bureau's database to find your credit card agreement www.consumerfinance.gov/credit-cards/agreements and learn which additional protections you have.

The Fair Credit and Charge Card Disclosure Act requires credit and charge card issuers to include this information on credit applications. You can also do your own research. There are many websites available to help you compare credit cards; some provide free credit card tips, reviews of credit cards, and calculators.

Visit www.federalreserve.gov/creditcard to view an interactive version of a sample credit card bill.

The Consumer Financial Protection Bureau (CFPB) provides useful information for consumers on selecting a credit card appropriate for their needs. See "How do I Shop for a Credit Card," on the CFPB website, www.consumerfinance.gov/blog/how-do-i-shop-for-a-credit-card.

Complaints

To complain about a problem with your credit card company, call the number on the back of your card or try to resolve it with the CFPB (p. 89). If you fail to resolve the issue, ask for the name, address, and phone number of the card company's regulatory agency. See the chart on page 8 to find the best federal or state regulatory agency to contact.

Contact the CFPB to complain about a credit bureau. For complaints about a department store that offers credit, or other Federal Deposit Insurance Corporation (FDIC)-insured financial institution, write to the agency's Consumer Response Center (p. 98). You may also file a complaint with the FTC at www.consumer.ftc.gov.

Credit Card Billing Disputes

Under the Fair Credit Billing Act, you have the right to dispute charges on your credit card that you did not make, are incorrect, or are for goods or services you did not receive. To dispute these charges:

- Send a letter to the creditor within 60 days of the statement date of the bill with the disputed charge.
- Include your name and account number, the date and amount of the disputed charge, and a complete explanation of why you are disputing the charge. To

ensure it is received, send your letter by certified mail, with a return receipt requested.

- The creditor or card issuer must acknowledge your letter in writing within 30 days of receiving it and conduct an investigation within 90 days of receiving your letter. You do not have to pay the amount in dispute during the investigation.
- If there was an error, the creditor must credit your account and remove any fees.
- If the bill is correct, you must be told in writing what you owe and why. You must then pay it, along with any related finance charges.

If you do not agree with the creditor's decision, file a complaint with the CFPB. You may also file a lawsuit against the creditor, unless your agreement includes a mandatory arbitration clause (p. 55).

CREDIT REPORTS AND SCORES

A credit report contains information on where you work and live, how you pay your bills, whether you have been sued or arrested, or have filed for bankruptcy. Credit reporting agencies (CRAs) gather this information and sell it to creditors, employers, insurers, and others. The most common type of CRA is the credit bureau. There are three major credit bureaus:

- Equifax: 1-800-685-1111 or www.equifax.com. To place a fraud alert on your credit report, call 1-888-766-0008.
- Experian: 1-888-397-3742 or www.experian.com.
- TransUnion: 1-800-888-4213 or www.transunion.com or 1-800-680-7289 to place a fraud alert.

The CFPB (p. 89) is responsible for overseeing the credit reporting agencies and receiving complaints about them.

Credit Scores

A credit score is a number that lenders and other companies use to evaluate your credit-worthiness. Scores generally range between 300 and 850. The higher your score, the less risk you pose to creditors.

Credit scores are based on the information in your credit reports. There is not just one universal credit score; there are different versions, created by different companies. Each credit score provider uses their own formula to create a score for you and places different amounts of emphasis on several factors, such as:

- **Payment history**. Do you pay your debt on time?
- **Available credit**. What is the total amount of credit available across all of your accounts?
- **Credit utilization**. How much of your available credit are you using?
- **Inquiries and new accounts**. Have you recently applied for credit or purchased items that required a company to review your credit reports?

ORDER YOUR FREE CREDIT REPORTS

You can request a free credit report once a year from each of the three major credit reporting agencies—Equifax, Experian, and TransUnion. If you ask the credit bureaus directly, they will charge you a fee to obtain your report. You may want to request your credit reports one at a time, every four months, so you can monitor your credit throughout the year without having to pay for a report. To order your free report, you must go through www. annualcreditreport.com or call 1-877-322-8228.

Check the accuracy of your credit report when you get it.

* Is your full name, social security number, and birthdate and address correct?
* Are employers, creditors, or home addresses listed that don't belong to you?
* Are account statuses correctly reported as open, closed, delinquent?
* Do judgements, such as liens or bankruptcies, appear correctly?

If there are any inaccuracies, contact the credit reporting agency and creditor that furnished that information to get it corrected. If they don't fix your report, you can file a complaint with the Consumer Financial Protection Bureau.

* **Type of accounts**. What is the mix between your mortgage, car loans, credit cards, and other credit accounts?
* **Length of your credit history**. What is the age of your oldest and newest accounts, along with the average across all accounts?

Although you can get your credit reports for free from www. annualcreditreport.com, you normally have to pay to get your credit score.

Tips for Building a Better Credit History
* Pay your bills on time. Delinquent payments and collections negatively affect your score.
* Keep balances low on credit cards and other "revolving credit." High outstanding debt lowers your score.
* Apply for and open new credit accounts only as needed. Don't open an account just to have a better credit mix; it probably will not raise your score.
* Pay off debt instead of moving it around.

You do not rebuild your credit score; you rebuild your credit history. Time is your ally in improving your credit. There is no "quick fix" for a bad credit score, so be suspicious of any deals that offer you a fast, easy solution.

Negative Information in Your Credit Report
Negative information concerning your use of credit can be kept in your credit report for seven years. A bankruptcy can be kept for 10 years, paid tax liens for seven years and unpaid tax liens indefinitely. Information about a lawsuit or

an unpaid judgment against you can be reported for seven years or until the statute of limitations runs out, whichever is longer. Inquiries remain on your report for two years.

Other negative items that can land on your credit report are outstanding parking fines and local government debts.

If a company denies you credit, housing, insurance, or a job as a result of a credit report it must give you the name, address, and telephone number of the CRA that provided the report. Under the Fair Credit Reporting Act (FCRA), you have the right to request a free report within 60 days if a company denies you credit based on the report.

If there is inaccurate or incomplete information in your credit report:

* Contact the CRA and the company that provided the information.
* Tell the CRA in writing what information you believe is inaccurate. Keep a copy of all correspondence.
* You can upload, mail, or fax any important documents (paid bill, letter stating that a bill has been paid) about your report to the major credit reporting agency's online dispute website when you submit your dispute.

Under the FCRA, the information provider is required to investigate and report the results to the CRA. If the information is found to be incorrect, the FCRA requires that company to notify all nationwide CRAs to correct your file. If the investigation does not solve your dispute, ask that your statement concerning the dispute be included in your file. A notice of your dispute must be included whenever the CRA reports the negative item.

If the information is accurate, only time, hard work, and a personal debt repayment plan will improve your credit history. Credit repair companies advertise that they can erase bad credit for a hefty fee. Don't believe it. Under the Credit Repair Organizations Act, credit repair companies cannot require you to pay until they have completed promised services. They must also give you:

* A copy of the *Consumer Credit File Rights Under State and Federal Law* before you sign a contract.
* A written contract that spells out your rights and obligations.
* Three days to cancel without paying any fees.

Some credit repair companies promise to help you establish a whole new credit identity. You can be charged with fraud if you use the mail or telephone to apply for credit with false information. It is also a federal crime to make false statements on a loan or credit application, to give a false Social Security number, or to obtain an Employer Identification Number from the Internal Revenue Service under false pretenses. Contact your state consumer affairs office (p. 102) if you were the victim of a credit repair scam.

DEALING WITH DEBT

If you want to reduce your amount of debt, you can do some work on your own. First, develop a realistic budget so you can see your income and expenses in one place and look for ways to save money. Contact your creditors and inform them that you are having difficulty making payments; they may be able to modify your payment plan. For help in creating a budget, visit www.mymoney.gov or www.consumer.gov/articles/1002-making-budget#!what-it-is.

Debt Collection

The Fair Debt Collection Practices Act applies to those who collect debts owed to creditors for personal, family, and household expenditures. These debts include car loans, mortgages, charge accounts, and money owed for medical bills. A debt collector is someone hired to collect money you owe.

Within five days after a debt collector first contacts you, the collector must send you a written notice that tells you the name of the creditor, how much you owe, and what action to take if you believe you do not owe the money. If you owe the money or part of it, contact the creditor to arrange for payment. If you believe you do not owe the money, contact the creditor in writing and send a copy to the collection agency with a letter telling it not to contact you.

A debt collector may not:

- Contact you at unreasonable times, for example, before 8 am or after 9 pm, unless you agree.
- Contact you at work if you tell the debt collector your employer disapproves.
- Contact you after you write a letter telling the collector to stop, except to notify you if the collector or creditor plans to take a specific action.
- Contact your friends, relatives, employer, or others, except to find out where you live and work.
- Harass you with repeated telephone calls, profane language, or threats to harm you.
- Make any false statement or claim that you will be arrested.
- Threaten to have money deducted from your paycheck or to sue you, unless the collection agency or creditor intends to do so and it is legal.

To file a complaint about a debt collection company, contact the Federal Trade Commission (p. 98) and your state or local consumer protection agency (p. 102).

Credit Counseling Services

Counseling services are available to help people budget money and pay bills. Credit unions, extension offices, military family service centers, and religious organizations are among those that may offer free or low-cost credit counseling.

Some local nonprofit agencies provide educational programs on money management and can help you develop debt payment plans. Make certain that the agency is accredited by a nationally recognized association of credit counselors.

Typically, a counseling service will negotiate lower payments with your creditors, and then make the payments using money you send to it each month. The cost of setting up this debt-management plan is paid by the creditor, not

you. Ask these questions to find the best counselor for you:

- What services do you offer? Look for an organization that offers budget counseling and money management classes as well as debt-management planning.
- Do you offer free information? Avoid organizations that charge for information or make you provide a lot of details about your problem first.
- What are your fees? Are there set-up and/or monthly fees? Beware of agencies that charge large up-front fees.
- How will the debt-management plan work? What debts can be included in the plan, and will you get regular reports on your accounts?
- Can they get creditors to lower or eliminate interest and fees? If the answer is yes, contact your creditors to verify this.
- Are the fees mandatory or is it possible to get services for a reduced price or for free? If an organization will not help you because you cannot afford to pay, go somewhere else for help.
- Will the counselor help you prevent future debt problems? Getting a plan for avoiding future debt is as important as solving the immediate debt problem.
- Ask for a contract. All verbal promises should be in writing before you pay any money.
- Are your counselors accredited or certified? Legitimate credit counseling firms are affiliated with the National Foundation for Credit Counseling (p. 133), Association of Credit Counseling Professionals (p.131), or the Association of Independent Consumer Credit Counseling Agencies (p. 131).

Check with your local consumer protection agency (p. 102) and the Better Business Bureau (p. 63) to see whether any complaints have been filed about the counseling service you are considering.

Contact the U.S. Trustee Program at www.justice.gov/ust or call 202-514-4100 if you have concerns about approved credit counseling agencies or credit counseling providers.

Personal Bankruptcy

Bankruptcy generally is considered the debt management option of last resort because the results are long-lasting and far-reaching. The Bankruptcy Abuse and Prevention Act of 2005 established more stringent rules for consumers and attorneys.

There may be multiple steps in the bankruptcy filing process:

- Debtors must file documents, including itemized statements of monthly net income, proof of income (pay stubs) for the last 60 days, and tax returns for the preceding year (four years for Chapter 13 bankruptcies).
- Debtors must take a pre-filing credit counseling and post-filing education course to have debts discharged. To find an approved credit counseling provider, visit www.justice.gov/ust.

- Debtors face increased filing fees, plus fees for credit counseling and education.
- The bankruptcy petition and process are complicated, so it is very difficult to file without an attorney.

LOANS

There are different types of loans. Some are secured loans, where you pledge collateral. Collateral is an item you already own, such as a house or car, that you promise to forfeit to the lender if you are unable to repay the loan. If you cannot pay back the loan, the lender will take your collateral to get their money back. Other types of loans, unsecured loans, do not use property as collateral. Lenders consider these as more risky than secured loans, so they charge a higher interest rate for them. Most credit cards are unsecured loans, although some consumers have secured credit cards. Two very common types of secured loans are home equity and installment loans.

Home Equity Loans

A home equity loan is a form of credit where your home is used as collateral for the loan. This type of loan is often used to pay for major expenses, such as education, medical bills, and home repairs. Consider carefully before taking out a home equity loan. If you are unable to make payments on time, you could lose your home.

Home equity loans can be either a revolving line of credit or a lump sum. Revolving credit lets you withdraw funds when you need them. A lump sum is a one-time, closed-end loan for a particular purpose, such as remodeling or tuition. Apply for a home equity loan through a bank or credit union first. These loans are likely to cost less than those offered by finance companies.

See Housing (p. 25) for helpful information about buying, leasing, renting, or repairing a home.

Installment Loans

Installment loans are loans that are repaid over time with a set number of scheduled payments; the most common installment loans are home or car loans. Before you sign an agreement for a loan to buy a house, a car, or other large purchase, make sure you fully understand all of the lender's terms and conditions, including:

- The dollar amount you are borrowing.
- The payment amounts and when they are due.
- The total finance charge, including all interest and fees you must pay to get the loan.
- The APR, the rate of interest you will pay over the full term of the loan.
- Penalties for late payments.
- What the lender will do if you cannot pay back the loan.
- Penalties if you pay the loan back early.

The Truth in Lending Act requires lenders to give you this information so you can compare different offers.

EDUCATION

The U.S. Department of Education's website, www.studentaid.ed.gov, provides information on preparing for and funding education beyond high school with details on federal aid programs. Another source of information on financial assistance is www.finaid.org. Both sites offer calculators to help you determine how much school will cost, how much you need to save, and how much aid you will need.

There are steps you can take as you plan for college expenses. Check the Department of Education's infographic that shows how to apply for financial aid and college at studentaid.gov/sites/default/files/financial-aid-process.png. Also, the National Association of Student Financial Aid Administrators provides advice, tips, and information on financing your education at www.nasfaa.org.

PAYING FOR COLLEGE 101

Many state governments have created 529 Plans that make it easier for families to save for their child's education. These plans, which can be sponsored by states or institutions of higher learning, encourage saving for future college costs, and the earnings grow tax-free. There are two main types: "prepaid tuition plans" and "college savings plans." Prepaid plans allow you to pay for your child's college tuition based on today's costs, and then pay out at the future (higher) cost once your child is in college. College savings plans allow you to invest money in several investment funds, ranging in

COLLEGE ACCREDITATION

Accreditation ensures that education provided by institutions of higher education meets acceptable levels of quality. The Secretary of Education is required by law to publish a list of nationally recognized accrediting agencies that it determines to be reliable authorities on the quality of education or training provided by the institutions of higher education and the higher education programs they accredit. You can access the list at ope.ed.gov/accreditation.

BEWARE: AUTOMATIC DEFAULT ON STUDENT LOANS

Private student loans can be a needed financial resource to pay for college. Lenders require borrowers to have a co-signer to qualify for a private loan and lower interest rates. Unfortunately, having a co-signer can cause problems for you down the road, if this person files for bankruptcy or dies. You could find yourself in automatic default, with the lender requiring you to pay the entire loan amount immediately.

An automatic default can place a strain on your budget, negatively impact your credit report, and prevent you from getting hired for jobs or being approved for a mortgage.

Some lenders state that they offer a co-signer release on their loans, after a set period of time or after you make a certain number of on-time payments. Contact your lender to see if you qualify for a co-signer release. The Consumer Financial Protection Bureau (CFPB) offers a sample co-signer release letter at files.consumerfinance.gov/f/201404_cfpb_inquiry-letter_how-to-release-cosigner.doc to help you with the request. If your lender will not help you, file a complaint with the CFPB (p. 89).

risk level, to pay for your child's college education. There may also be tax benefits, such as credit and deductions, when you contribute to some college savings plans. Visit www.collegesavings.org for more information about the different types of 529 Plans and the plans available in each state.

Financial Aid

Student financial aid is available from a variety of sources, including the federal government, individual states, colleges and universities, and other public and private agencies and organizations. The four basic types of college aid are:

- **Grants.** Gift aid that does not have to be repaid and is generally awarded according to financial need.
- **Work-Study.** The Federal Work-Study Program (FWS) is a federally funded source of financial assistance used to offset financial education costs. Students who qualify earn money by working while attending school. This money does not have to be repaid.
- **Loans.** Funds are borrowed and must be repaid with interest. As a general rule, federal student loans have more favorable terms and lower interest rates than traditional consumer loans.

MY COLLEGE CLOSED - NOW WHAT?

If your college or university closes permanently while you are enrolled or shortly after you withdraw, you could be stuck with student loan debt and no degree to make it worthwhile.

There is consoling news. If you have federal student loans you may be eligible for a student loan discharge. However, you are not eligible for a loan discharge if you transfer to another college to complete your degree.

You will still be required to repay the full amount of the loan, if you have private student loans. Check with your state's department of education or your lender for information about programs to help you in this situation. Visit studentaid.ed.gov/repay-loans/forgiveness-cancellation/closed-school for more information.

- **Scholarships.** Funds are offered by the school, local or community organizations, private institutions, and trusts. Scholarships do not have to be repaid and are generally awarded based on specific criteria.

Applying for Aid

You must complete and submit a Free Application for Federal Student Aid (FAFSA℠) to apply for federal student aid. FAFSA on the Web is the quickest and easiest method of applying. Go to www.fafsa.gov to apply.

Some companies offer to help you find scholarships or complete your FAFSA application, for a fee. If the company asks you for money up front, but does not deliver on its promises to find scholarships, it could be a scam. Learn more about financial aid scams at www.studentaid.ed.gov/types/scams.

Federal Student Aid Information Center

The Federal Student Aid Information Center (FSAIC) can answer your federal student financial aid questions and can give you all the help you need for free. You can also use the FSAIC automated response system to find out whether your FAFSA℠ has been processed and to request a copy of your Student Aid Report (SAR). For FSAIC contact information, see page 90.

Federal Loan Program Repayment Information

- **Public Service Loan Forgiveness Program.** Offers forgiveness for outstanding federal loans for individuals working full time in public service jobs.
- **Income-Based Repayment Plan.** Helps to make repaying education loans more affordable for low-income borrowers.

Both programs offer generous benefits, but the rules may seem complex, so it is important to get all of the details. For more information on these programs as well as other repayment options:

- U.S. Department of Education/Federal Student Aid: www.studentaid.ed.gov/repay-loans
- National Association of Student Financial Aid Administrators: www.nasfaa.org

Comparing Student Loans

Not all student loans are the same, especially federal and private loans. Federal student loans are offered through the U.S. Department of Education. Private loans are offered by banks, credit unions, or schools. Federal loans tend to offer loans at lower interest rates than private loans. While federal loans don't require you to have a co-signer, many private loans make this a requirement. Visit studentaid. ed.gov/types/loans/federal-vs-private for more information about the difference between these loans.

The Consumer Financial Protection Bureau (CFPB) has a Know Before You Owe Student Loan website, www. consumerfinance.gov/paying-for-college/compare-financial-aid-and-college-cost. This financial aid tool lets you compare financial aid offers from multiple colleges.

Defaulting on Student Loans

Take steps to avoid defaulting on your student loan. Before you get the loan, determine how much money you need to borrow and only borrow that amount. When you get the loan, make certain that you understand the details such as the payment terms and what type of loan you have. Once your student loan becomes due:

- Maintain accurate records of your loan, including the loan agreement, interest rates, and account numbers.
- Track your loans to stay updated on how much you owe.
- Make certain that the loan servicer has your current contact and bank account information (if payments are withdrawn automatically).

If you default, it means you failed to make payments on your student loan as scheduled. Your loan becomes delinquent the first day after you miss a payment. However, the loan is not in default until 270 days have passed without a payment. The consequences of default can be severe, including:

- The entire unpaid balance of your loan and any interest is immediately due and payable.
- Your loan account is assigned to a collection agency.
- The loan will be reported as delinquent to credit bureaus, damaging your credit rating.
- Your federal and state taxes may be withheld through a tax offset. This means that the Internal Revenue Service can take your federal and state tax refund to collect any of your defaulted student loan debt.
- Your employer can withhold money from your pay and send the money to the government. This process is called wage garnishment.

Contact your loan servicer immediately if you are having difficulty making your payments. The servicer may be able to help by changing your repayment plan, switching the due date, getting a deferment or forbearance, or consolidating your student loans.

Visit www.studentaid.ed.gov/repay-loans/default for information to help you avoid defaulting on your student loan.

EMPLOYMENT

Times have changed for job searching, and numerous websites are now available that post private industry jobs. Many companies also offer a way to apply online. However, these sites and new methods do not replace traditional and proven job-hunting approaches such as networking, personal contacts, business organizations, and interviewing.

EMPLOYMENT AGENCIES AND RECRUITERS

If you are looking for a job, you may come across ads from employment agencies or receive calls from recruiters that promise wonderful opportunities. While some companies honestly want to help you, others are more interested in taking your money. Be wary of:

- Promises to get you a job and a guaranteed income
- Up-front fees, even when you are guaranteed a refund if you are dissatisfied
- Employment agencies whose ads read like job ads
- Promotions of "previously undisclosed" government jobs. All federal jobs are announced to the public at www.usajobs.gov.

PRE-EMPLOYMENT CREDIT CHECKS

Potential employers are not just reading your résumé; they are also reviewing your credit history to find out:

- If you pay your bills on time.
- How much money you owe.
- If someone has sued you.

Potential employers must notify you and ask your permission before they request your credit report.

Visit www.annualcreditreport.com to get a copy of your report before you begin your job search, so you can see and correct inaccuracies.

If a company decides not to hire you because of your credit report, it must tell you so. It must also inform you of your rights to get a free report, and your rights to dispute the accuracy of the report.

Get a copy of the employment agency contract and review it carefully before you pay any money. Check with your local consumer protection agency (p. 102) and the Better Business Bureau (p. 63) to see whether any complaints have been filed about a company.

The Federal Trade Commission (p. 98) investigates businesses that fraudulently advertise employment openings and guarantee job placement. Contact the FTC if you have a complaint.

WORK-AT-HOME COMPANIES

Not all work-at-home opportunities deliver on their promises. Some classic work-at-home schemes are medical billing, envelope stuffing, and assembly or craftwork. Ads for these businesses say, "Be part of one of America's Fastest-Growing Industries. Earn thousands of dollars a month from your home!". Legitimate work-at-home program sponsors should tell you, in writing, what is involved in the program they are selling. Here are some questions you might ask a promoter:

- What tasks will I have to perform? Ask the program sponsor to list every step of the job.
- Will I be paid a salary, or will my pay be based on commission?
- Who will pay me?
- When will I get my first paycheck?
- What is the total cost of the work-at-home program, including supplies, equipment, and membership fees? What will I get for my money?

The answers to these questions may help you determine whether a work-at-home program is appropriate for your circumstances and whether it is legitimate.

Multilevel Marketing

Some multilevel marketing plans are legitimate; however, others are illegal pyramid schemes. In pyramids, commissions are based on the number of distributors recruited, rather than actual products that are sold.

If you are thinking about joining what appears to be a legitimate multilevel marketing plan, take time to learn about the plan:

- What is the company's track record?
- What products does it sell?
- Does it sell products to the public at large?
- Does it have the evidence to back up the claims it makes about its product?
- Is the product competitively priced?
- Is the product likely to appeal to a large customer base?
- How much does it cost to join the plan?
- Are monthly minimum sales required to earn a commission?
- Will you be required to recruit new distributors to earn your commission?

Unemployment

The government's Unemployment Insurance Program provides benefits to eligible workers who become unemployed through no fault of their own and who meet other eligibility requirements. Each state administers its own program under federal guidelines. Eligibility requirements, benefit amounts, and length of benefits are determined by the states. Go to www.dol.gov/dol/topic/unemployment-insurance/index.htm for more information.

In addition, some states are extending unemployment benefits for eligible recipients. The length of the extensions vary by state. Visit www.workforcesecurity.doleta.gov for the latest information regarding your state's benefit programs.

FOOD AND NUTRITION

Consumers have a wide variety of food choices available. You want food that is safe, nutritious, and will not break your budget.

HEALTHY FOOD CHOICES

To help you make healthy food choices, the federal government posts dietary guidelines at www.health.gov/dietaryguidelines. Federal regulations also require many foods to identify fat content, fiber, and nutrients on their labels. Visit www.fda.gov/Food/ResourcesForYou/Consumers for more information about food labels.

Check out these resources for advice, tips, and information on food shopping and nutrition:

- U.S. Department of Agriculture (p. 89)
- U.S. Food and Drug Administration (p. 92)
- Nutrition.gov (www.nutrition.gov)
- MedlinePlus.gov (www.medlineplus.gov)
- Center for Nutrition Policy and Promotion (www.cnpp.usda.gov)
- Choose My Plate (www.choosemyplate.gov)

FOOD SAFETY

Food safety in the home revolves around three main functions: food storage, food handling, and cooking. By practicing a few simple rules for cleaning, separating, cooking, and chilling, you can prevent most foodborne illness in the home. The website www.foodsafety.gov is your gateway to government food safety information, including publications you can download or request. You can also visit www.recalls.gov for the latest food safety alerts and recalls.

For more information, here are some additional resources:

- Centers for Disease Control and Prevention (p. 91) www.cdc.gov/foodsafety
- FDA's Food Information Hotline, www.fda.gov/Food 1-888-723-3366
- Partnership for Food Safety Education, www.fightbac.org
- USDA Food Safety and Inspection Service, www.fsis.usda.gov
- USDA Meat and Poultry Hotline, 1-888-674-6854

SAVING MONEY ON GROCERIES

It can be a challenge to make healthy food choices and stay within your food budget. Follow these tips to help you get the most from your grocery budget:

- Take an inventory of the food you already have in your home. Plan your meals for the week, keeping in mind what you already have.
- Make a shopping list and stick to it.
- Use apps to compare prices between grocery stores so that you can get the best deal.
- Compare unit prices (cost per ounce or pound) to get the best deal.
- Buy the generic store brand versions of foods.
- Take advantage of store loyalty savings programs, as well as clipping coupons and online discounts.
- Only take advantage of the deal if you know you will eat the discounted item. It is not a deal if the food goes to waste.
- Check the amount of food in the packaging. Some food manufacturers have reduced the amount of food in the can or box of food, but charge the same price. This is basically the same as a price increase.
- Visit your local farmers market to find fresh produce. Find your local farmers market at search.ams.usda.gov/farmersmarkets.
- Shop for foods that are in season. When the supply is plentiful, the prices tend to be lower.
- Bring bags. Some stores charge a fee to customers who do not bring their own bags.

If you need assistance with food expenses, you may qualify for assistance from the Supplemental Nutrition Assistance Program (SNAP). Learn more at www.fns.usda.gov/snap/supplemental-nutrition-assistance-program-snap. The Senior Farmers Market Nutrition Program issues coupons to low-income seniors for use at farmers markets. Details are available at www.fns.usda.gov/sfmnp/overview.

ORGANIC FOODS

Buying organic food is a way to eat in a healthy manner and protect the environment. These foods are grown and processed according to USDA regulations and follow specific rules concerning pest control, raising animals, and the use of additives. Keep in mind that organic and natural foods tend to be more expensive than conventionally grown foods, and that the USDA does not claim that organic food is safer or more nutritious than other foods.

To make sure a product is certified organic, look for the USDA organic seal. You can also tell whether produce was grown organically by checking the price look up code (PLU); if the first number starts with a 4, then the food was grown conventionally, if it starts with a 9, it was grown organically.

Other common labels that help you choose certain types of food products include:

Free-Range or Cage-Free. This means the flock was provided shelter in a building, room, or area with unlimited access to food, fresh water, and the outdoors.

Natural. As required by the USDA, meat, poultry, and egg products labeled as "natural" must be minimally processed and contain no artificial ingredients.

Grass-Fed. Grass-fed animals receive a majority of their nutrients from grass throughout their life, while organic animals' pasture diet may be supplemented with grain.

Visit www.ams.usda.gov for more information about organic foods.

GOING GREEN

"Going Green" means practicing an environmentally friendly and ecologically responsible lifestyle, as well as making decisions to help protect the environment and sustain natural resources. There are lots of reasons to consider going green—too much trash, greenhouse gases, air and water pollution, damage to the ozone layer, and saving money. You can make choices that protect the environment and possibly help you save money, such as:

- Turn your thermostat down two degrees in winter and up two degrees in summer.
- Make sure your walls and ceilings are well insulated.
- Replace bathroom and kitchen faucets with low-flow models.
- Participate in the curbside recycling program. Check with your local government to get more information on recycling services.

For more ideas to help the environment and your wallet, visit www.epa.gov/epahome/home.htm.

BUYING GREEN

The U.S. Environmental Protection Agency (EPA) has a green products web portal (www.epa.gov/greenerproducts) to help you navigate the complex world of green products. The EPA also has a number of eco-labeling partnership programs to help you identify greener, safer, and more efficient products. Look for these EPA program labels when buying:

- **Energy Star**—For energy-efficient electronics and appliances (www.energystar.gov).
- **WaterSense®**—For water-efficient products (www.epa.gov/watersense).
- **Design for the Environment (DfE)**—For household cleaners and other products that have been determined to be safer for both your health and the environment (www.epa.gov/dfe).
- **SmartWay Certified Vehicle**—For cleaner, more fuel-efficient cars and trucks (www.epa.gov/smartway).

You can also choose to buy organic or locally produced food and eco-friendly clothing. Go to the U.S. Department of Agriculture's Agricultural Marketing Service at www.ams.usda.gov/AMSv1.0 for more information about national standards covering organic food and fiber. There are no national standards for organic clothing, but some fabrics to consider include organic cotton, bark cloth, bamboo, and organic wool.

By making greener product choices, you are saving money on utilities and fuel, and protecting public health and the environment.

HEALTH CARE

There are plenty of resources available to help you make health care decisions. Be wary of websites sponsored by companies that are trying to sell you a particular treatment. It is better to contact reputable associations or visit sites run by government agencies and recognized organizations. This information should complement, not replace, what you receive from a doctor. Here are some sites that are generally recognized as reliable information sources:

- **HealthCare.gov** (www.healthcare.gov)—Learn about, and apply for, the Health Insurance Marketplace online.
- **HealthFinder.gov** (www.healthfinder.gov)—Provides information and tools to help you stay healthy.
- **Mayo Clinic** (www.mayoclinic.org)—Offers an index of symptoms, diseases and procedures.
- **Medical Library Association** (www.mlanet.org)— Provides links to websites suggested by librarians.
- **MedlinePlus®** (www.medlineplus.gov)—Provides information on illnesses, diseases, and wellness issues.

CHOOSE A DOCTOR

When searching for a primary care doctor, dentist, specialist, or other health care professional:

- Find out whether the health care professional is licensed in your state. A state or local occupational and professional licensing board will be able to give you this information.
- Research whether the health care professional is board-certified in the appropriate specialty. Visit www.ama-assn.org and www.abms.org for more information.
- Ask how often the health care professional has performed the procedure you need or has treated your condition. You may be able to find some of this information online.
- Check whether there have been any complaints or disciplinary actions taken against the provider you are researching. Visit www.docboard.org for more information. There are also pay-for-use sites with similar information. Visit www.healthfinder.gov and www.ahrq.gov/consumer for more advice on identifying providers.

- Find out what doctors participate in your health insurance plan. If you are having surgery, check that all providers (radiologists, anesthesiologists) are also covered by your plan, to avoid surprise bills.

Consider these questions regarding your health care provider and his or her practice:

- Does the doctor participate in your insurance plan?
- Is the office in an area that you can get to easily, or does it have office hours during times when you can make an appointment?
- Does the doctor have privileges to practice medicine at the hospital you prefer?
- Do you get along well with the doctor? Do you feel that you communicate well with each other? Does the doctor listen to your concerns and explain diagnoses and benefits of new treatments and prescriptions clearly?
- What is the doctor's appointment cancellation policy? Will you have to pay for a cancelled appointment?

Filing a Complaint

If you have a complaint about the medical services you received from a physician, you may file a complaint with your state medical board. For a complete directory from the Federation of State Medical Boards, visit www.fsmb.org/directory_smb.html. You can also call the Federation at 817-868-4000 to get the phone number of your state's medical board.

CHOOSE A HEALTH CARE FACILITY

Online report cards can help you compare health care facilities. Compare doctors and health care facilities at www.healthgrades.com. In addition, www.usnews.com rates hospitals based on information collected from Medicare records and other sources. The Affordable Care Act requires all hospitals to report performance publically.

When determining the best health care facility for you, consider these factors:

- Does the facility accept payment from your insurance plan?
- Does your doctor have practice privileges to provide treatment to patients at the facility?

MEDICAL CREDIT CARDS

Some health care providers offer deferred-interest credit cards that give you more time to pay for medical and dental procedures.

If you pay off the entire bill before the promotional period ends, you will not be responsible for paying any interest on the credit card balance. But beware: if you are unable to pay off the credit card balance by the end of the promotional period or make any late payments, you will have to pay all the accrued interest during the loan (usually at higher than 25% APR), on top of the credit card balance.

The staff at medical offices are not required to (and often are not trained to) clearly explain the terms of these cards to you. Before you apply for a medical payment plan or credit card, do some research:

- Read any disclosures and terms of services before applying for a medical credit card. Get them in writing, not just orally from staff members.
- Check for the interest rates and when a promotional period would end.
- Comparison shop. Your doctor's office may offer one plan, but if you have time, shop around to determine if there are better offers available.
- Can you use the card for other medical expenses? If so, find out if interest becomes due on future purchases immediately or if it is also deferred.
- Determine how much you would have to pay each period in order to finish paying the balance before interest comes due.

- What is the quality of the facility?
- Does the facility specialize in services and procedures that fit with your medical needs?
- Is the facility in an area you can travel to and from easily? Find health care facilities in your area at findahealthcenter.hrsa.gov/Search_HCC.aspx.

Patient Portals

A patient portal is a website, sponsored by a health care facility or health insurer, that gives you electronic access to your medical information. You may access notes from recent doctor's appointments, lab test results, prescriptions, and more. Some portals also provide medical advice or have staff that help them to provide medical care or diagnose symptoms remotely. Visit www.HealthIT.gov or contact your health providers for more information.

Elder Care

The need for services for seniors has become more important. The Eldercare Locator (www.eldercare.gov), a public service of the Administration for Community Living, U.S. Department of Health and Human Services, is a nationwide service that connects older Americans and

BEWARE: HEALTH INSURANCE SCAMS

Scam artists take advantage of consumers that are looking to save money on their health care. However, their scams could hurt both your wallet and health care coverage. Take these steps to protect yourself from frauds:

- Don't pay anyone to help you navigate the Health Insurance Marketplace. There are official navigators that can help you for free.
- Don't give personal information to someone who calls you, claiming to be from the government or Medicare.
- Ask questions if anything is unclear. Double check information that is confusing.

If you suspect fraud, file a complaint with your local police department and with the FTC at www.ftc.gov/complaint. If the fraud involves the Health Insurance Marketplace, call 1-800-318-2596. Read more about signs of health scams at www.consumer.ftc.gov/articles/0394-suspect-health-care-scam.

their caregivers with information on senior services. Visit acl.gov/Get_Help/Help_Older_Adults/Index.aspx for a list of resources to connect older persons, caregivers, and professionals with important federal, national, and local programs.

If you are looking for a nursing home or other assisted-living facility, these organizations can help:

- Nursing Home Compare, operated by the U.S. Department of Health and Human Services, will help you compare facilities in many states. Go to www.medicare.gov/nhcompare/home.asp or call 1-800-633-4227.
- Eldercare Locator (www.eldercare.gov) provides information and referral services for those seeking local and state support resources for the elderly (p. 92).
- LeadingAge (www.leadingage.org) helps you locate nonprofit organizations that meet the needs of the elderly.
- The Assisted Living Federation of America (www.alfa.org) represents both for-profit and nonprofit assisted-living facilities; call 703-894-1805.
- The Commission on Accreditation of Rehabilitation Facilities (www.carf.org) gives its seal of approval to qualifying facilities; call 1-888-281-6531 (p. 132).
- The Joint Commission accredits hospitals, nursing homes, and other health care organizations. Check out a local facility at their website www.qualitycheck.org.

PRESCRIPTION DRUGS

Your pharmacist oversees an important part of your health care by providing the medications prescribed by other health care professionals. It is important that you are proactive and communicate honestly with your pharmacist.

Make certain that your pharmacy has your current health and prescription insurance information on record so you get the best price possible.

If you have difficulty paying for your medications, contact the manufacturer; some pharmaceutical companies have patient assistance programs to help you afford your medication.

You may decide to replace a trip to the pharmacy with a visit to an online pharmacy. While there are legitimate online pharmacies, there are also some fraudulent ones that advertise prescription drugs for low prices. Beware: they can cause you more harm than good, by selling you medications that are counterfeit and do not treat your condition.

Fraudulent online pharmacies can also hurt your wallet. They may not have security processes in place to protect your personal information such as your credit card numbers and your home address, putting your privacy at risk. They may also charge you for medicines you never received. Be suspicious if an online pharmacy:

- Allows you to buy medication without a prescription from your doctor.
- Offers medication at deep discounts that seem too good to be true.
- Is not licensed and has no physical address in the U.S.
- Sends unsolicited emails (spam) offering cheap drugs.
- Does not have a licensed pharmacist available to answer your questions.

Check the Food and Drug Administration's (FDA) database of safe online pharmacies and get more tips to protect yourself at www.fda.gov/BeSafeRx or call 1-888-463-6332. If you suspect that a pharmacy is fake, report it to the FDA at www.fda.gov/Safety/ReportaProblem/ucm059315.htm.

MEDICARE PRESCRIPTION DRUG COVERAGE

Medicare offers prescription drug coverage to senior citizens and others who need financial assistance get the prescription drugs they need. Prescription coverage is available under Part D of the program or Part C if you are enrolled in the Medicare Advantage Plan. Everyone with Medicare can join a drug plan to get this coverage. Not all Medicare drug plans are the same. If you are not sure whether a drug plan is approved by Medicare, call 1-800-633-4227. Look for the "Medicare Approved" seal on drug discount cards to make sure you are getting the best deal.

Medicare prescription drug coverage pays expenses up to $2,960; once your prescription costs exceeds that amount, you will no longer have coverage and will be responsible for the full cost of your drugs. However, once your out-of-pocket spending reaches $4,700, your prescription coverage

MEDICAL IDENTITY THEFT

Medical identity theft can occur when someone steals your personal information to obtain medical care, buy medication, or submit fake claims to your insurer or Medicare in your name. To prevent medical identity theft, you can:

- Guard your Social Security, Medicare, and health insurance identification numbers.
- Review your explanation of benefits or Medicare Summary Notice. Report errors to your insurer.
- Request and carefully review a copy of your medical records for inaccuracies and conditions that you don't have.

If you believe you have been a victim of medical identity theft, file a complaint with the FTC at 1-877-438-4338 or online at www.ftccomplaintassistant.gov and your health insurance company's fraud department.

will kick back in. Any amount of prescription drug spending between $2,960 and $4,700 is called the coverage gap or Medicare "donut hole." In 2015, if you reach the coverage gap, you will automatically get a 55% discount on covered brand-name drugs and a 35% discount on generic drugs. If you have limited income and resources, you may get extra help to cover prescription drugs for little or no cost. Contact the Centers for Medicare & Medicaid Services (p. 92) for more information.

Visit www.medicare.gov for more information about Medicare benefits.

ADVANCE MEDICAL DIRECTIVES

Advance directives are written documents that tell your doctors what kind of treatment you want if you become unable to make medical decisions (for example, if you are in a coma). Forms and laws vary from state to state, so it is a good idea to understand the laws of the state where you live when you write advance directives. It is also a good idea to make them before you become very ill. Federal law requires hospitals, nursing homes, and other institutions that receive Medicare or Medicaid funds to provide written information regarding advance medical directives to all patients upon admission.

A living will is one type of advance directive that goes into effect when a person is terminally ill. A living will does not give you the opportunity to select someone to make medical decisions for you, but it does allow you to specify the kind of treatment you want in specific situations. For example, you might choose to specify that you do not want to be treated with antibiotics if death is imminent. You can, if you choose, include an advance directive that you do not wish to be resuscitated if your heart stops or if you stop breathing. In this case, a Do Not Resuscitate (DNR) order would be entered on your medical chart.

Naming a Durable Power of Attorney for Health Care

A durable power of attorney for health care (sometimes called a durable medical power of attorney) specifies the person you have chosen to make medical decisions for you.

It is activated when you are unconscious, or unable to make medical decisions. You need to choose someone who meets the legal requirements in your state for acting as your agent. State laws vary, but most states disqualify anyone under the age of 18, your health care provider, or employees of your health care provider.

The person you choose as your agent must:

- Be willing to speak and advocate on your behalf.
- Be willing to deal with conflict among friends and family members, if it arises.
- Know you well and understand your wishes.
- Be willing to talk with you about these issues.
- Be someone you trust with your life.

HOUSING

Housing is one of the most significant expenses that you have as a consumer. There are many decisions to make, such as choosing the best housing option for you, how to finance it, and choosing movers and contractors for home repairs. Use the resources from the U.S. Department of Housing and Urban Development at www.hud.gov, the Consumer Financial Protection Bureau at www.consumerfinance.gov/owning-a-home, as well as your local housing departments so you know your rights and responsibilities.

BUY A HOME

Buying a home is one of the most complex financial decisions you will ever make. In addition to the financial and legal issues involved, real estate agents and lenders may not be acting in your best interest.

- Real estate agents represent the seller, not the buyer. Consider hiring a buyer's agent who works for you, not for the seller.

- Get prices on other homes. Knowing the price of other homes in a neighborhood will help you avoid paying too much.
- Have the property inspected. Use a licensed home inspector to inspect the property carefully before you agree to buy it.
- Check to see if a particular home requires you to pay any ongoing homeowners association (HOA) or condo fees.

Mortgages

When shopping for a home mortgage, make sure you obtain all of the relevant information:

- Research current interest rates. Check the real estate section of your local newspaper, use the Internet, or call several lenders for information.
- Check the rates for 15-year, 20-year, and 30-year mortgages. You may be able to save thousands of dollars in interest charges by getting the shortest-term mortgage you can afford.
- Ask for details on the same loan amount, loan term, and type of loan from multiple lenders so you can compare the information. Be sure to get the APR, which takes into account not only the interest rate, but also points, broker fees, and other credit charges expressed as a yearly rate.
- Ask whether the rate is fixed or adjustable. The interest rate on adjustable-rate mortgages (ARMs) can vary a

great deal over the lifetime of the mortgage. An increase of several percentage points might raise payments by hundreds of dollars per month.

- If a loan has an adjustable-rate, ask when and how the rate and loan payment can change.
- Find out how much of a down payment is required. Some lenders require 20% of the home's purchase price as a down payment. But many lenders now offer loans that require less. In these cases, you may be required to purchase private mortgage insurance (PMI) to protect the lender if you fall behind on payments.
- If PMI is required, ask what the total cost of the insurance will be. How much will the monthly mortgage payment be when the PMI premium is added, and how long will you be required to carry PMI?
- Ask whether you can pay off the loan early, and whether there is a penalty for doing so.

There is a long list of sources for mortgage loans: mortgage banks, mortgage brokers, banks, thrifts and credit unions, home builders, real estate agencies, and Internet lenders.

Visit www.hud.gov for more information on home buying and mortgages. The Consumer Financial Protection Bureau's Owning a Home at www.consumerfinance.gov/owning-a-home is another resource.

Fixed-rate and adjustable-rate mortgages are the two main types of mortgages, but there is a wide variety of other mortgage products available. Below are pros and cons of some of the mortgage products you want to consider:

TYPE OF MORTGAGE	PROS	CONS
Adjustable-rate (ARM) or variable-rate mortgage	Usually offers a lower initial rate of interest than fixed-rate loans.	After an initial period, rates fluctuate over the life of the loan. When interest rates rise, generally so do your loan payments.
Balloon mortgage	Usually a fixed-rate loan with relatively low payments for a fixed period.	After an initial period, the entire balance of the loan is due immediately. This type of loan may be risky for some borrowers.
Federal Housing Administration (FHA) loans	Allows buyers who may not qualify for a home loan to obtain one with a low down payment.	The size of your loan may be limited.
Fixed-rate mortgage	No surprises. Interest rate stays the same over the entire term, usually 15, 20, or 30 years.	If interest rates fall, you could be stuck paying a higher rate.
Interest-only	Borrower pays only the interest on the loan in monthly payments for a fixed term.	After an initial period, the balance of the loan is due. This could mean higher payments, paying a lump sum, or refinancing.
Reverse mortgage	Allows seniors to convert equity in their homes to cash; you don't have to pay back the loan and interest as long as you live in the house.	The entire loan amount is due immediately once the borrower no longer resides in the home. This can cause problems for borrower's estate.
Veterans Administration (VA) loan	Guaranteed loans for eligible veterans, active duty personnel, and surviving spouses. Offers competitive rates, low or no down payments.	The size of your loan may be limited.

To contact an organization, use the directory beginning on page 60.

Mortgage Transfers

Mortgage companies must notify you when your loan is sold to another company. The rules ensure that you know who owns your loan, which is important information if you have questions or payment disputes or want to discuss loan modifications. Under these rules, the company that takes over your loan must send you a notice within 30 days of acquiring it. Even with a new loan owner, the company that "services" or handles your loan might not change, and you might continue to send your mortgage payments to the same address. If that loan servicer changes, you will receive a separate notice.

Read CFPB's overview of your rights at www.consumerfinance.gov/askcfpb/215/what-happens-if-my-servicer-changes-what-do-i-do.html.

MORTGAGE RULES TO PROTECT YOU

The Consumer Financial Protection Bureau (CFPB) created rules to ensure that you get a mortgage that you can afford. Some protections include:

Ability to Repay

- Lenders must verify your ability to pay back a mortgage. They may review your credit history, proof of your income and assets, your other debt and living expenses, and how much money you have left each month after paying your expenses.

- If you're applying for an adjustable-rate mortgage, your ability to repay must be based on the highest interest rate you would be charged, rather than teaser rates.

Increased Information

- You must receive appraisal reports at least 3 days before closing on the house.

- Once you have a mortgage, your servicer must send you a statement each billing cycle that shows your balance, the amount you have paid, how much of your payment went to the principal, interest, or escrow.

- Your servicer must inform you 2 months in advance of an interest rate increase.

High Cost Loans

- If you apply for a mortgage with high fees, points, or APR, you have additional consumer protections.

- A lender must inform you that you have a high cost loan and state all the fees and costs upfront.

- You must receive counseling from a housing counselor and certify to the lender that you received counseling about this high cost mortgage.

- Your lender is limited from charging some fees, like prepayment penalties, late fees that are more than 4% of your regular payment amount, or balloon payments due at the end of the loan.

Contact the Consumer Financial Protection Bureau (p. 89) for a more information on mortgage rules.

AVOID FORECLOSURE

If you miss your mortgage payments, foreclosure may occur. This is the legal means your lender can use to repossess your home. If you owe more than your property is worth, a deficiency judgment is pursued. A deficiency judgement would require you to pay the difference between the amount you owe and your home's value. Both foreclosures and deficiency judgments have a negative impact on your credit history.

These steps can help:

- Do not ignore letters from your lender. If you are having problems making your payments, call or write to your lender's Loss Mitigation Department immediately. Explain your situation. Be prepared to provide financial information, such as your monthly income and expenses. Without this information, the lender may not be able to help you.

- Stay in your home for now; you may not qualify for assistance if you abandon your property.

- Contact a HUD-approved housing counselor. Call 1-800-569-4287 or TDD 1-800-877-8339 for the housing counseling agency nearest you. These agencies are valuable resources.

- Contact Making Home Affordable for help. Call 1-888-995-4673, or 1-877-304-9709 for hearing-impaired homeowners, to talk to a HUD-approved credit counselor who will guide you through your options for free.

Beware of offers and sales pitches that target homeowners who are struggling to make mortgage payments. Additional advice, resources, and tips for homeowners can be found under Home Equity Loans (p. 17) and Homeowners and Renters Insurance (p. 31).

MOVING COMPANIES

Not all moving companies are the same. Although many are legitimate, some attempt to take advantage of their clients. Follow these guidelines to help you choose the right mover:

- Get a written estimate from several movers. Be wary of very low estimates. Some companies quote a low price to get a contract and later ask for more money before they will remove your belongings from their truck.

- Make sure the mover has an operating license. For moves from one state to another (inter-state), visit www.protectyourmove.gov to verify a mover's license. For moves within a state (intra-state), check your state, county, or local consumer affairs agency (p. 102).

- Make sure the mover has insurance. If furniture is damaged during the move, the mover's insurance should cover it. Ask how to file a complaint if there are limits to the coverage. Visit www.protectyourmove.gov/consumer/awareness/valuation/valuation-insurance.htm for more information about the levels of mover's insurance coverage.

MORTGAGE REFINANCING

Refinancing your mortgage can help you save money or make your monthly payments more affordable. Some factors that make it a good idea, include:

- A decrease in interest rates.
- A change in the length of your mortgage.
- A change in the type of mortgage (fixed-rate vs adjustable-rate).

Do some research before you decide to refinance.

- Research interest rates offered by several lenders to compare your options.
- Research options available through the Federal Housing Administration (FHA), Home Affordable Refinance Program (HARP), or your local housing agency.
- Read your current mortgage to see if there are any fees or penalties for early cancellation.
- Gather information about refinancing expenses: appraiser, broker fees, real estate attorney, changes in taxes. Determine if those expenses are greater than the benefits of refinancing.

For an overview, review the Federal Reserve's publication www.federalreserve.gov/pubs/refinancings/default.htm or consult a HUD certified housing counselor.

- Check the mover's record. Contact your state or local consumer protection agency (p. 102) or the Better Business Bureau (p. 63) to see whether there is a history of complaints.

If you have a dispute with a moving company, you can file a complaint with the Federal Motor Carrier Safety Administration by calling 1-888-368-7238 or by visiting www.fmcsa.dot.gov.

HOME IMPROVEMENT AND REPAIRS

Home improvements and repairs can cost thousands of dollars and are the subject of frequent complaints.

When selecting a contractor:

- Get recommendations and references. Talk to friends, family, and others who have used the contractor for similar work.
- Get at least three written estimates. Insist that contractors come to your home to evaluate what needs to be done. Be sure the estimates are based on the same work so you can make meaningful comparisons.
- Check contractor complaint records with your state or local consumer protection agency (p. 102) or the Better Business Bureau (p. 63).
- Make sure the contractor meets licensing and registration requirements. Your state or local consumer protection agency (p. 102) can help you determine the necessary requirements.

- Get the names of suppliers and ask them whether the contractor makes timely payments.
- Contact your local building inspection department to check for permit and inspection requirements. Be wary if the contractor asks you to get the permit; it could mean the firm is not licensed.
- Be sure your contractor is insured. The contractor should have personal liability, property damage, and workers' compensation insurance for workers and subcontractors.
- Insist on a written contract that states exactly what work will be done, the quality of materials that will be used, warranties, timetables, the names of any subcontractors, the total price of the job, and the schedule of payments.
- Try to limit your down payment. Some states have laws limiting the amount of down payment required.
- Understand your payment options. Compare the cost of getting your own loan versus contractor financing.
- Don't make a final payment or sign a final release until you are satisfied with the work and know that subcontractors and suppliers have been paid. Beware: some state laws allow unpaid subcontractors and suppliers to put a lien on your home for bills the contractor failed to pay.
- Pay by credit card when you can. You may have the right to withhold payment to the credit card company until problems are corrected (p. 14).

Be especially cautious if the contractor:

- Comes door-to-door or seeks you out.
- Happens to have material left over from a recent job.
- Offers you discounts for finding other customers.
- Quotes a price that is out of line with other estimates.
- Pressures you for an immediate decision.
- Can only be reached by leaving messages with an answering service.
- Has no physical address for the business.
- Has out-of-state license plates.
- Asks you to pay for the entire job up front.

With most home improvements, federal law gives you three business days to cancel without penalty. See the 3-Day Cooling-Off Rule (p. 4). You would be liable for any benefit already received. State laws may also provide some protection. And remember, if you finance home improvements with a home equity loan (p. 17) and do not make your payments, you could lose your home.

RENTING AND LEASING

A lease is an agreement that outlines the obligations of the owner and the tenants of a house or apartment. It is a legally binding document that courts will generally uphold in legal proceedings, so it is important for you to know the exact terms of the lease agreement before you sign it. Before agreeing to lease an apartment to you, a landlord may review your credit report, so you may want to get a copy before you start your apartment search. Some things to look for in a lease:

- Clauses that allow the landlord to change the terms of the lease after it is signed.

- Requirements and responsibilities of the tenants to do routine repairs such as lawn maintenance, cleaning, or notification about needed repairs.

- Restrictions that would prevent you from living normally or comfortably in the home.

- Terms of the lease and any important dates such as when the rent is due or garbage pickup days.

- Extra fees for parking spaces or storage, garbage collection, water, and pets.

- Information regarding utility providers, how to arrange for service, and whether the landlord or tenant is responsible for paying the bills (see Utilities, page 49).

Read the lease carefully and discuss anything you do not understand or any issues you might have. All landlord responsibilities should be stated clearly. Always get a copy of the signed lease to keep in your records. Any clause or terms in the agreement affects ALL parties who sign.

Check with the Better Business Bureau (p. 63) or your local consumer protection office (p. 102) to determine if your prospective landlord has any existing complaints from previous tenants.

The Fair Housing Act protects tenants who lease or rent property. If you think your rights have been violated, you may write a letter to, or call, the HUD office nearest you (p. 94). You have one year after the alleged violation to file a complaint with HUD, but you should file as soon as possible.

Each state has its own set of tenant rights, laws, and protections. For a state-by-state directory, visit www.hud.gov/local. You can also find available public housing at www.hud.gov. HUD (p. 94) offers several housing assistance programs for tenants and landlords as well as information on rights of residents and displaced tenants.

Take these steps and be prepared when you meet with a prospective landlord:

- Bring a completed rental application with you; written references from previous landlords, employers, friends, and colleagues; and a current copy of your credit report and rental history report (see Specialty Consumer Reports box, p. 39).

- Carefully review the lease before you sign.

- Get all promises in writing.

- Know your rights to live in a habitable rental unit—and don't give them up.

- Keep communication open with your landlord.

- Purchase renters insurance to cover your valuables. See more information under Homeowners and Renters Insurance (p. 31).

- Make sure the security deposit refund procedures are spelled out in your lease or rental agreement.

INSURANCE

Insurance protects you from financial loss in the event of a disaster or other hardship. By purchasing insurance policies, you can receive reimbursement for losses due to car accidents, property theft, natural disasters, medical expenses, and loss of income due to disability or death.

General sources of insurance information include the American Council of Life Insurers (p. 131), the Insurance Information Institute (p. 132), the National Association of Insurance Commissioners (p. 133), and your state insurance department (p. 119). You can also visit www.insure.com.

When buying any type of insurance (home, life, auto, rental, or other), you should:

- Find out whether your state insurance department (p. 119) offers any information concerning insurance companies and rates.

- Check several sources for the best deal. Try getting quotes online, but be aware that many online services may provide prices for just a few companies. An independent insurance agent who works with several insurers in your area may be able to get you a better deal.

- Make sure the insurance company is licensed and covered by the state's guaranty fund. The fund pays claims in case the company defaults. Your state insurance department (p. 119) can provide this information.

- Ask your insurance agent about discounts. You may be able to get a lower premium if you have safety features in your home, such as dead-bolt locks, smoke detectors, an alarm system, storm shutters, or fire-retardant roofing material. Similarly, you may save on car insurance based on the safety features, the number of miles you drive, your age (turning 25 or 50), your good grades (if you are a student) and/or your driving record (no moving vehicle violations or accidents in three years). You might also be able to get discounts if you are member of civic or alumni associations, or insure your vehicle and home with the same company.

- Consider a higher deductible. Increasing your deductible by just a few hundred dollars can make a big difference in your premiums.
- Check the financial stability and soundness of the insurance company. Ratings from A.M. Best (www.ambest.com), Standard & Poor's (www.standardandpoors.com), and Moody's Investors Service (www.moodys.com) are available online and at most public libraries.
- Research the complaint record of the company. Contact your state insurance department (p. 119), or visit the website of the National Association of Insurance Commissioners (www.naic.org), which has a database of complaints filed with state regulators.
- Find out what others think about the company's customer service. Consumers can rate homeowner insurance companies at www.jdpower.com/industry/insurance.
- Make sure you receive a written policy. This tells you that the agent forwarded your premium to the insurance company. If you do not receive a policy within 60 days, contact your agent and the insurance company.

PAY AS YOU GO CAR INSURANCE

Auto insurance companies' 'pay as you drive' policies allow you to only pay for the amount of insurance you actually need, based on your driving habits.

Most of these programs offer an initial discount for registering with the program. However, in order to participate, you may be required to install a device in your car that records your driving behavior and reports it to your insurer. These devices track activities such as the number of miles driven, frequency of use, and times of day that you drive. These factors are combined to determine your car insurance rates.

While the discounts can be helpful to your wallet, it is important to know the facts of what you are signing up for. Before using this type of policy ask:

- Are the advertised discount amounts guaranteed? If not, how widely do they vary?
- Can your insurer increase your rates based on your actual driving habits?
- How often will the rates change?
- Will the insurer use your driving data for other purposes than just setting your insurance rates? Will your data be sold to third parties?
- How will your privacy be protected?
- Does the device include a GPS? If so, how does your insurer protect and use that data?

If you suspect fraud, call the National Insurance Crime Bureau's hotline, 1-800-835-6422. Check out www. insurancefraud.org for more information.

AUTO INSURANCE

Every state requires that you carry minimum levels of auto insurance coverage, or the equivalent in financial responsibility waivers, to ensure that you can cover the cost of damages to people or property in the event of a car accident. Auto insurance requirements vary from state to state. Check with your state insurance regulator (p. 119) to learn more about individual requirements as well as insurers you may be considering for your policy.

There are multiple factors that can affect your car insurance rates, including:

- your gender
- your age
- marital status
- credit history
- the make and model of your car
- city and neighborhood where you live

To get the best coverage at the best price, get several quotes from insurance companies; it may save you hundreds of dollars a year. You could also raise your deductible on collision and comprehensive coverage. If you have an older car, you might want to drop this coverage altogether.

You can also find valuable information about car ownership in the cars section (p. 8), as well as information about insurance for rental cars (p. 12).

DISABILITY INSURANCE

Disability insurance helps you replace lost income, if you are unable to work due to sickness or injury. Many employers offer some type of disability insurance coverage for employees, or you can get an individual disability insurance policy. There are two types of disability policies: short-term disability (STD) and long-term disability (LTD). Short-term disability policies have a maximum benefit of two years, while long-term disability policies have benefits that can last the rest of your life.

When purchasing disability insurance, ask:

- **How is disability defined?** Some policies consider you disabled if you are unable to perform the duties of any job. Better plans pay benefits if you are unable to do the usual duties of your own occupation.
- **When do benefits begin?** Most plans have a waiting period after an illness before payments begin.
- **How long do benefits last?** After the waiting period, LTD payments are usually available until you reach age 65, though shorter or longer terms are also available.
- **What dollar amount is promised?** Can benefits be reduced by Social Security disability and workers' compensation payments? Are the benefits adjusted

for inflation? Will the policy provider continue making contributions to your pension plan so you have retirement benefits when the disability coverage ends?

Visit www.iii.org for more information.

HEALTH INSURANCE

Group Policies

Many consumers have health care coverage from their employers. Others have medical care paid through a government program such as Medicare (p. 92), Medicaid (p. 92), or the Veterans Health Administration (p. 97). You may also purchase health insurance through the Health Insurance Marketplace, at www.healthcare.gov.

If you have lost your group coverage from an employer as the result of unemployment, death, divorce, or loss of "dependent child" status, you may be able to continue your coverage temporarily under the Consolidated Omnibus Budget Reconciliation Act (COBRA). You, not the employer, pay for this coverage. When one of these events occur, you must be given at least 60 days to decide whether you wish to purchase the coverage.

Medicare and Medicaid

There are also health insurance programs for people who are seniors, disabled, or have low incomes.

- **Medicaid** provides health insurance for people with low incomes, children, and pregnant women. Eligibility is determined by your state.
- **Medicare** provides health insurance for people who are 65 years or older, some younger people with disabilities, and those with kidney failure.

Contact the Centers for Medicare & Medicaid Services (p. 92) for more information on benefits.

Most states also offer free or low-cost coverage for children who do not have health insurance. Visit www.insurekidsnow.gov or call 1-877-543-7669 for more information.

Health Care Plans

When purchasing health insurance, your choices typically will fall into one of three categories:

- **Traditional** fee-for-service health insurance plans are usually the most expensive choice, but they offer you the most flexibility in choosing health care providers.
- **Health maintenance organizations (HMOs)** offer lower co-payments and cover the costs of more preventive care, but your choice of health care providers is limited. The National Committee for Quality Assurance evaluates and accredits HMOs. You can find out whether one is accredited in your state by calling 1-888-275-7585. You can also get report cards on HMOs by visiting www.ncqa.org.
- **Preferred provider organizations (PPOs)** offer lower co-payments like HMOs, but give you more flexibility in selecting a health care provider. A PPO gives you a list of providers you can choose from.

If you go outside the HMO or PPO network of providers, you may have to pay a portion or all of the cost. When choosing among different health care plans, you will need to read the fine print and ask lots of questions, such as:

- Do I have the right to go to any doctor, hospital, clinic, or pharmacy I choose?
- Are specialists such as eye doctors and dentists covered?
- Does the plan cover special conditions or treatments such as pregnancy, psychiatric care, and physical therapy?
- Does the plan cover home care or nursing home care?
- Will the plan cover all medications my physician may prescribe?
- What are the deductibles? Are there any co-payments? Deductibles are the amount you must pay before your insurance company will pay a claim. These differ from co-payments, which are the amount of money you pay when you receive medical services or a prescription.
- What is the most I will have to pay out of my own pocket to cover expenses?
- If there is a dispute about a bill or service, how is it handled? In some plans, you may be required to have a third party decide how to settle the problem.

HOMEOWNERS AND RENTERS INSURANCE

Homeowners or renters insurance protects your personal property against damage or loss, and insures you in case someone gets hurt while on your property.

Homeowners or renters insurance may pay claims for:

- Damage to your home, garage, and other outbuildings.
- Loss of furniture and other personal property due to damage or theft.

BEWARE: WHEN COVERAGES COLLIDE

When a disaster strikes, your home may be damaged by several factors at the same time or one right after the other. You may think that your insurance policy will protect you, but that isn't always the case.

Many home insurance policies include an anti-concurrent causation clause. These clauses give your insurer the right to reject your claim if your home is damaged by several factors, such as wind and rain. If these two or more factors together cause damage to your home, your insurer may deny your entire claim because they can't determine which factor came first and actually caused the damage. You can face a serious shock if you thought your policy protected you from such disaster.

Before disaster strikes, read your home insurance policy closely for anti-concurrent causation clauses. Ask your agent if you may opt out of that clause or pay an increased premium to have full coverage.

SHARING SERVICES, SHARED RISKS

The sharing economy is popular. You may rent out your home, drive others around in your personal cars, or use car sharing services. Your insurance policy may limit your protection for accidents or damages that happen in these transactions.

Before you rent your home or drive your car as a service, ask your insurance company if you need to add to your policy, since you will be using your personal property for commercial purposes. Also, the shared service company may offer insurance coverage for damages or injuries.

Contact the home or car sharing service to find out if you are protected in the case of injury or theft. Also contact your own insurance company to understand your coverage options.

- Additional living expenses if you rent temporary quarters while your house is being repaired.

Homeowners or renters insurance may also:

- Include liability for bodily injury and property damage that you cause to others through negligence.
- Include liability for accidents happening in and around your home, as well as away from home, for which you are responsible.
- Pay for injuries occurring in and around your home to anyone other than you or your family.
- Provide limited coverage for money, gold, jewelry, and stamp and coin collections.
- Cover personal property in storage or away in dorm rooms.

Keep these tips in mind when shopping for homeowners insurance:

- Insure your house, not the land under it. If you don't subtract the value of the land when deciding how much homeowners insurance to buy, you will pay more than you should.
- Make certain you purchase enough coverage to replace what is insured. "Replacement" coverage gives you the money to rebuild your home and replace its contents. An "Actual Cash Value" policy is cheaper but pays the difference between your property's worth at the time of loss minus depreciation for age and wear.
- Ask about any special coverage you might need. You may have to pay extra for computers, cameras, jewelry, art, antiques, musical instruments, or stamp collections.
- Remember that flood and earthquake damage are not covered by a standard homeowners policy. The cost of a separate earthquake policy will depend on the likelihood of earthquakes in your area. Homeowners who live in areas prone to flooding should take advantage of the National Flood Insurance Program (p. 94).
- If you are a renter, do not assume your landlord carries insurance on your personal belongings. Purchase a separate policy for renters.

PROTECT YOUR PROPERTY IN STORAGE

Storage units are a common way to store items that you do not have room for or use infrequently. Take these steps to protect your possessions from theft and damage:

- **Get insurance.** Contact your insurance provider to find out whether or not the contents of your storage unit are covered under your homeowner policy. If so, ask if there is a monetary limit for the coverage. Is the coverage for the depreciated cash value or the replacement value? The storage company may also offer insurance policies.

- **Maintain an inventory.** Use an online home inventory system, such as the Insurance Information Institute's "Know Your Stuff" tool (www.knowyourstuff.org), to keep track of the items in your storage unit.

- **Be selective.** Avoid keeping documents with your personal information (social security numbers, birthdates) that can be stolen and used by ID thieves. Keep important documents in a place with more controlled access.

LIFE INSURANCE

A life insurance policy is a contract between you and an insurance company. The contract states that you will pay premiums over time, and, in exchange, the company will pay a lump sum amount upon your death to a designated beneficiary. The proceeds from your life insurance policy can help pay bills and help support your surviving family members' living expenses.

There are two main types of life insurance policies:

- Whole (or universal) life insurance policies are considered permanent. As long as you pay the premium, the policy is in effect. Whole life insurance policies also have an investment or savings component. This means that you accumulate cash value over the life of the policy, so you can borrow money from these policies if you need to.

- Term life insurance policies are in effect for a certain period of time, or term. If you have this type of policy and pass away during the policy's term then the insurance company will pay a benefit. If you live past the time that the policy is in effect, the insurance company won't pay a benefit or give you a refund.

Term life insurance policies are usually less expensive than whole life insurance policies. This is because term life insurance policies only cover a set amount of time, while whole life insurance policies are intended to be permanent and because part of your premium is put away for savings.

If you have misplaced a life insurance policy, your state's insurance commission may be able to help you locate it. Or you can search for it at www.policylocator.org. If the insurance company knows that an insured person has died, but cannot locate the beneficiaries, the company must turn the benefits over to the state's unclaimed property office.

Check with that office at www.unclaimed.org if you believe that you are due a benefit.

Avoid losing your life insurance policy benefits by alerting the policy beneficiaries and filing a copy with your will.

LONG-TERM CARE INSURANCE

Medical advances have resulted in greater need for nursing home care and assisted-living. Most health insurance plans and Medicare severely limit or exclude long-term care. You should consider these costs as you plan for your retirement.

Here are some questions to ask when considering a separate long-term care insurance policy:

- **What qualifies you for benefits?** Some insurers say you must be unable to perform a specific number of the following activities of daily living: eating, walking, getting from bed to a chair, dressing, bathing, using the restroom, and remaining continent.

- **What type of care is covered?** Does the policy cover nursing home care? What about coverage for assisted-living facilities that provide less client care than a nursing home? If you want to stay in your home, will it pay for care provided by visiting nurses and therapists? What about help with food preparation and housecleaning?

- **What will the benefit amount be?** Most plans are written to provide a specific dollar benefit per day. The benefit for home care is usually about half the nursing home benefit, but some policies pay the same for both forms of care. Other plans pay only for your actual expenses.

- **What is the benefit period?** It is possible to get a policy with lifetime benefits, but this can be very expensive. Other options for coverage are from one to six years. The average nursing home stay is about 2.5 years.

- **Is the benefit adjusted for inflation?** If you buy a policy before age 60, you face the risk that a fixed daily benefit will not be enough by the time you need it.

- **Is there a waiting period before benefits begin?** A 20 to 100-day period is not unusual.

Visit www.longtermcare.gov for more information.

OTHER INSURANCE

- **Catastrophic Health Care Insurance.** A health plan that only covers certain types of expensive care, like hospitalizations.

- **College Tuition insurance.** Get a refund of college tuition if you must withdraw because of a serious injury or illness.

- **Dental and Vision Insurance.** Some companies that offer health insurance plans may also allow employees to purchase separate dental and vision plans, which are not part of most standard health plans.

- **Identity Theft Insurance.** This type of insurance provides reimbursement to crime victims for the cost of restoring their identity and repairing credit reports. This insurance may be part of your homeowner insurance policy or as a stand-alone policy.

- **International Health Care Insurance.** A policy that provides health coverage no matter where you are in the world. The policy term is flexible, so you can purchase it only for the time you will be out of the country.

- **Liability Insurance.** Insurance for what the policyholder is legally obligated to pay because of bodily injury or property damage caused to another person.

- **Shared Services Insurance.** Find out what insurance you need if you rent your home out or use your car to drive others for a fee.

- **Travel Insurance.** There are four kinds of travel insurance: Travel Cancellation Insurance, Baggage or Personal Effects Coverage, Emergency Medical Coverage, and Accidental Death. Visit www.insuremytrip.com to learn more. See page 14 for travel insurance perks provided by your credit card issuer.

- **Umbrella Insurance.** A policy that supplements the insurance you already have for home, auto, and other personal property. Umbrella insurance can help cover costs that exceed the limits of other policies.

Contact your current insurance provider or state insurance commission for more information on these insurance policies.

INVESTING

If you have a financial goal in mind, such as saving for retirement, paying for college, or buying a new house, then you may decide to invest your money to earn enough to fund your goals. Before you invest, make sure you have answers to all of these questions:

- **How quickly can you get your money back?** Stocks, bonds, and shares in mutual funds usually can be sold at any time, but there is no guarantee you will get back all the money you invested. Other investments, such as limited partnerships, certificates of deposit (CDs), or IRAs, often restrict your ability to cash out your holdings.

- **What can you expect to earn on your money?** While bonds generally promise a fixed return, earnings on most other securities go up and down with market changes. Keep in mind that just because an investment has done well in the past, there is no guarantee it will do well in the future.

- **What type of earnings can you expect?** Will you get income in the form of interest, dividends, or rent? Some investments, such as stocks and real estate, have the potential for earnings and growth in value. What is the potential for earnings over time?

- **How much risk is involved?** With any investment, there is always the risk that you will not get your money back or the earnings promised. There is usually a trade-off between risk and reward—the higher the potential return, the greater the risk. While the federal government backs U.S. Treasury securities, it does not protect against loss on any other investments.

- **Are your investments diversified?** Some investments perform better than others in certain situations. For example, when interest rates go up, bond prices tend to go down. One industry may struggle while another prospers. Putting your money in a variety of investment options can reduce your risk.

- **Are there any tax advantages to a particular investment?** U.S. Savings Bonds are exempt from state and local taxes. Municipal bonds are exempt from federal income tax and, sometimes, state income tax as well. Tax-deferred investments for special goals, such as paying for college and retirement, are available that let you postpone or even avoid paying income taxes.

Check out the Securities and Exchange Commission's (SEC's) website, www.investor.gov for more information about investing. Be sure to note specific tips at www.investor.gov/Saving-and-Investing. The SEC requires public companies to disclose financial and other information to help you make sound decisions. View the text of these files at www.sec.gov/edgar.shtml. Contact the SEC's Investor Information Service at 1-800-732-0330 to ask your investment related questions, get alerts, and learn how to file a complaint.

TYPE OF INVESTMENT	WHAT IS IT?	RISK LEVEL
Bonds and Bond Funds	Also known as fixed-income securities because the income they pay is fixed when the bond is sold. Bonds and bond funds invest in corporate or government debt obligations.	Low risk.
Commodities	Physical commodities, such as an agricultural product (grains) or a natural resource (like gold). A futures contract is an agreement to purchase or sell a commodity for delivery in the future.	High risk.
Index Funds	Invest in a particular market index such as the S&P 500 or the Russell 2000. An index fund is managed passively and mirrors the performance of the designated stock or bond index.	Risk level depends on which index the fund uses. A bond index fund involves a lower risk level than an index fund of emerging markets overseas.
Market-linked CDs (or structured CDs)	Returns are linked to the future performance of a market index and may include stocks, bonds, foreign currency, or other assets. These are designed for long-term commitment (up to 20 years).	Medium to high risk.
Money Market Funds	Mutual funds that invest in short-term bonds. Usually pay better interest rates than a savings account but not as much as a certificate of deposit (CD).	Low risk.
Mutual Funds	Invest in a variety of securities, which may include stocks, bonds, and/or money market securities. Costs and objectives vary.	Risk levels vary according to the holdings in the mutual fund.
Roth IRA	A personal savings plan where earnings that remain in the account are not taxed. Investments may include a variety of securities. Contributions are not tax-deductible.	Risk levels vary according to the holdings in the IRA.
Stocks	Stocks represent a share of a company. As the company's value rises or falls, so does the value of the stock.	Medium to high risk.
Traditional IRA	Traditional IRA is a personal savings plan that gives tax advantages for savings for retirement. Investments may include a variety of securities. Contributions may be tax-deductible; earnings are not taxed until distributed.	Risk levels vary according to the holdings in the IRA.

BEWARE: VIRTUAL CURRENCIES

Virtual currencies, a type of electronic money, are created through online mining or purchased on exchanges. The money is stored in a virtual wallet and can be used to transfer money to friends, make purchases, or to invest in exchanges. Investing in virtual currency comes with additional risks that you don't have to worry about with cash, credit and debit cards, or regular stocks, such as:

- **Fluctuating value.** The value of virtual currencies can change drastically, even in just one day.

- **Currency exchanges.** Virtual currency exchanges can shut down at any time, without notice to investors. If this happens, it would be very difficult to get your money back.

- **No link to other currencies.** The values of virtual currencies are not tied to the value of any country's currency or banking system.

- **Unregulated.** There are no regulations in place to protect investors. The currencies, the issuers, and exchanges, are not regulated by any government and the funds are not insured from loss, if the exchange shuts down or the value plummets.

- **Hackers.** The virtual wallets, which are stored on your computer, are targets for hackers.

- **High risk for fraud.** Scammers target investors with promises of high returns, fake opportunities, and other schemes. If fraud or theft happens, you have limited recovery options.

All virtual currency exchanges and kiosks (like an ATM for virtual currencies) must register with the Department of Treasury. Look up virtual currency companies, exchanges, and kiosks in the Department of Treasury's database at www.fincen.gov/financial_institutions/msb/msbstateselector.html.

The SEC (p. 99) or the National Association of Attorneys General (p. 133) have more information on this topic. Contact the CFPB (p. 89) to file a complaint about these virtual currencies.

The Financial Industry Regulatory Authority (FINRA) also provides up-to-date market data and information for a wide range of stocks, bonds, mutual funds, and other securities through its Market Data Center at www.finra.org/marketdata.

The following companies rate the financial condition of corporations and municipalities issuing bonds. Their ratings are available online and at many public libraries:

- Standard & Poor's (www.standardandpoors.com)
- Moody's Investors Service (www.moodys.com)

For ratings of mutual funds, consult personal finance magazines.

FINANCIAL BROKERS AND ADVISORS

A financial professional can have multiple titles and be authorized to provide multiple services, including investment, financial planning, and insurance products. Keep in mind that a professional title is not the same as a license. When researching a financial professional, find out what the titles and licenses mean, as well as the educational, work experience, and ethical requirements. Check FINRA's Investment Professional tool at www.finra.org/Investors/ToolsCalculators/ProfessionalDesignations to understand the designations and the organizations that offer them. Remember, that the SEC, FINRA, and state regulators do not grant or endorse any professional titles.

When selecting a broker or investment advisor, research the person's education and professional history as well as the firm the person works for. Ask:

- Has the person worked with others who have circumstances similar to yours?

- Is the person licensed in your state? Your state securities regulator (p. 123) lists individuals and firms that are registered in your state. Ask whether the regulatory office has any other background information. You can find out how to reach your state securities regulator by visiting www.nasaa.org.

- Has the person had any run-ins with regulators or received serious complaints from investors? Call your local state securities regulator or the SEC (p. 99). Check out www.finra.org/brokercheck to find licensing, employment, and disciplinary information.

- How is the person paid? Is it an hourly rate, a flat fee, or a commission that depends on the investments you make? Does the person get a bonus from his or her firm for selling you a particular product?

- What are the fees for setting up and servicing your account?

Additional organizations that could be helpful are:

- The Commodity Futures Trading Commission (CFTC) offers free tools to check the background of financial professionals and stay informed on the latest fraud schemes at www.smartcheck.cftc.gov. The CFTC oversees the Reparations Program that resolves disputes between commodity customers and commodity professionals. Contact the CFTC (p. 99) to ask a question, report information, or submit a complaint.

- Both the North American Securities Administrators Association and the National Futures Association (p. 133) can offer helpful information.

- FINRA (p. 132) provides a dispute resolution program among investors, brokers, and brokerage firms.

BEWARE: AFFINITY FRAUD

Affinity frauds are investment scams that target specific groups, such as the elderly, religious, or ethnic communities. The investment promoters often are (or pretend to be) members of the group.

Affinity fraud usually involves either a fake investment or an investment where the scammer lies about the investment's risk of loss, earnings or historical performance. Many affinity frauds are Ponzi or pyramid schemes.

Take these steps to avoid being a victim of affinity fraud:

- Research the investment opportunity, separately from the information the promoter provides.
- Verify that the promoter is licensed with the SEC (p. 99) and your state's securities administrator (p. 123).
- Beware of promises of spectacular profits or "guaranteed" returns, with little risk.

Contact the SEC (p. 99) or your state's securities administrator (p. 123) if you have questions about investments or to file a complaint about investment fraud.

- SaveAndInvest.org offers unbiased information and strategies to help you avoid investment fraud.

INVESTING IN GOLD AND COMMODITIES

Some financial experts recommend buying precious metals as part of a balanced portfolio. Some suggest buying only a small amount because values can drastically fluctuate, while others recommend larger investments.

There are a number of ways to invest in precious metals; common ones include bullion, certificates, and coins. Most people depend on an investment advisor or company to help them choose. Make sure the person and company you choose is licensed with a government agency. If you are considering investing in coins, check the U.S. Mint website at www.usmint.gov. Before you purchase coins or coin-related products, research the seller with your state consumer protection office (p. 102) or the Better Business Bureau (p. 63).

Trading in commodity futures is different from investing. Commodity futures are an agreement to buy or sell a specific quantity of a variety of commodities such as precious metals, grains, or other natural resources. Trading commodity futures and options is a volatile, complex and risky venture that is rarely suitable for individual investors or "retail customers." Before participating in the commodities market, check the registration status and background of the person and company at www.nfa.futures.org/basicnet. Anyone who trades or gives advice to the public about futures must be registered with the National Futures Association (p. 133). The CFTC also provides additional information about how to protect yourself before and during trading in the commodities and options markets at www.cftc.gov/ConsumerProtection.

RETIREMENT PLANNING

As you approach retirement, there are many factors to consider. Experts advise that you will need about 80% of your pre-retirement income in your retirement years. The exact amount, of course, depends on your individual needs. For example:

- At what age do you plan to retire?
- Will your spouse or partner retire when you do?
- Where do you plan to live? Will you downsize, own, or rent your home?
- Do you expect to work part time?

CROWDFUNDING

Crowdfunding is a way for companies, entrepreneurs, or artists to raise money to complete a project. After setting a fundraising goal and deadline to reach that goal, the creator markets the campaign to potential backers, or investors. There are several websites that help connect creators with backers. While fundraising websites conduct a background check on the company, you should still do your own research before contributing:

- **Research the company.** Is there any information available about the product or service they want to offer? Are there complaints related to the company or campaign creator with the state attorneys' general about fraud?
- **Type of campaign.** Is the campaign an "all or nothing" or "flexible funding"? If it is an "all or nothing" campaign, the creator only gets the money that has been pledged if they reach their fundraising goal. If the campaign is a "flexible funding" campaign, the creator will receive all the donations, even if they did not reach the fundraising goal.
- **Timing of payments.** Does the fundraising website charge your credit card immediately after you pledge your support or wait until the funding deadline has arrived?
- **Additional fees.** Does the fundraising platform charge backers additional credit card processing fees?
- **Rewards.** What rewards, or returns, will you receive in exchange for your investment? Do you get to pre-order the product that the company is producing? Are there different rewards, based on how much you invested?
- **Ownership control.** If you invest, do you have an ownership stake or any control in the project?
- **Refunds.** Are you able to get a refund if the company does not reach their fundraising goal or complete the project? If so, do you need to get the refund from the website or directly from the campaign creator?

- Will you have the same medical insurance you had while working? Will coverage change?
- Do you want to travel or pursue a new hobby that might be costly?
- If you have a financial advisor, talk to him or her about your plans.

In addition to planning to maintain your lifestyle during retirement, you may need to purchase long-term health insurance (p. 33) or to pay for assisted-living services (p. 24).

For more information go to:

- AARP (www.aarp.org)
- American Savings Education Council (www.asec.org)
- Certified Financial Planner Board of Standards (www.cfp.net)
- Investopedia (www.investopedia.com/university/retirement)
- U.S. Department of Labor: (www.dol.gov/ebsa)
- The Investor's Clearinghouse (www.investoreducation.org)
- MyMoney.gov (www.mymoney.gov)
- MyRA (www.MyRA.treasury.gov)
- Securities and Exchange Commission (www.sec.gov or www.investor.gov)
- Social Security Administration (www.socialsecurity.gov)

PRIVACY AND IDENTITY THEFT

Your personal information is a valuable resource for identity thieves, scammers, and even to corporations. Data breaches of customer databases and payment processing systems at retailers highlight the importance of protecting your privacy, and making sure companies with which you do business do the same.

Identity thieves steal your personal information to commit fraud. They can damage your credit status and cost you time and money to restore your good name. You may not know that you are the victim of ID theft until you experience a financial consequence (mystery bills, credit collections, denied loans) down the road from actions that the thief has taken with your ID. Follow these tips to protect yourself:

BEWARE: SYNTHETIC ID THEFT

Synthetic identity theft is a new version of identity theft. In traditional ID theft, the thief steals all of the personal information of one person to create a new identity. However, with synthetic ID theft, a thief steals pieces of information from different people to create a new identity. For example, the thief may steal one person's social security number, combine it with another person's name, and use someone else's address to create a brand new identity. The thief can then use this fraudulent identity to apply for credit, rent an apartments, or make major purchases.

Unfortunately, synthetic ID theft is difficult to detect because the fraud isn't directly tied to just one person. Fraud alerts and monitoring services would not be able to stop or prevent these scams. Also, children's social security numbers are often targeted in these frauds, because no one would be checking their credit scores until they are much older.

While you cannot prevent synthetic ID theft, you should still get copies of your credit report to check for accounts you did not open. Also, contact the credit reporting agencies to ask if there is a fragmented file (a sub-account that uses your social security number but not your name) attached to your main credit file. If this is the case, you may be the victim of synthetic identity theft. Report all cases of identity theft to the Federal Trade Commission (p. 98).

- **Secure your Social Security card.** Don't carry it in your wallet or write your number on your checks. Only give out your social security number (SSN) when absolutely necessary.
- **Protect your PIN.** Never write a PIN on a credit or debit card or on a slip of paper kept in your wallet.
- **Watch out for "shoulder surfers."** Shield the keypad when typing your passwords on computers and at ATMs.
- **Be skeptical.** Don't respond to unsolicited requests for personal information (your name, birthdate, social security number, or bank account number) by phone, mail, or online.
- **Collect mail promptly.** Ask the post office to put your mail on hold when you are away from home for more than a day or two.
- **Pay attention to your billing cycles.** If bills or financial statements are late, contact the sender.
- **Keep your receipts.** Ask for carbons and incorrect charge slips as well. Promptly compare receipts with account statements. Watch for unauthorized transactions.

PRIVACY AND IDENTITY THEFT

SPEAR PHISHING

"Spear phishing" is another version of phishing where the scammer already has some of your personal information, often a result of hacking another company's network. The scammer will then send you an urgent email that seems to be from a company that you already do business. The message will require you to click on a link that directs you to a fake, but realistic, webpage to confirm an account number, or install malware on your computer. Remember, legitimate companies never ask for your password or account number via email. If you are not sure whether the email is trustworthy, call the company directly and forward the email to spam@uce.gov.

- **Tear up or shred** unwanted receipts, credit offers, account statements, and expired cards, to prevent "dumpster divers" (p. 7) from getting your personal information.
- **Store personal information in a safe place** at home and at work.
- **Install firewalls** and virus-detection software on your home computer.
- **Create complex passwords** that identity thieves cannot guess easily.
- **Order your credit report once a year.** Check it more frequently if you suspect someone has gained access to your account information. See "Order Your Free Credit Reports" (p. 15).

REPORT IDENTITY THEFT

If you are a victim of identity theft, follow these steps:

- **Report it to your financial institutions.** Call the phone number on your account statement or on the back of your credit or debit card.
- **Report the fraud to your local police.** Keep a copy of the police report, which will make it easier to prove your case to creditors and retailers.
- **Contact the credit reporting agencies** (p. 14) and ask them to flag your account with a fraud alert, which asks merchants not to grant new credit without your approval.

The Federal Trade Commission recommends that you create an ID theft report, if your ID is stolen. This report will help you deal with the credit reporting agencies and companies that extended credit to the identity thief using your name. First, report the crime to the FTC and print a copy of the details. This detailed report is also called an ID theft affidavit. Then file the crime with your local police department; get a copy of that report. Together, your ID theft affidavit and your police report make up your ID theft report. Visit www.consumer.ftc.gov/articles/0277-create-identity-theft-report for more information about creating an ID theft report. You can file your complaint with the FTC at www.ftccomplaintassistant.gov or by calling toll free 1-877-438-4338.

PROTECT YOUR PRIVACY

Your personal data is always being shared. Companies, known as data brokers, compile information about your income, family size, email addresses, stores and websites you visit, the brands you buy, credit cards used, hobbies, and your demographic information to create a profile about you and your lifestyle. Some of the information you give willingly, but other bits of your personal information are collected in ways you may not realize. Data brokers often collect location-based data from the GPS on your mobile phone, the fitness tracking bracelets you wear, or from certain apps. These brokers then analyze all your information, develop scoring and models to help them understand your behavior, and sell thes consumer profiles to retailers and marketers.

Retailers use your information to offer targeted special promotions, customize the ads you see, and even the prices you are charged for items. While this can be a bonus and help you get good deals, it all comes at the cost of your personal privacy. Unlike credit reports or scores, you cannot access or review the data files that have been created about you, or even know the data brokerage companies you should contact to correct inaccuracies. These data reports can also result in discrimination, where some consumers are only targeted with high interest loans or inferior financial products. Take these steps to protect your privacy:

- If you apply for store loyalty cards, do not your include your full name so that it, and your purchase behavior, cannot be connected to your other consumer profiles.
- If you want to keep your purchase behavior private, consider using cash rather than electronic payment options.
- Maintain a separate email address for your coupons and promotions from retailers.
- Be careful about what you post on social media. Data brokers may scrape information you post to enhance the information that they have in your consumer profile.
- Disable cookies when shopping online, to prevent companies from tracking your online browsing behavior.
- Beware of using cell phones in stores or using the public Wi-Fi in a store. By using these networks, stores may know which items you looked at and which aisles you visited.
- Look for privacy statements on websites, sales materials, and forms you fill out. If a website claims to follow a set of established voluntary standards, read the standards. Don't assume it provides the level of privacy you want.
- Ask how your personal information will be stored and used.
- Only provide the purchase date, model and serial numbers, and your contact information on warranty registration forms.
- Opt-out if you do not want the company to share your email address with other companies.

Check with your state or local consumer agency (p. 102) to find out whether any state laws help protect your privacy.

Some companies and industry groups have also adopted voluntary policies that address privacy concerns.

FINANCIAL PRIVACY

The Federal Deposit Insurance Corporation (p. 98) and other federal regulators require banks, insurance companies, brokerage firms, and certain businesses that share financial information to inform you of their privacy policies. They must give you this information when you open an account and at least once every year. This includes:

- The kinds of information being collected.
- How the confidentiality and security of your information will be protected.
- What types of businesses may be provided this information.

If a business is going to share the information with anyone outside its corporate family, it must also give you the chance to "opt-out" or say "no" to information sharing. Even if you do not opt-out, your account numbers may not be shared with third parties for marketing purposes.

You cannot prevent certain types of information from being shared, including information needed to conduct normal business or protect against fraud, or information that is already publicly available. Also, a bank can share your information with a partner company to market products.

Your credit information has additional privacy protections under the Fair Credit Reporting Act. Only people with a legitimate business need can get a copy of your report. An employer can only get your report with your written consent. See Credit Reports and Scores on page 14 for more information on your rights under this federal law, and to find out how you can get a copy of your credit reports.

SPECIALTY CONSUMER REPORTS

Credit reports are not the only reports that you can get for free (see "Order Your Free Credit Reports", page 15). The same law that allows you to get a free credit report each year also allows you to get a copy of specialty consumer reports. Just as Equifax, Experian, and TransUnion collect your credit information, there are other consumer reporting agencies that collect information about your medical, insurance, rental, tenant, and alternative credit histories.

Since there is no centralized place to order these reports, you must contact each agency individually. If you find a mistake on your report, you have the right to correct it.

Visit files.consumerfinance.gov/f/201207_cfpb_list_consumer-reporting-agencies.pdf, for a list of specialty consumer agencies. If you need to file a complaint about a consumer reporting agency, contact the Consumer Financial Protection Bureau (p. 89).

ID THEFT

Here are some common schemes that ID thieves use to steal your identity.

Telemarketing. An ID thief may call, making fraudulent offers for products, benefits or medical services. The caller will require you to provide personal information, such as your social security number, birth date, or Medicare ID number.

Tax ID theft. Phony tax preparers steal your social security number and sell it to scammers. For more information contact the IRS' Taxpayer Advocate Service at 1-877-275-8271 or visit www.irs.gov/uac/Taxpayer-Advocate-Service-6.

Medical ID theft. Medical service providers can take advantage of access to your insurance information to get medical services in your name, or to issue fraudulent billing to you and your health insurer.

Child ID theft. Children's IDs are vulnerable because children don't need to file taxes or use their social security numbers to apply for loans for many years. By the time they are adults, the damage has already been done.

Follow the steps listed in "Reporting Identity Theft" (p. 38) to report ID theft.

MEDICAL PRIVACY

Personal information you give to your doctor is shared with insurance companies, pharmacies, researchers, and employers based on specific regulations. The privacy of your health records is protected by federal law, specifically under the Health Insurance Portability and Accountability Act, also known as HIPAA. The Act:

- Defines your rights over your health information.
- Sets rules and limits on who is allowed to receive and/or see your health information.

The Department of Health and Human Services, Office for Civil Rights (p. 91) is a resource for complete details and advice about the HIPAA ruling. The Office for Civil Rights also provides a listing of resources for consumers, providers, and advocates, along with fact sheets and other educational materials.

You can request a copy of your medical records from your medical provider or from the hospital where medical services were provided, for a fee.

If you believe that a person, agency, or organization covered under the HIPAA Privacy Rule violated your health information privacy rights or committed another violation of the Privacy Rule, file a written complaint with the Department of Health and Human Services, Office for Civil Rights (p. 91).

Visit the U.S. Department of Health and Human Services, Office for Civil Rights website at www.hhs.gov/ocr/privacy

BEWARE: FARCING

A primary component of using social media is connecting with friends. Unfortunately, scammers are taking advantage of this in order to steal your identity. Known as "farcing", these scams start when you receive a friend request from someone who supposedly shares mutual friends with you. Once you accept the request the scammers search your online profile to collect personal data about you, such as your hometown, schools you attended, employers, siblings, and vacation spots. They often go a step further by contacting you directly through the site's direct messaging feature to ask more questions about you, based on the information you've already posted. After you have accepted their request, they continue their scheme by sending friend requests to your friends, and then their friends.

Take these steps to protect your social media identity:

- Use the privacy settings on social media websites to manage who can access your profile.

- If you get a friend request from someone you don't know, don't accept it. If you are interested in accepting it, ask the mutual friends that you supposedly have in common who the person is. If they can't give you definite answers about the person, ignore the request.

- Be cautious if you receive direct messages from new friends that request details or your personal information.

- Notify the website if your profile has been hacked or images have been stolen.

Visit www.OnguardOnline.gov for more online safety tips.

for more information on how the federal government protects your personal health information.

ONLINE PRIVACY

In addition to following the general advice on protecting your privacy, make sure you only use websites with acceptable privacy policies.

- Look for a privacy policy statement or seal that indicates the site abides by privacy standards. Take the time to read how your privacy is protected.

- Look for signals that you are using a secure web page. A secure site encrypts or scrambles personal information so it cannot be intercepted easily. Signs include a screen notice that says you are on a secure site, a closed padlock or unbroken key in the bottom corner of your screen, or a change in the first letters of the Internet address you are viewing from "http" to "https."

Another threat to your privacy is spyware, software that is secretly installed when you download games, music, and other applications. Spyware sends information about your online activities to a third party, usually to target you with pop-up ads. You can install anti-spyware software to stop this threat to your privacy. See the Internet section on page 40 for more information.

TELECOMMUNICATIONS

Choices for phone service, Internet, and television have never been greater. As devices have multiple functions, such as the ability to watch television shows on your computer or surf the Internet using your phone, your decisions about each of these services may overlap. Most consumers are now able to bundle phone, TV, and Internet service for a discount; however, buying a bundle of services could make it more difficult to change providers for any one service if you are tied into a long-term contract. Before you buy, it is important to compare service providers and options to make sure you are getting what you want, as well as the best deal possible to meet your needs.

INTERNET

Choosing Service Providers

To connect your computer to the Internet, you will need an Internet Service Provider (ISP). Some companies limit their service to providing Internet access only. Others, such as a telephone or cable company, may offer Internet access as part of a larger package of services.

Consider these factors when selecting a provider:

- **Speed.** If you only want to check email and view web pages, a dial-up connection may be enough. But if you want to download music or television shows, or watch videos, you will need a faster connection with broadband access, such as a digital subscriber line (DSL), cable modem, or satellite.

- **Availability.** Which companies offer service in your area?

- **Wireless access.** Can you get a wireless connection for other computers in your home?

- **Email.** Do email accounts come with the service? What will be the storage limit on your mailbox?

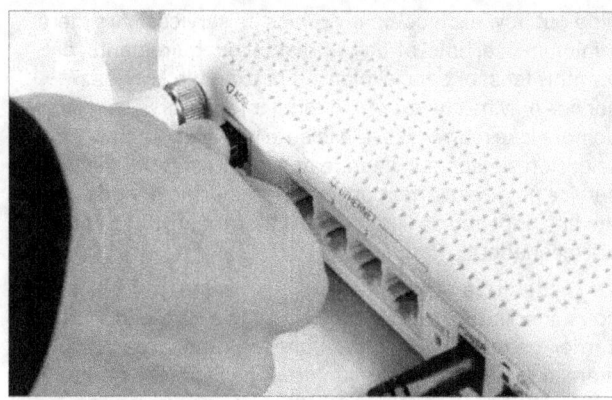

- **Software**. Is any software required to activate the service?

- **Support**. What kinds of support are available—phone, email, chat? Is the support free?

- **Special features**. What services are provided for spam blocking, virus protection, instant messaging, and chat rooms?

- **Terms of service**. Is there a limit to the amount of data you can use per month?

- **Cost**. What is the monthly fee for the service? Are there fees for renting a modem or set up?

Wi-Fi (Wireless)

Going wireless provides you with the freedom to use your computer in multiple locations. However, with this increased freedom comes the danger of increased vulnerability. Wireless Internet requires that you have access to a wireless network via a wireless router. It is important that you secure your network so strangers (or neighbors) cannot use your network without your knowledge (also known as "piggybacking"). Also, computer hackers could use your network to access personal information you save on, or send from, your computer. This is particularly important if you conduct financial transactions online. If you use the wireless (Wi-Fi) network at bookstores, airports, coffee shops, or other public places, there are other precautions you should take to protect your privacy.

At home:

- **Turn on encryption.** When you buy a wireless router, it is important to turn on the encryption feature. This scrambles information that you send over the Internet so other people cannot access it.

- **Rename your router.** Change the name from the manufacturer's default name to something only you would know.

- **Change the password.** Routers come with a standard password. Create a new one with a mix of letters, numbers, and special characters.

- **Turn off your router** when you are not using it.

- **Be aware of cookies.** Cookies are small text files that some websites place on your computer to collect information about the pages you view and your activities on the site. They also allow the site to recognize you when you return. Visit www.ftc.gov/ftc/cookies.shtm for more information.

On public wireless networks:

- **Don't assume the network is secure.** Most public wireless networks do not encrypt information you send. Avoid sending private information from public locations. Or, consider using a virtual private network (VPN) to secure information you send via public networks.

- **Use encrypted websites.** If you must send sensitive information from a public network, make certain that URL starts with "https" ("s" means secure). Look for that on every page you visit.

- **Log off** sites after you finish using them rather than using "remember me" features.

Visit www.OnGuardOnline.gov for more information about wireless computing.

Spam

Email spam is not just unwanted; it can be offensive. Decrease the number of spam emails you receive by making it difficult for spammers to get, and use, your email address:

- Don't use an obvious email address, such as JaneDoe@isp.com. Instead use numbers or special characters, such as Jane4oe6@isp.com.

- Use one email address for close friends and family and another for everyone else.

BILL CREEP

Have you ever wondered how your Internet service bill jumped from $30 to $50 a month in just a few years? If so, then you have experienced "bill creep", where the costs of a monthly expense creeps up. In some cases, the costs crept up because you added features. However, it may be due to higher prices charged by service providers for the same level of service. The price increases are usually small dollar amounts, but over time those climbing prices can take a toll on your budget. Take these steps to protect yourself from bill creep:

- Review your monthly statements to know what you're really paying.

- Cut out services that you are not actually using.

- Consider unbundling services.

- Contact companies to negotiate lower rates.

- Find out if the service providers have deals to reward loyal customers rather than just get new customers.

- Research cheaper options that meet your needs.

- If your discount prices are going to expire at a certain date, mark the date on your calendar and make an active decision to cancel your service or see if you can get a better deal.

- Don't post your email address on a public web page. Spammers use software that harvests text addresses. Substitute "jane4oe6 at isp dot com" for "jane4oe6@isp.com," or display your address as a graphic image, instead of the text.
- Don't enter your address on a website before you check its privacy policy.
- Uncheck any checked boxes. Otherwise, you may be giving permission for the website and its partners to contact you.
- Don't click on an email's "unsubscribe" link unless you trust the sender. This action tells the sender you are there.
- Never forward chain letters, petitions, or virus warnings. It could be a spammer's trick to collect addresses.
- Disable your email "preview pane." This stops spam from reporting to its sender that you have received it.
- Choose an ISP that filters email. If you get lots of spam, your ISP may not be filtering effectively.
- Use spam-blocking software. Web browser software often includes free filtering options. You can also purchase special software that will accomplish this task.
- Report spam. Alert your ISP that spam is slipping through its filters. The FTC also wants to know about "unsolicited commercial email." Forward spam to spam@uce.gov. Visit www.OnGuardOnline.gov/articles/0038-spam for more information.

PHONES

The choices for phone service have never been greater. Most consumers are now able to buy local and long-distance phone service from their telephone company, cable or satellite TV provider, or ISP. Services such as voice mail, call waiting, caller ID, and wireless may be offered as a package deal or sold separately. Before you buy, compare services and prices and think about what you really need:

- Whom do you call most often?
- What time of day or day of the week do you call?
- Do you want call waiting and/or caller ID?

Find out how each company prices its services. Are there minimum use, time-of-day, or distance requirements; flat monthly fees; or special plans? For example, wireless service may be cheaper than regular local service if you do not make many calls. Make sure you are comparing prices on similar plans and features. Understand that many service providers offer contracts for specific periods. Read the fine print and ask questions if there is anything you are not clear about.

The Federal Communications Commission (p. 98) offers consumer information about choosing a long-distance carrier, understanding new phone fees and taxes, and more at www.fcc.gov/consumers. The FCC also offers information to help you understand phone charges at transition.fcc.gov/cgb/consumerfacts/understanding.pdf.

Slamming and Cramming

"Slamming" occurs when a phone company illegally switches your phone service without your permission. If you notice a different company's name on your bill or see phone charges that are higher than normal, contact the company that slammed you and ask to be switched back to your original company. Tell the company you are exercising your right to refuse to pay charges, then report the problem to your original company and ask to be re-enrolled in your previous calling plan.

"Cramming" occurs when companies add charges to your phone bill without your permission. These charges may be for services such as voice mail, ringtones, or subscriptions. You may not notice these monthly charges because they are relatively small ($5 to $30) and look like your regular phone charges.

Take These Steps to Avoid Slammers and Crammers:

- **Block changes to your phone service.** Ask your telephone service provider if it offers a blocking or account protection service, which usually requires the company to notify you before making any changes to your service.
- **Read the fine print** on contest entry forms and coupons. You could be agreeing to switch your phone service or to buy optional services.
- **Watch out for impostors.** Companies could falsely claim to be your regular phone company and offer some type of discount plan or change in billing. They may also say they are taking a survey or they may pretend to be a government agency.
- **Beware of "negative option notices."** You can be switched or signed up for optional services unless you say "NO" to telemarketers.
- **Examine your telephone bill** carefully, including pages that show the details, and look for suspicious charges.

Your phone service cannot be shut off for refusal to pay for unauthorized services. Contact your local or state consumer protection agency (p. 102), state public utilities commission (p. 127), or the FCC (p. 98) for help.

LOST OR STOLEN CELL PHONES

Mobile phones are a vital part of life. You may store passwords, account numbers, phone numbers, and addresses all in this one device. However, if your phone is lost or stolen, your privacy, identity, and bank accounts could be in jeopardy.

Cell phone carriers manage stolen phone databases, where they can record your phone's unique ID number when you report it missing. This makes it impossible for your lost or stolen phone to be reactivated on their network (also called "bricking"). Take steps to protect your phone's content and your privacy:

- Set up a PIN or password to access your phone's home screen and settings.
- Export and backup your sensitive information onto an external device, like a USB drive.
- Report your lost or stolen phone to your cell phone carrier and the police immediately. Keep your cell phone provider's phone number in a separate place so that you can report your lost phone. Ask for written confirmation from your carrier to verify that you reported your phone missing.
- If you report your phone lost or stolen to your carrier, you are responsible for all fees incurred before you report it, but no charges after you report it missing.
- Ask your carrier to remotely delete the content, contacts, and apps on your phone.

Get more information on this topic from the FCC www.fcc.gov/guides/stolen-and-lost-wireless-devices.

Cell Phones

Before you sign a contract and choose a plan and a company that meets your needs, you should ask these types of questions:

Where can you make and receive calls? Most providers now offer a choice of local or national plans. A local plan offers low-cost options if most of your calls are made near your home or specific calling areas. National plans are the most expensive, but they let you use your phone anywhere in the country for a single per-minute price.

How frequently will you use the phone? If you don't use your phone often, a few minutes a month may be all you need. On the other hand, if your cell phone is your primary phone, a plan with the lowest airtime rate is a wiser choice.

Is a family plan option available? You can share one cellular service plan and a pool of monthly usage minutes among several phone lines. The cost of the additional lines per month is usually less than if you purchased individual accounts.

Is there a trial period? There are "dead spots" where a cell phone does not work in certain calling areas. A trial period lets you test your service and try the features of the phone

without incurring a termination fee.

Upgrades. How often can you upgrade your smart phone, under your contract? What fees do you pay for this service?

What if you want to cancel your service? Read your contract to see if you have to pay a termination fee or if there is a clause that allows you to cancel for free.

Be sure to keep track of your usage and understand your cell phone bill to avoid "bill shock." Visit www.fcc.gov/encyclopedia/bill-shock to learn how to better monitor your usage.

Smart Phones

Smart phones are like miniature computers; they provide basic phone functions, along with advanced features, including browsing the Internet, accessing email, interacting on online social networks, listening to music, watching videos, uploading pictures, and using apps.

When shopping for a smart phone, consider these tips:

- Compare the cost of data plans. These plans govern use and costs associated with mobile access for email, web browsing, social networking, and applications.
- Take advantage of special pricing and promotions.
- Is there a limit on the amount of data you can use each month?
- Be wary of buying phone insurance, which may sound tempting; consumer groups generally advise against it.

Since smart phones are like miniature computers, many of the same privacy and safety concerns apply. See Online Privacy (p. 40) and Internet (p. 40) for more information on how to protect yourself from these concerns.

Pay-As-You-Go Plans

If you want cell phone service only for emergencies, or you are not sure how much you will actually use a cell phone once you get it, you may want to consider a prepaid cell phone before you commit to a long-term wireless contract. With a prepaid cell phone, there is no contract to sign and no monthly bill. You will know exactly how much you spend. The downside of prepaid plans is that you pay more per minute and, if you do not use the phone for an extended period, you may lose the money in your account.

UNLOCKED CELL PHONES

Have you ever wanted to move your cell phone from one cellular service provider to another? You probably were not able to do so, because your phone provider had your phone's software locked, making it impossible for it to work on another phone provider's network. Well those days are gone. You can now use your phone on any carrier's network. This gives you the freedom to switch cellular service providers and prevents you from having to buy a new phone. You may still be required to complete a contract or pay a fee for early termination of a contract.

HOW SMART IS YOUR TV?

Smart TVs, part TV and part computer, allow you to access the Internet, online apps, use streaming video services, and even chat via video. These TVs advanced features may recommend other shows and apps that you may enjoy.

Your TV may track your viewing behavior and online browsing behavior. Many manufacturers of Smart TVs include terms and conditions when you first turn on the TV. If you decline, your access to the smart and interactive features may be limited or completely stripped away. Before you buy a Smart TV, find out:

- How long will the licenses between the TV manufacturer and content providers last? If licenses expire, you won't be able to access those features with the TV anymore.

- Can you access the services that you prefer? Will there be updates to the software to allow new services and apps to be added in the future?

- Is your Internet connection fast enough to provide a smooth video connection?

- How comparable are the features of smart TVs with those available from gaming systems, Blu-ray players or set-top streaming devices?

- What data does the TV model collect about you? Who is it shared with?

- Can you turn off tracking and targeted advertisements on your Smart TV?

- Are you able to use any of the functions of the Smart TV if you decline the manufacturer's terms and conditions?

TV

There are many choices for consumers looking to buy new televisions today. Before buying a new TV, do your homework. It is important to see the screens in person before buying to make sure the one you select will meet your needs. For independent ratings and reviews, check out *Consumer Reports* at www.consumerreports.org. Additional information is also available at www.energystar.gov. Once you have a television, there are several options for tuning into the channels. In addition to free television, you can subscribe to cable, satellite or Internet TV.

Cable

You can start with a basic lineup of channels and additional tiers of channels. The more channels you want, the more it will cost. You may want to consider video on demand so you can order movies and sports events and watch them when you like (usually within a 24-hour window). You can also buy a bundle of services that includes digital TV, digital phone, and broadband Internet access at discounted rates. Keep in mind, however, that you may be asked to sign a contract for bundled services.

Satellite

This service requires a dish that is mounted outside (service requires an unobstructed view of the satellite) and a receiver that is placed by your television. Satellite TV offers comparable channels to cable TV, and you can add a digital video recorder to record shows for viewing later. Check with your satellite TV provider for channel options and prices. As with cable TV, you may be asked to sign a contract for a package of services. One downside to satellite TV is occasional interference during periods of rain or snow. Find out if there are additional fees for the repositioning of a satellite dish due to bad weather, or for damages due to falling tree limbs.

Internet TV

If you have a high-speed Internet connection, you are already able to watch thousands of videos on your computer. Movies and TV shows are also available and becoming more prevalent as large online companies start distributing TV programming. You may even be able to connect your computer to your television so that shows you would normally watch online can project on a larger screen. Several services allow Internet streaming for a fee, along with free access to shows on network websites.

TELEMARKETING AND UNWANTED MAIL

What can you do about the growing pile of unwanted mail in your mailbox and unwelcome telemarketers on your phone? Actually, there are several things you can do:

- Tell companies you do business with to remove your name from customer lists they rent or sell to others. Look for information on how to opt-out of marketing lists on sales materials, order forms, and websites.

- Use the services provided by the Direct Marketing Association (p. 132) to remove your name from most national telemarketing, mail, and email lists.

TELEMARKETING

SHOP WITH A DIRECT SELLER

Direct sellers offer many unique and quality products at home parties or person-to-person. The Direct Selling Education Foundation recommends that you ask these questions to protect yourself before you buy:

- Is the company that the seller represents a member of the Direct Selling Association (DSA)? If so, do they have a copy of and adhere to DSA's enforced Code of Ethics? The Code of Ethics were written to protect you.
- When will your order be delivered?
- Can the seller explain the return policy or how to cancel an order?
- Does the seller have documentation for any claims he or she makes about products or services?
- How does the seller protect your credit card and personal information?
- Do you like and will you use the products? This is especially important before you sign up for an automatic monthly shipping program.

Contact the DSA for more information at www.dsa.org or www.directselling411.com.

- Call the credit reporting agencies' notification system at 1-888-567-8688. This will reduce the number of unsolicited credit and insurance offers you get. All three major credit bureaus (p. 14) participate in this program.
- Under U.S. Postal Service (USPS) rules, it is illegal to send mail that looks like it is from a government agency when it is not. It is also illegal to send mail that looks like a bill when nothing was ordered, unless it clearly states that it is not a bill. Report violations of this rule to the USPS (p. 99).

NATIONAL DO NOT CALL REGISTRY

The federal government's Do Not Call Registry allows you to restrict telemarketing calls permanently by registering your phone number at www.donotcall.gov or by calling 1-888-382-1222. If you receive telemarketing calls after your number has been in the national registry for 31 days, you can file a complaint using the same web page and toll free number. Contact your state's consumer protection office (p. 102) to find out if your state has its own Do Not Call (DNC) list and how you can add your number to it.

Placing your number on this national registry will stop most telemarketing calls, but not all of them. Calls that are still permitted include those from political organizations, charities, telephone surveyors, and some organizations with which you have a relationship.

Cell phone numbers can also be added to the Do Not Call Registry (www.donotcall.gov), but it is not necessary, since telemarketers are already forbidden to call them.

PRE-RECORDED MESSAGES

Pre-recorded sales calls or robocalls are illegal. Companies cannot transmit these messages or send text messages to consumers who have not agreed, in writing, to accept such messages. A company cannot contact you based on a prior business relationship. Pre-recorded calls may only be made to residential telephone numbers in the following cases:

- Emergency calls needed to ensure your health and safety.
- Calls that do not include any unsolicited advertisements.
- Calls by, or on behalf of, tax-exempt nonprofit organizations.
- Calls for which you have given prior consent.

If you receive pre-recorded telemarketing calls but have not agreed to get them, file a complaint with the FCC at www.donotcall.gov or by calling 1-888-225-5322.

TELEMARKETING SALES CALLS

The FTC Telemarketing Sales Rule defines what telemarketers can and cannot do when making a sales call. Callers must:

- Provide the seller's name.
- Disclose that the call is a sales call.
- Tell you exactly what they are trying to sell.
- Disclose the total cost and other terms of sale before you make any payment for goods or services.
- Tell you if they do not allow refunds, exchanges, or cancellations.

If a prize is involved, the caller must give you the odds of winning, inform you that no purchase is necessary, and tell you how to get instructions for entering without buying anything. It is illegal for telemarketers to:

- Misrepresent what they are offering.
- Call before 8 am or after 9 pm.
- Threaten, intimidate, or harass you, or call again if you ask them not to.

OPTING OUT

Tired of unwanted email filling up your inbox? You can opt-out of most unsolicited email lists by going to the "unsubscribe" button, usually found at the bottom of the message. Some senders make the button difficult to find, so you may have to do some searching.

In addition, the Direct Marketing Association (p. 132) lets you opt-out of receiving unsolicited commercial mail from many national companies for three years. You can register with this service for a small fee, but your registration only applies to organizations that use the association's Mail Preference Service. To register, go to www.dmachoice.org. If you would like to opt-out of credit and insurance offers, you can call 1-888-567-8688 or go online at www.optoutprescreen.com, which is managed by the major credit reporting companies.

This FTC rule applies even when you receive a call from a telemarketer in another state or country. It also applies when you make a call to a company in another state or country in response to a mail solicitation.

The rule generally does not apply when you call to order from a catalog or in response to an ad on television or radio, or in a magazine or newspaper. It also does not apply to solicitations you receive by fax or email. Beware that certain types of businesses, including nonprofit organizations, investment brokers and advisors, and banks and financial institutions, are exempt from the rule.

TRAVEL

Whether reserving a hotel room, buying plane tickets, or making other travel arrangements, these tips will help you get the deal you have been promised:

- **Plan as far ahead as you can.** Special deals on hotel rooms and airline seats often sell out very quickly.
- **Be flexible in your travel plans.** Hotels usually offer better rates on days when they expect fewer guests. Once you get a fare quote from an airline, ask if you can save money by leaving a day earlier or later, by taking a different flight on the same day, or by using a different airport. Changing planes during your trip is sometimes cheaper than a nonstop flight.
- **Check out the seller.** Ask tour operators and travel agents whether they belong to a professional association, then check to see if they are members in good standing. Contact your state or local consumer protection agency (p. 102) and the Better Business Bureau (p. 63) to find their complaint history.
- **Comparison shop.** Determine the complete cost of the trip in dollars, including all service charges, baggage fees, taxes, and processing fees.
- **Beware of unusually cheap prices and freebies.** These could be a scam, and you could end up paying more than the cost of a regular package tour. See When Prices Aren't Final on page 3.

- **Make sure you understand the terms of the deal.** If you hear you have won a free vacation, ask whether you have to buy something in order to get it. If the destination is a beach resort, ask the seller how far the hotel is from the beach. Then ask the hotel.
- **Ask about cancellation policies.** You may want to look into travel insurance for added protection (p. 33). There are websites that offer pricing and policy information on plans from different companies and describe the different forms of policies available.
- **Insist on written confirmations.** Ask for written proof of reservations, rates, and dates.
- **Ask for the total price.** Some airlines may sell each item separately, so the advertised price is much less than what you have to pay.
- **Pay by credit card.** It's not unusual to make a deposit or even pay in full for travel services before the trip. Paying by credit card gives you the right to dispute charges for services that were misrepresented or never delivered. If a travel agent or service provider says you cannot leave for at least two months, be very cautious—the deadline for disputing a credit card charge is 60 days, and most scam artists know this. (See Credit Card Billing Disputes, page 14).
- **Chip and PIN credit card.** Do you have a credit card that uses embedded chip and PIN technology instead of a magnetic strip? If travelling internationally, you will

TRAVEL FEES

Fees have become more common for all aspects of travel. While the reason for some fees are easy to understand, others have become more confusing, such as:

- **Seat selection fee.** You may pay a fee for the privilege of choosing your seat when you book your flight.
- **Car rental fees.** Beware of other costs, such as energy surcharges, concession fees, and facility fees.
- **Resort fees.** These fees give you access to fitness centers, golf courses, and other amenities. These may be charged to your account, whether or not you use them.
- **Mini-bar fees.** Some hotels charge you a restocking fee for replacing the items you purchased.
- **Valet parking.** Some hotels advertise valet parking as if it is an optional service, but some hotels make it mandatory.
- **Wi-Fi.** Does the hotel charge a fee for access to their Wi-Fi network?

Before you book your travel, contact airlines, car rental companies, and hotels to get an explanation of fee policies. Also, when you check out or complete your rental, review your receipt carefully. Speak up if you have been charged for something that you don't understand or services you didn't purchase.

VACATION HOME RENTALS

Private home and room rentals are common housing choices for a vacation. Before you decide to take part in a home rental agreement, know your consumer rights.

As a guest:

- Examine pictures of the rental and maps of the area. Does it have features that the description stated? Is it actually located as close to the tourist sites, beach, and other attractions that you want to visit during your vacation?
- Read reviews from past guests that have rented from this person or company.
- Find out about refund and cancellation policies.
- Pay with a credit card so that you can dispute the charge for the rental if there is a problem.

- Are you required to pay a deposit for damages? Will it be refunded if you don't break or damage anything in the rental?
- Find out whether or not the home owner will be in the house during your stay.

As a home owner or host:

- Make sure that renting out your private home is permitted in your city, homeowners associations, or leasing office.
- Take pictures and describe your home that accurately show your home's features and the location for potential renters.
- Contact your insurance company to make sure your homeowner's insurance policy covers renting out your house, or certain rooms.
- Find out if you have to collect taxes from guests, and if you have to do so directly or if a third party service will do that for you.

probably need it, since magnetic strip credit cards are not accepted in some countries.

In some states, travel sellers must be registered and insured. Advance payments for travel must be placed in an escrow account until services are provided. Prizes or "free" gifts may also be regulated. Contact your state or local consumer protection agency (p. 102) to find out about your rights and how to file complaints.

RESOLVE AIR TRAVEL PROBLEMS

No matter how well you plan, you might encounter these common air travel hassles.

Delayed and Canceled Flights

Airline delays caused by bad weather, traffic control problems, and mechanical repairs are hard to predict. If your flight is canceled, most airlines will rebook you on the earliest flight possible to your destination, at no additional charge. If you are able to find another flight on another airline, ask the first airline to endorse your ticket to the other carrier. This could save you from a fare increase, but there is no rule requiring the airline to do so.

Each airline has its own policies about what it will do for delayed passengers; there are no federal requirements. If your flight is delayed or canceled, ask the airline whether it will pay for meals, lodging, or a phone call. Contrary to what many people believe, airlines are not required to do so.

Delayed or Damaged Bags

If your bags are not on the conveyor belt when you arrive, file a report with the airline before you leave the airport:

- Insist the airline fill out a form and give you a copy, even if personnel say the bags will be on the next flight.

REVAMPED FLYER REWARD PROGRAMS

Traditionally, airline frequent flyer programs awarded points based on the number of miles that you flew on a trip. However, starting in 2015, many airline reward programs will give you mileage points based on the price of the ticket.

The number of miles you earn for a trip may vary, from three to eleven miles per dollar that you spend. The number of miles you earn for a trip can increase if you booked the flight on the airline's website, using the airline's branded credit card, or if you have preferred status in the rewards program. These changes can limit the ability of some travelers, like those who shop for deeply discounted flights, to earn points. If you are a member of a frequent flyer program that has changed it's operations, find out:

- How will your current points transfer to the new system?
- Will the points you already have expire?
- Is there a minimum or maximum number of miles you can earn on a trip?
- Are the rewards tickets redeemed on a tiered system?

Contact airlines' customer service offices for specific information about the programs.

BEWARE: TIMESHARE RESALE SCHEMES

Fraudulent timeshare resale companies take advantage of people that want to sell their property by charging large upfront fees and urging owners to act fast. Before you sell, consider these tips to avoid being scammed:

- Don't fall for promises and guarantees of a quick sale
- Be leery of pressure to act immediately or claims that "we've got a buyer right here."
- Research complaints against the reseller with the state's attorney general or consumer protection office (p. 102) and the Better Business Bureau (p. 63)in the state where the timeshare property is located.

- Ask if the reseller is licensed to sell real estate in the state where the property is located. Verify with that state's real estate commission.
- Don't pay upfront fees, based on a promise.
- Get everything in writing.
- Only pay for fees after your timeshare is sold, as if you were selling your primary home.

Visit www.ftc.gov/travel for more information about timeshare scams. File a complaint with the Federal Trade Commission (p. 98) and the state regulators (p. 102) if you have been the victim of this type of fraud.

- Get the name of the person who filled out the form and a phone number.
- Confirm that the airline will deliver the bag to you without charge when it is found.

Some airlines will give you money to purchase a few necessities. If they do not provide you with cash, ask what types of articles are reimbursable and keep all receipts.

If a suitcase arrives damaged, the airline may pay for repairs if you file a claim immediately (before you leave the airport). If an item cannot be fixed, the airline will negotiate to pay you its depreciated value. The same is true for belongings packed inside a suitcase. However, airlines may refuse to pay for damage if it was caused by your failure to pack something properly rather than by the airline's handling.

Lost Bags

If your bag is declared officially lost, you will have to submit a second, more detailed form within a time period set by the airline. The information on the form is used to estimate the value of your lost belongings. Airlines can limit their liability for delay, loss, and damage to baggage; however, they must prominently display this information (on the website and/or at the ticket counter) that explains the limit. According to the Department of Transportation (www.dot.gov/briefing-room/news-digest-75), the maximum an airline pays on lost bags and their contents is limited to $3,400 per passenger on domestic flights, and approximately $1,500 per passenger for baggage on international flights. See www.thetravelinsider.info/travelaccessories/lostbaggagerights.htm for more information on maximum liability, including special rates that change daily.

If the airline's offer does not cover your loss fully, check your homeowner's or renter's insurance to see whether it covers losses away from home. Some credit card companies and travel agencies also offer optional or even automatic supplemental baggage coverage.

On those trips when you know you are carrying more than the liability limits, you may want to ask about purchasing "excess valuation" insurance from the airline when you check-in. Of course, there is no guarantee the airline will sell you this protection. The airline may refuse, especially if the item is valuable or breakable.

Overbooked Flights

Selling more tickets than there are seats is not illegal. Most airlines overbook their flights to compensate for "no-shows." If there are more passengers than seats just before a plane is scheduled to depart, you can be "bumped" or left behind against your will. Whether you are bumped may depend on when you officially checked in for your flight, so check-in early. The U.S. Department of Transportation requires airlines to ask people to give up their seats voluntarily, in exchange for compensation. Airlines decide what to offer volunteers, such as money, a free trip, food, or lodging.

Passengers who are bumped involuntarily on most flights within the United States and on outbound international flights. are protected under Federal Aviation Administration guidelines (www.faa.gov). If you volunteer to be bumped, your agreement with the airline is not regulated and will depend on negotiating at the gate.

The airline must give you a written statement describing your rights as well as the airline's boarding priority rules and criteria. If the airline is able to get you to your final destination within two hours of your original arrival time, there is no monetary compensation. If that is not possible, the airline must pay you an amount equal to 200% of your one-way fare, with a maximum of $650. To receive this payment, you must have a confirmed reservation. You must also meet the airline's deadlines for ticketing and check-in. An airline may offer you a free ticket on a future flight in place of a check, but you have the right to insist on a check.

CRUISES

Taking a cruise can be a fun way to travel and enjoy an all-inclusive vacation. Before you sail, you should know that your ticket is also a binding contractual agreement between you and the cruise ship company, so it is important to read all of the terms and conditions in the ticket contract. You must agree to the terms, exactly as they are written, or you cannot take the cruise. Before you book tickets on a cruise,

To contact an organization, use the directory beginning on page 60.

research the company and the ship's history.

Some things to look out for when reading the contract:

- **Cancellation policy.** Some cruises require you to cancel 50 or more days in advance of the departure date. What are your rights if you have to cancel your trip? How far in advance do you have to cancel in order to get a refund? Will it be a partial or a full refund?

- **Understand your legal rights.** Your contract may limit your ability to sue the company or specify the time frame and location where a court case must be filed.

- **Itinerary changes.** The itinerary and ports of call can be changed at the captain's discretion.

- **Refunds.** Are you able to get a refund if you depart early? If so, what portion of the cruise price will be refunded?

Visit www.dot.gov/mission/safety/passenger-cruise-ship-information for more cruise safety resources.

TRAVEL SAFETY

Several federal agencies offer advice and information on the Internet or mobile apps that can help you have a safe trip. For advice on:

- **Airline, highway, and rail safety information:** Check out the U.S. Department of Transportation (p. 96) at www.dot.gov to look up crash-safety reports on cars and road conditions. Find out how weather is affecting air travel at www.fly.faa.gov and www.faa.gov/passengers.

- **Safe travel by air, land, and sea:** Refer to the Transportation Security Administration (p. 93) at www.tsa.gov/travelers. This site posts tips on dealing with airline security checks, traveling with kids, and warnings on prohibited items.

- **What to do before, during, and when returning from a trip overseas:** Visit the U.S. Department of State (p. 96) at www.state.gov/travel. You can also get warnings on locations to avoid, and tips on what to do in an overseas emergency.

- **Health-related travel information:** Consult the Centers for Disease Control and Prevention (p. 91) at www.cdc.gov/travel. Research vaccination requirements, find information on how to avoid illnesses caused by food and water, and review sanitation inspection scores on specific cruise ships.

UTILITIES

In many states, consumers can choose their telephone and energy service provider. Contact your state utility commission (p. 127) to find out whether you have a choice. Some commissions will provide a list of service providers and advice on making a choice, and most state utility commissions will take any complaints you have concerning utility sales and service.

STARTING UTILITY SERVICE

When you move into a new home or apartment, you may also be required to have the utility services (electricity, gas, water, waste removal, and cable) started in your name. Your city or county government may handle some services, such as water, sewer, and garbage collection. If you live in an apartment or are leasing a house from a homeowner, the landlord may handle this for you, but that is not required. Notify the utility provider in advance of the date you need service to start. If you are moving, remember to have service turned off at your old address.

Each company may require you to pay a fee to start service. You may also be required to pay a deposit or allow the company to check your credit to establish service at your home. If any of these companies fails to meet its service requirements, file a complaint with the company. If that does not work, contact your state's utility commission (p. 127).

BILLING

Once you have established service, you should start receiving your bills at regular intervals, normally monthly or quarterly. Utility bills are based on the amount of energy or water you actually use. However, if you live in an apartment complex, the amount you pay for some utilities may be prorated or split, based on a mathematical formula among all of the residents in your community. If the amount of energy varies by season, you may decide to sign up for a budget billing program. These programs allow you to smooth out your monthly payments by paying more in lighter-use months, so your bills are still manageable in months with heavier use. Contact your utility company to

SWITCHING UTILITY PROVIDERS

Your state's public utilities commission may allow you to "un-bundle" your electric (or gas) service, so that you purchase your electricity from one company and the delivery of the electricity from a separate company. The electricity supplier will generate your electricity, but your local utility company will still deliver the electricity to your home. Some suppliers may call you or advertise specials to encourage you to switch your service. Before you decide which option is best for you, ask these questions:

- How do the supplier's rates compare to the rates of your utility company?
- Is the energy rate fixed or does it vary from month to month?
- What other fees or taxes will be charged?
- How long does the contract last? Are there penalties if you cancel early?
- Will you receive one combined bill that includes charges from both the supplier and utility company?
- Is there a special offer or incentive for signing up?
- Is the company licensed by your state's public utility commission?

Contact your state's public utilities commission (p. 127) for more information on switching utility suppliers.

sign up for these programs. To learn ways to save on your energy bill, see Going Green (p. 21).

In addition to your actual service, you may have other fees on your bill, such as administrative fees, public surcharges, or local taxes. Contact the service provider if you see charges you do not understand or did not authorize, or if you have difficulty making timely payments.

If you have difficulty paying your bills, especially for electricity or gas, help is available. Contact the company to find out if it has a program in place to help consumers. Also, your state's utility commission (p. 127) may sponsor a program to either reduce your bill or make your payments based on a set amount of your income each month. Programs like these from utility companies and local government are usually based on your income. You may also consider applying for help through the Low Income Home Energy Assistance Program (LIHEAP). The benefits vary from state to state. Visit www.acf.hhs.gov/programs/ocs/programs/liheap or call 1-866-674-6327 for more information.

WILLS AND FUNERALS

People at all economic levels benefit from an estate plan. Upon death, an estate plan legally protects and distributes property based on your wishes and the needs of your family and/or survivors with the fewest tax consequences.

WILLS

A will is the most practical first step in estate planning. It makes clear how you want your property to be distributed after you die. Writing a will can be as simple as typing out how you want your assets to be transferred to loved ones or charitable organizations. If you do not have a will when you die, your estate will be handled in probate, and your property could be distributed differently from what you would like. When writing your will, remember:

- In most states, you must be 18 years of age or older.
- To be valid, a will must be written when you are of sound judgment and have adequate mental capacity.
- The document must clearly state that it is your will.
- An executor of your will, who ensures your estate is distributed according to your wishes, must be named.
- It is not necessary to notarize or record your will, but doing so can safeguard any claims that it is invalid. For it to be valid, it must be signed in the presence of at least two witnesses.
- A financial will and testament will always supersede a last will and testament when bestowing financial assets.

It may help to get legal advice when writing a will, particularly when it comes to understanding all of the rules of the estate disposition process in your state. For information about legal issues, see page 55. Some states, for instance, have community-property laws that entitle your

WHAT IS PROBATE?

Probate is a legal process that takes place after you die. It involves proving that your will is valid, identifying all of your property, paying debts and taxes, and distributing your remaining property as the will directs.

WRITE A DIGITAL ASSET PLAN

More and more the things you buy and own are intangible items, like digital books, music, and photos stored online. You may have online accounts with retailers, financial institutions, or digital media subscriptions for streaming TV and movies. In addition, some things are stored by companies on your behalf, like social media profiles, email accounts, airline frequent flyer miles, and credit card reward points.

What happens to these assets once you die? You should consider creating a digital asset plan. This document should state how you would like these assets and online accounts to be handled. You should appoint someone you trust as an digital asset executor. This person will be responsible for closing your online accounts, subscriptions, social media profiles, and handling all of your electronic assets after you are deceased. Take these steps to help you write a digital asset plan:

- Review the terms and conditions of each company where you have digital assets and profiles to know their policies when a customer dies.
- State how you would like your profiles to be handled. You may want to cancel your accounts or profiles completely or keep it open for friends and family to use.
- Include a list all of the companies where you have digital accounts, along with your usernames and passwords with your will.
- If the account is for a fee based service, include the credit card or bank account numbers that are used to pay for the service so that the executor can contact the companies to stop the charges.
- Stipulate in your will that the executor of your digital asset plan should have a copy of your death certificate. He or she may need this as proof for websites and service providers to take any actions on your behalf.
- Check to see if the companies have account management features that let you assign access to friends and family, ahead of time.

surviving spouse to keep at least half of your wealth after you die, no matter what percentage you leave him or her in your will. Fees for the execution of a will vary according to its complexity.

Choose an Executor

An executor is the person who is responsible for settling the estate after your death. Duties of an executor include:

- Taking inventory of property and belongings.
- Appraising and distributing assets.
- Paying taxes.
- Settling debts owed by the deceased.

Most important, the executor is legally obligated to act in the interests of the deceased, following the wishes stated in the will. Here again, it can be helpful to consult an attorney to help with the probate process or offer legal guidance. In most states, any person over the age of 18 who has not been convicted of a felony can be named executor of a will. Some people choose a lawyer, accountant, or financial consultant based on his or her professional experience. Others choose a spouse, adult child, relative, or friend. Since the role of executor can be demanding, it is often a good idea to ask the person if he or she is willing to serve.

If you have been named executor in someone's will but are not able or do not want to serve, you need to file a "declination," which is a legal document that declines your designation as an executor. The contingent executor named in the will then assumes responsibility. If no contingent executor is named, the court will appoint one.

Choose Beneficiaries

As you write your will, you need to decide who you want to inherit your assets to ensure that your possessions are dispersed as you want. Primary beneficiaries are your first choice to receive your assets. You should also consider choosing secondary or contingent beneficiaries. If your primary beneficiary dies before you do or does not meet a condition (ex. age) for inheritance, your secondary beneficiaries will receive your assets. Designating a secondary beneficiary can also prevent going through probate, which can be time consuming and expensive. Use specific names instead of broad categories like "nieces and nephews" when naming beneficiaries in your will.

You should also add primary and secondary beneficiaries on your individual bank accounts, the deeds to your homes and cars, contents of your safe deposit boxes, investments, and insurance policies to make it easier to transfer the assets. Also, remember that giving someone power of attorney does not automatically make this person a beneficiary of your assets. After you die, this person will not have the right to the money or even the right to access your account. If you want this person to be a beneficiary, you must state it in your will.

FUNERALS

One of the largest expenses many consumers will face is arranging for a funeral. A traditional burial, including a casket and vault, costs about $7,000. Extras such as flowers, obituary notices, cards, and limousines can add thousands of dollars more. At such a highly emotional time, many people are easily swayed to believe that their decisions reflect how they feel about the deceased and wind up spending more than may be necessary.

Most funeral providers are professionals who work to serve their clients' needs and best interests. Unfortunately, some do not and may take advantage of clients by insisting on unnecessary services and overcharging consumers. The Funeral Rule is a federal rule that regulates the actions of funeral directors, homes, and services.

Many funeral providers offer a variety of package plans that include products and services that are most commonly sold. Keep in mind, you are not obligated to buy a package plan; you have the right to buy the individual products and services you prefer. As outlined by the Funeral Rule:

- You have the right to choose the funeral goods and services you want (with some exceptions).
- The funeral provider must state this "Rule" in writing on the general price list.
- If state or local law requires you to buy any particular item, the funeral provider must disclose it on the price list, with a reference to the specific law.
- The funeral provider may not refuse, or charge a fee, to handle a casket that you bought elsewhere.
- A funeral provider who offers cremations must make alternative urns available.
- When prepaying for funeral services, do not agree to give the check from the life insurance company directly to the funeral home. You are paying for specific goods and services, and signing over the life insurance check might result in a significant overpayment for services rendered.

Visit www.ftc.gov/bcp/edu/microsites/funerals for more information about the Funeral Rule.

Planning ahead is the best way to make informed decisions about funeral arrangements. An advance plan also spares your family from having to make choices in the middle of grief and under time constraints. Every family is different, and funeral arrangements are influenced by religious and cultural traditions, budgets, and personal preferences.

You are not legally required to use a funeral home to plan and conduct a funeral, but most people find that the services of a professional funeral home make the process easier. Comparison shopping, either in person or by phone, can save you money and is much easier when done in advance. Visit www.funerals.org to learn more about how to select a funeral home and research its history. Many funeral homes will also send you a price list by mail, but this is not required by law.

If you have a problem concerning funeral matters, it is best to try to resolve it first with the funeral home director. If you are dissatisfied, the Funeral Consumers Alliance (p. 101) may be able to advise you on how best to resolve your issue. You can also contact your state or local consumer protection agencies (p. 102) or the Funeral Service Consumer Assistance Program at 1-800-662-7666. Most states have a licensing board that regulates the funeral industry. You can contact the board in your state for information or help.

Prepaying

Millions of Americans have entered into contracts to prearrange their funerals and prepay some or all of the expenses involved. Various states have laws to help ensure that these advance payments are available to pay for the funeral products and services when they are needed; however, protections vary widely from state to state. Some state laws require the funeral home or cemetery to place a

percentage of the prepayment in a state-regulated trust or to purchase a life insurance policy with the death benefits assigned to the funeral home or cemetery. For a list of questions to consider before prepaying for a funeral, visit www.consumer.ftc.gov/articles/0305-planning-your-own-funeral.

52 www.USA.gov

To contact an organization, use the directory beginning on page 60.

FILE A COMPLAINT

Even the savviest consumer has problems with a product or service at one time or another. It is your right to complain if you have a genuine consumer problem. It is also your responsibility. A problem cannot be fixed if no one knows it exists.

CONTACT THE SELLER

The first step in resolving a consumer problem is contacting the seller. You can solve most consumer problems by talking to a local salesperson or representative. If this fails, try going higher up to the national headquarters of the seller or the manufacturer of the item.

Many companies have a special customer relations or consumer affairs division whose primary function is solving consumer problems. You can often contact this division by toll free number, postal mail, online form or contact information listed on the product label or warranty. If this is not the case:

- Check the Corporate Consumer Directory portion of this *Handbook* for the contact information of several hundred corporations (p. 68).

- Visit the company's website and look for a "Contact Us", "About Us", Customer Service", or "Privacy Policy" link.

- Dial the directory of toll free numbers at 1-800-555-1212 to see whether the company has a toll free number listed.

- Ask your local librarian to assist you. Most public libraries have reference books with corporate contact information.

- As you do your search, keep in mind that the name of the manufacturer or parent company is often different from the brand name. ThomasNet, an online database of manufacturers, may be helpful.

- With each person you contact, calmly and accurately explain the problem and what action you would like to be taken. A written letter is a good strategy because you will have a record of your communication with the company. The sample letter (p. 54) will help you prepare a written complaint.

- Be brief and to the point. Note all important facts about your purchase, including what you bought, serial or model numbers, the name and location of the seller, and when you made the purchase.

- State exactly what you want done about the problem and how long you are willing to wait for a response. Be reasonable.

- Don't write an angry, sarcastic, or threatening letter. The person reading your letter probably was not responsible for your problem but could be very helpful in resolving it.

- Send your letter by certified mail or request delivery confirmation.

- Include copies of all documents regarding your problem. Keep the originals.

- Provide your name, address, and phone numbers. If an account is involved, be sure to include the account number.

- Keep a record of your efforts to contact the seller; include the name of the person with whom you spoke and what was done, if anything. You should also keep a record of the dates and times of your contact.

- If you use a company's online complaint form, print the screen or take a sceenshot before you click "submit" so that you have a record of your complaint.

CONTACT THIRD PARTIES

Don't give up if you are not satisfied with the seller's response to your complaint. Once you have given the seller a reasonable amount of time to respond, consider filing a complaint with one or more of these outside organizations:

State or local consumer protection offices (p. 102). These government agencies mediate complaints, conduct investigations, and prosecute those who break consumer laws.

State regulatory agencies that have jurisdiction over the business. For example, banking (p. 115), insurance (p. 119), securities (p. 123), and utilities (p. 127) are regulated at the state level.

State and local licensing agencies. Doctors, lawyers, home improvement contractors, auto repair shops, realtors, debt collectors, and child care providers are required to register or be licensed. The board or agency that oversees this process may handle complaints and have the authority to take disciplinary action. Your state or local consumer protection office (p. 102) can help you identify the appropriate agency.

Better Business Bureaus (p. 63). This network of nonprofit organizations supported by local businesses tries to resolve buyer complaints against sellers. Records are kept on unresolved complaints as a source of information for the seller's future customers. The umbrella organization for the BBBs assists with complaints concerning the truthfulness of national advertising and helps to settle "lemon law" disputes with automobile manufacturers through the BBB AUTO LINE program (p. 62).

Trade associations. Companies that sell or produce similar products or services often belong to an industry

FILE A COMPLAINT

Keep copies of all of your letters, emails, warranties, work orders, order confirmation numbers, receipts, owner's manuals and related documents.

Your Address
Your City, State, ZIP Code
Date

Name of Contact Person, if available
Title, if available
Company Name
Consumer Complaint Division (if you have no specific contact)
Street Address
City, State, ZIP Code

Dear (**Contact Person**):

Re: (**account number, if applicable**)

On (**date**), I (**bought, leased, rented, or had repaired/serviced**) a (**name of the product, with serial or model number or service performed**) at (**location, date and other important details of the transaction**).

- describe purchase
- name of product, serial/model number
- include date and place of purchase

Unfortunately, your product (**or service**) has not performed well (**or the service was inadequate**) because (**state the problem**). I am disappointed because (**explain the problem: for example, the product does not work properly, the service was not performed correctly, I was billed the wrong amount, something was not disclosed clearly or was misrepresented, etc.**).

- state problem
- give history

To resolve the problem, I would appreciate if you would (**state the specific action you want—money back, charge card credit, repair, exchange, etc.**). Enclosed are copies (**do not send originals**) of my records (**include receipts, guarantees, warranties, canceled checks, contracts, model and serial numbers, and any other documents**).

- ask for specific action
- enclose copies of documents

I look forward to your reply and a resolution to my problem and will wait until (**set a time limit**) before seeking help from a consumer protection agency or Better Business Bureau. Please contact me at the above address or by phone at (**home and/or office numbers with area code**).

- allow time for action
- state how you can be reached

Sincerely,

Your name

Enclosure(s)

Download a copy of the sample complaint letter at:
www.usa.gov/topics/consumer/complaint/complaint-letter.shtml

association that will help resolve problems between its members and consumers (p. 131).

National consumer organizations. Some of these organizations assist consumers with complaints (p. 100).

Media programs. Local newspapers, radio stations, and television stations often have action lines or hotline services that try to resolve consumer complaints they receive. Call for Action, Inc. (p. 100) is a nonprofit network of consumer hotlines that educate and assist individuals with consumer problems.

DISPUTE RESOLUTION PROGRAMS

Some companies and industries offer programs to address disagreements between buyers and sellers. The auto industry (p. 62) has several of these programs. The Financial Industry Regulatory Authority (p. 132) offers a program to resolve investment-related disputes.

Mediation, arbitration, and conciliation are three common types of dispute resolution. During mediation, both sides involved in the dispute meet with a neutral third party and create their own agreement jointly. In arbitration, the third party decides how to settle the problem. Conciliation is similar; however, you and the other party meet with the conciliator separately (not a group meeting). Request a copy of the rules of any program before deciding to participate. You will want to know beforehand whether the decision is binding; some programs do not require both parties to accept the decision. Also ask whether participation in the program places any restrictions on your ability to take other legal action.

SMALL CLAIMS COURT

Small claims courts resolve disputes over small amounts of money. Court procedures are generally simple, inexpensive, quick, and informal. Additionally court fees are minimal. You probably will not need a lawyer. Even though the court is informal, the judge's decision must be followed.

If you file a case and win, the losing party should give you what the court says you are owed without further action on your part. If the losing party refuses to follow the court's decision, you can go back to court and ask for the order to be enforced. Depending on local laws, law enforcement officials might sell a person's property, or take money from a bank account or business cash register.

Check your local telephone book under the municipal, county, or state government headings for small claims court offices. If you have more questions, the court's clerk may be able to answer your questions.

LEGAL HELP AND INFORMATION

If you need an attorney to advise or represent you, ask friends and family for recommendations. You can also contact the Lawyer Referral Service of your state, county, or city bar association listed in your local phone directory. Websites such as www.americanbar.org (American Bar Association) and www.nolo.com can help you with answers to general legal questions.

Choosing an Attorney

Many lawyers who primarily serve individuals and families are general practitioners with experience in frequently needed legal services, such as divorce and family matters, wills and probate, bankruptcy and debt problems, real estate, and criminal and/or personal injury. Be sure the lawyer you are considering has experience in the area for which you are seeking help.

Once you have identified some candidates:

- Call each attorney and describe your legal issue to find out whether they handle your situation.
- Ask if you will be charged for an initial consultation.
- Ask for an estimate of what the lawyer usually charges to handle your kind of case.
- Ask whether there are hourly charges, or if your attorney accepts a percentage of the settlement as a contingency fee. If the lawyer is paid by a contingency fee, then the or she will only receive a payment if they win your case.

The initial consultation is an opportunity for you and the lawyer to get to know each other. After listening to the description of your case, the lawyer should be able to outline your rights and liabilities, as well as alternative courses of action. The initial consultation is the lawyer's opportunity to explain what he or she can do for you and how much it will cost. You should not hesitate to ask about the attorney's experience in handling matters such as yours. Also, do not hesitate to ask about the lawyer's fees and the likely results. If you are considering going beyond the initial consultation and hiring the lawyer, request a written fee agreement before proceeding.

MANDATORY ARBITRATION CLAUSES

Mandatory arbitration clauses in contracts prevent you from filing a lawsuit against a company. These clauses are fairly common in automotive, credit card, and cell phone contracts. But now, they are appearing in website terms and conditions statements, coupons, or corporate social media profiles. While arbitration can be less expensive, it is sometimes seen as unfair to make arbitration a requirement before a negative incident has happened or knowing how serious the problem is. Also, the decisions are binding, so you can't appeal the decision, even if the company was severely negligent.

Before you sign a contract or even use a website, read the contract or terms of service for mentions of "arbitration", "binding arbitration" or "resolution programs"; this language is often in the fine print of the contract and can be easily missed. Also, note that some companies may let you opt-out of these clauses, if you do so within 30 days.

What If You Cannot Afford a Lawyer?

If you cannot afford a lawyer, you may qualify for free legal help from a Legal Aid or Legal Services Corporation (LSC) office. These offices generally offer legal assistance for such things as landlord-tenant relations, credit, utilities, family matters (for example, divorce and adoption), foreclosure, home equity fraud, Social Security benefits, welfare, unemployment, and workers' compensation. If the Legal Aid office in your area does not handle your type of case, it may refer you to other local, state, or national organizations that can provide help.

- To find the Legal Aid office nearest to you, check a local telephone directory or contact:

  National Legal Aid & Defender Association
  1901 Pennsylvania Ave., NW Suite 500
  Washington, DC 20006
  Phone: 202-452-0620
  www.nlada.org

- To find the Legal Services Corporation (LSC) office nearest to you, check a local telephone directory or contact:

  Legal Services Corporation Public Affairs
  3333 K St., NW, 3rd Floor
  Washington, DC 20007
  Phone: 202-295-1500
  www.lsc.gov

Free assistance may also be available from a local law school program where students, supervised by attorneys, handle a variety of legal matters. Some of these programs are open to all; others limit their service to specific groups, such as senior citizens or low-income persons.

REPORT FRAUD AND SAFETY HAZARDS

If you suspect a law has been violated, contact your local or state consumer protection agency (p. 102). This agency may take action or refer you to another state organization that has authority where you live. A local law enforcement officer may also be able to provide advice and assistance.

Violations of federal laws should be reported to the federal agency responsible for enforcement. While federal agencies are rarely able to act on behalf of individual consumers, complaints are used to document patterns of abuse, allowing the agency to take action against a company or industry.

If you suspect fraud, there are some additional steps to take:

- Report it to the Federal Trade Commission (p. 98).
- Report scams that use the mail or interstate delivery service to the U.S. Postal Inspection Service (p. 99). It is illegal to use the mail to misrepresent or steal money.
- Report scams that are Internet-based to the Internet Crime Complaint Center at www.ic3.gov.

Reporting fraud promptly improves your chances of recovering what you have lost and helps law enforcement authorities stop scams or safety hazards before others are victimized.

If you suspect you have a product that poses a health or safety hazard, report the problem to the appropriate federal agency:

- **Animal Products.** Food and Drug Administration (p. 92)
- **Automobiles.** National Highway Traffic Safety Administration (p.96)
- **Consumer Household Products.** U.S. Consumer Product Safety Commission (p. 89)
- **Drugs, Cosmetics, and Medical Devices.** Food and Drug Administration (p. 92)
- **Food.** Food and Drug Administration (p. 92), U.S. Department of Agriculture (p. 89)
- **Household Chemicals.** Environmental Protection Agency (p. 97)
- **Seafood.** Food and Drug Administration (p. 92), U.S. Department of Commerce (p. 90)
- **Toys, Baby Products, and Play Equipment.** U.S. Consumer Product Safety Commission (p. 89)

KEY INFORMATION RESOURCES

Federal Citizen Information Center (FCIC)

FCIC is a one-stop source that provides government information and services directly to the public. FCIC offers information across various channels, including the websites

USA.gov and GobiernoUSA.gov (in Spanish). Order print publications at Publications.USA.gov and through the *Consumer Information Catalog.* You can also get answers to your government questions by telephone at 1-844-872-4681, and via social media on Facebook at www.facebook.com/USAgov and Twitter @USAgov.

Center for the Study of Services
Evaluates quality and price for local services in major metropolitan areas. Visit www.checkbook.org or see page 100.

Consumer Reports
Researches and tests goods and services such as automobiles, appliances, food, clothing, luggage, and insurance. Visit www.consumerreports.org or see page 100.

Consumer World
A public service website with links to hundreds of consumer resources, corporations, and government agencies. Visit www.consumerworld.org.

National Institute of Food and Agriculture (NIFA)
Programs cover food and nutrition, housing, gardening, budgeting, using credit, saving for retirement, and more. Visit www.nifa.usda.gov or www.extension.org or see page 89.

Libraries
Publications from the organizations mentioned on this page are available at your local public library or by visiting www.publiclibraries.com.

EMERGENCY PREPAREDNESS

Disasters can strike in many forms—fires, floods, hurricanes, tornadoes, and even national emergencies. Protecting yourself, your family, your pets, and your home or your business requires advance planning. It is equally important to know where to turn for help and information. You may even be eligible for government assistance.

There are numerous sources of information to help you prepare. To get started, check out these websites:

- www.disasterassistance.gov
- www.fema.gov
- www.ready.gov
- www.redcross.org

Visit www.ready.gov/financial-preparedness to get resources to help you make a pre-disaster financial plan. It is also helpful to have a home inventory of your belongings; you can create one online that you can access anywhere at www.knowyourstuff.org. In case of a disaster, make certain that you have your ID, cash, debit and credit cards, and a list of your account numbers and insurance policy numbers.

FOR TEACHERS

Teachers often use the *Consumer Action Handbook* to teach essential information about credit, insurance, major purchases, complaint letters, saving and investing, and other consumer topics. For classroom copies of the *Handbook*, email action.handbook@gsa.gov; include the name and address of your school and the number of copies you would like to receive.

FOR PERSONS WITH DISABILITIES

National Council on Disability
A federal agency whose mission is to improve the quality of life for Americans with disabilities and their families. Visit www.ncd.gov.

National Disability Rights Network
Provides legally based advocacy services for people with disabilities. Visit www.ndrn.org.

Department of Education
Provides training and information to parents of disabled children and to people who work with them. See page 90 or visit www.ed.gov.

Department of Housing and Urban Development
Learn more about the housing rights of people with disabilities, and the responsibilities of housing providers and building and design professionals. Visit www.hud.gov/offices/fheo/disabilities or see page 94.

SERVICES AND RESOURCES FOR PERSONS WITH DISABILITIES

Relay Services: Telecommunications relay services link telephone conversations between individuals who use standard voice telephones and those who use text telephones (TTYs). Calls may be made from either type of telephone to the other type through the relay service.

Local Relay Services: States provide relay services for local and long-distance calls. Consult your local telephone directory for information on use, fees (if any), services, and dialing instructions for that area.

Federal Relay Service: The FRS, a program of the U.S. General Services Administration (GSA), provides access to TTY users who wish to conduct official business nationwide with, and within, the federal government. The toll free number is 1-800-877-8339. For more information on relay communications, or to obtain a brochure on using the FRS, call 1-800-877-0996.

Other Services: Consumers who are deaf or hard of hearing, or who have a speech impairment and use a TTY, may receive operator and directory assistance for calls by calling 1-800-855-1155. Check the introductory pages of your local telephone directory for additional TTY services.

KEY INFORMATION RESOURCES

National Library Service for the Blind and Physically Handicapped

Administers a free loan service of recorded and Braille books and magazines, music scores in Braille and large print, plus specially designed playback equipment. Visit www.loc.gov/nls.

FOR MILITARY PERSONNEL

Today's military families face many common consumer challenges as well as the additional stress associated with frequent moves and separation. To ease such difficulties, Family Centers, along with the other programs described below, provide help and support for military families.

U.S. Military Family Centers

Located on most military installations, Family Centers provide information, life skills education, and support services to military members and their families. Family Centers link people with appropriate services available in the local community and/or through state and federal assistance programs in health and human services, school systems, employment assistance, law enforcement, and recreation.

Air Force Community Readiness and Family Support

Airman and Family Readiness Centers (A&FRC) are located on every Air Force Installation and offer a wealth of resources to airmen and their families. They provide consultations on topics such as financial management, transition assistance, spouse employment, readiness, deployment, family life and relocation assistance.

Fleet and Family Support Programs

www.ffsp.navy.mil

The Fleet and Family Support Program provides support, references, information, and a wide range of assistance for members of the Navy and their families to meet the unique challenges of the military lifestyle.

Marine Corps Community Services (MCCS)

www.usmc-mccs.org

The Personal and Family Readiness Division (MR) provides a number of Marine Corps personnel service programs,

including casualty assistance, DEERS dependency determination, voting assistance, postal services, and personal claims.

U.S. Army Family and Morale, Welfare and Recreation

www.armymwr.com

This office provides support to Army personnel and families, including resources to strengthen home and family life, finances, employment, and other key resources.

U.S. Coast Guard

www.uscg.mil

The U.S. Coast Guard offers key resources, including core publications, career information and related news. It also covers background about its mission, community services, history, photos, and reports.

FedsHireVets

Veterans Employment Program Office
U.S. Office of Personnel Management
1900 E St., NW
Washington, DC 20415-0001
Phone: 202-606-5090
www.fedshirevets.gov

FedsHireVets is a one-stop resource for federal veteran employment information.

Military OneSource

Phone: 1-800-342-9647
www.militaryonesource.mil

Military OneSource is a comprehensive resource for military members and their families, relating to nearly every aspect of personal and professional life. Topics include health and wellness, finances, family matters, and resiliency. The website features blogs, discussion boards, and podcasts.

RESOURCES FOR MILITARY FAMILIES

Check with family readiness centers on your installation to get access to financial help. The Consumer Financial Protection Bureau's Office of Servicemember Affairs offers resources to plan your financial future and prevent being a victim of fraud at www.consumerfinance.gov/servicemembers. The Better Business Bureau also offers consumer education and advocacy to service members through their Military Line® at www.bbb.org/council/programs-services/bbb-military-line/. If you need to file a complaint, you can file it with the FTC (p. 98) or the CFPB (p. 89).

58   www.USA.gov

To contact an organization, use the directory beginning on page 60.

BEWARE: FRAUDS AGAINST SERVICEMEN

Servicemembers, many of whom are young and making major financial decisions for the first time, are appealing targets for scammers. They receive a steady paycheck, plus reenlistment bonuses and deployment pay. In addition, military families move frequently and do not know which sellers to avoid. Scam artists also know that military personnel are required to keep their finances in good shape and may be more likely to pay a fake debt, to keep their finances in good standing.

Take steps to protect yourself and your finances:

- Be wary of sellers or "investment professionals" that use their connection to the military to make a sale. See "Beware: Affinity Fraud" (p. 36).
- Protect yourself from identity theft by changing your mailing address when you are restationed.
- Contact the credit reporting agencies (p. 14) to place an active duty alert on your accounts. This limits the ability of ID thieves to apply for credit while a servicemember is deployed.
- Know your rights. The Servicemember Civil Relief Act extends consumers rights to service personnel; there is added protection from default judgements as well as the ability to cancel contracts and leases. Visit www.dmdc.osd.mil/appj/scra for more information.

Consumer Sentinel
www.ftccomplaintassistant.gov

Consumer Sentinel allows members of the military to enter consumer complaints directly into a database. Law enforcement agencies, members of the Judge Advocate General's staff, and the Department of Defense can access the database to help protect armed services members and their families from consumer protection–related problems.

Commissaries and Exchanges
Consumers who shop at military commissaries and exchanges and who have a question or problem should contact the local manager before contacting the regional office. If your problem is not resolved at the local level, write or call the regional office nearest you.

eBenefits National Resource Directory
www.nationalresourcedirectory.gov

The National Resource Directory is a partnership of the Departments of Defense and Veterans Affairs. This online directory connects service members and veterans with resources to benefit them and their families.

SaveandInvest.org
www.saveandinvest.org/militarycenter

Whether on base or deployed overseas, it is crucial that military personnel have access to financial education information that enables them to make prudent saving and investing decisions for themselves and their families. This site offers online and on-the-ground training to support military personnel at key financial milestones.

VETERANS CEMETERIES

All veterans are entitled to a free burial in a national cemetery and a grave marker. This eligibility also applies to some civilians who have provided military-related service and some Public Health Service personnel.

Spouses and dependent children also are entitled to a lot and marker when buried in a national cemetery. There are no charges for opening or closing the grave, for a vault or liner, or for setting the marker in a national cemetery. For more information, visit the Department of Veterans Affairs, National Cemetery Administration (p. 97) at www.cem.va.gov.

BEWARE: PENSION POACHING

Unfortunately, the scams don't stop after you retire from the military. Veterans, particularly those aged 65 and over, are targeted with financial scams. Fraudulent financial advisors may offer to help you qualify for both your VA Aid and Attendance (A&A) benefits and Medicaid services, by moving your money into a trust. However, you could lose your eligibility for Medicaid services and have to pay back the A&A benefits if this shift does not meet Medicaid's rules. Plus, this advisor could run off with the money that you have placed in the trust account.

If you are approached with this offer, beware of a financial planner that:

- Calls, mails, or comes to your door offering their services.
- Charges you a fee (from $100 to $1000) to help you apply for benefits; there is no cost for the forms or to apply for VA benefits.
- Urges you to transfer money to a trust, or invest in certain financial products, in order to qualify for pension benefits.

For more information on these scams read the FTC's article at www.consumer.ftc.gov/articles/0349-veterans-pensions. If you have been the victim of a veterans' benefit scheme, file a complaint with your state's consumer protection office (p. 102) and the Federal Trade Commission (p. 98).

☽ SOCAP INTERNATIONAL

Many of the companies listed in this *Handbook* are members of the Society of Consumer Affairs Professionals International (SOCAP). Formed in 1973, SOCAP is composed of over 2,000 best-in-class customer care executives and professionals from over 100 brand name companies throughout the U.S. and Canada. SOCAP is committed to promoting customer care and engagement as competitive advantages. However, SOCAP International does not investigate or accept individual consumer complaints. SOCAP members are identified in the automotive and corporate directories by the SOCAP logo (see Key at right). For more information, contact SOCAP (p.133).

KEY:

✉   E-mail

☽   SOCAP International Member

◆   Provided financial support for the publication of the *Consumer Action Handbook*.

TTY   Numbers for people with hearing disabilities. For more information see the box on page 57.

Acura
1919 Torrance Blvd.
Mail Stop 500-2N7E
Torrance, CA 90501-2746
Toll free: 1-800-382-2238
✉: acr@ahm.acura.com
www.acura.com

American Honda Motor Company, Inc. ⟳
1919 Torrance Blvd.
Mail Stop 500-2N-7A
Torrance, CA 90501-2746
Toll free: 1-800-999-1009
www.honda.com

American Suzuki Motor Corporation
PO Box 1100
Brea, CA 92822
714-572-1490 (Motorcycle/ATV/Marine)
Toll free: 1-800-934-0934 (Automotive)
www.suzuki.com

Audi of America, Inc.
3800 Hamlin Rd.
Auburn Hills, MI 48326
Toll free: 1-800-822-2834
www.audiusa.com

BMW of North America, LLC
300 Chestnut Ridge Rd.
Woodcliff Lake, NJ 07677-7731
Toll free: 1-800-831-1117
✉: customerrelations@bmwusa.com
www.bmwusa.com

Buick
PO Box 33136
Detroit, MI 48232-5136
Toll free: 1-800-521-7300
www.buick.com

Cadillac
PO Box 33169
Detroit, MI 48232-5169
Toll free: 1-800-458-8006
www.cadillac.com

Chevrolet
PO Box 33136
Detroit, MI 48232-5136
Toll free: 1-800-222-1020
www.chevrolet.com

Chrysler Group, LLC ⟳
PO Box 21-8004
Auburn Hills, MI 48321-8004
Toll free: 1-800-247-9753
www.chrysler.com

Dodge
See: Chrysler Group, LLC
Toll free: 1-800-423-6343
www.dodge.com

Contact Your Automotive Manufacturer

If you have a problem with a car you purchased from a local dealer, first try to work it out with the dealer. Contact the manufacturer's regional or national office. Ask for the Consumer Affairs Office If the problem is not resolved.

If you are still unsuccessful, consider contacting the automotive dispute resolution resources listed at the end of this section. The method used to resolve your dispute may be mediation, arbitration, or conciliation. Decisions of arbitrators are usually binding and must be accepted by both the customer and the business. Ask for a copy of the rules of the program before you file your case. See page 55 for an overview of dispute resolution programs.

A local or state consumer agency (p. 102) could also be a useful resource in resolving problems with your vehicle. If you have a new vehicle, be sure to ask whether you have any protection under a state "lemon" law (p. 11).

Fiat
See: Chrysler Group, LLC
Toll free: 1-888-242-6342
www.fiatusa.com

Ford Motor Company ⟳
PO Box 6248
Dearborn, MI 48126
Toll free: 1-800-392-3673
TTY: 1-800-232-5952
www.ford.com

GMC ⟳
PO Box 33172
Detroit, MI 48232-5172
Toll free: 1-800-462-8782
www.gmc.com

Harley-Davidson
3700 W. Juneau Ave.
Milwaukee, WI 53208
Toll free: 1-800-258-2464
www.harley-davidson.com

Hyundai Motor America ⟳
PO Box 20850
Fountain Valley, CA 92728-0850
Toll free: 1-800-633-5151
✉: consumeraffairs@hmausa.com
www.hyundaiusa.com

Infiniti
See: Nissan North America, Inc.
Toll free: 1-800-662-6200
www.infiniti.com

Isuzu Motors America, LLC
1400 S. Douglass Rd., Suite 100
Anaheim, CA 92806
714-935-9300
Toll free: 1-800-255-6727
www.isuzu.com

Jaguar Cars ⟳
Customer Relationship Center
555 MacArthur Blvd.
Mahwah, NJ 07430
Toll free: 1-800-452-4827
www.jaguarusa.com

Jeep
See: Chrysler Group, LLC
Toll free: 1-877-426-5337
www.jeep.com/en

Kawasaki Motors Corporation, USA
PO Box 25252
Santa Ana, CA 92799-5252
Toll free: 1-866-802-9381
www.kawasaki.com

Kia Motors America, Inc. ⟳
PO Box 52410
Irvine, CA 92619-2410
Toll free: 1-800-333-4542
www.kia.com

Land Rover ⟳
Customer Relationship Center
555 MacArthur Blvd.
Mahwah, NJ 07430
Toll free: 1-800-637-6837
www.landroverusa.com

Lexus
PO Box 2991
Mail Drop L201
Torrance, CA 90509-2991
Toll free: 1-800-255-3987
www.lexus.com

Lincoln
See: Ford Motor Company
Toll free: 1-800-521-4140
www.lincoln.com

Mazda North American Operations
PO Box 19734
Irvine, CA 92623-9734
Toll free: 1-800-222-5500
www.mazdausa.com

Mercedes-Benz USA, LLC
Three Mercedes Dr.
Montvale, NJ 07645
Toll free: 1-800-367-6372
www.mbusa.com

Mercury
PO Box 6128
Dearborn, MI 48121
Toll free: 1-800-521-4140
www.mercuryvehicles.com

Mitsubishi Motors North America, Inc.
PO Box 6400
Cypress, CA 90630-9998
Toll free: 1-888-648-7820
www.mitsubishicars.com

Nissan North America, Inc.
PO Box 685003
Franklin, TN 37068-5003
Toll free: 1-800-647-7261
www.nissanusa.com

Oldsmobile
PO Box 33171
Detroit, MI 48232-5171
Toll free: 1-800-442-6537
✉: cac@oldsmobile.com
www.oldsmobile.com

Pontiac
See: GMC
Detroit, MI 48232-5172
Toll free: 1-800-762-2737
✉: cac@pontiac.com
www.pontiac.com

Porsche Cars North America, Inc.
Owner Relations
980 Hammond Dr., Suite 1000
Atlanta, GA 30328
Toll free: 1-800-767-7243
www.porsche.com/usa

Saturn
PO Box 33173
Detroit, MI 48232-5173
Toll free: 1-800-553-6000
✉: cac@saturn.com
www.saturn.com

Smart USA
See: Mercedes-Benz USA, LLC
Toll free: 1-800-762-7887
www.smartusa.com

Subaru of America, Inc.
Subaru Plaza
PO Box 6000
Cherry Hill, NJ 08034-6000
Toll free: 1-800-782-2783
www.subaru.com

Tesla Motors
3500 Deer Creek
Palo Alto, CA 94304
650-681-5000
Toll free: 1-877-798-3752
www.teslamotors.com

Toyota Motor Sales U.S.A., Inc.
Dept. WC 11
19001 S. Western Ave.
Torrance, CA 90501
Toll free: 1-800-331-4331
www.toyota.com

Volkswagen Group of America, Inc.
3800 Hamlin Rd.
Auburn Hills, MI 48326
Toll free: 1-800-822-8987
✉: VWCustomerCARE@vw.com
www.vw.com

Volvo Cars of North America
One Volvo Dr.
PO Box 914
Rockleigh, NJ 07647
Toll free: 1-800-458-1552
www.volvocars.com

Winnebago Industries, Inc.
PO Box 152
Forest City, IA 50436-0152
641-585-3535
Toll free: 1-800-537-1885
www.winnebagoind.com

Yamaha Motor Corporation
6555 Katella Ave.
Cypress, CA 90630
Toll free: 1-800-962-7926 (Customer Relations)
Toll free: 1-800-252-5265 (Yamaha Card)
www.yamaha-motor.com

Automotive Dispute Resolution Programs

BBB AUTO LINE
Council of Better Business Bureaus, Inc.
3033 Wilson Blvd., Suite 600
Arlington, VA 22201
703-276-0100
Toll free: 1-800-955-5100
www.bbb.org/us/auto-line-lemon-law
The BBB AUTO LINE is a dispute resolution program for consumers with "lemon law" complaints. The program covers car warranty issues against participating manufacturers.

Consumer Financial Protection Bureau (CFPB)
PO Box 4503
Iowa City, IA 52244
Toll free: 1-855-411-2372
TTY: 1-855-729-2372
✉: info@consumerfinance.gov
www.consumerfinance.gov
The CFPB supervises and accepts complaints related to your vehicle loans and financing problem, or if you encountered problems while shopping for your vehicle loan.

DOT Auto Safety Hotline
1200 New Jersey Ave., SE
West Building
Washington, DC 20590
Toll free: 1-888-327-4236
TTY: 1-800-424-9153
www.nhtsa.gov/Contact
Contact the DOT Auto Safety Hotline to report safety defects in vehicles, tires, and child safety seats.

National Center for Dispute Settlement (NCDS)
12900 Hall Rd., Suite 401
Sterling Heights, MI 48313
586-226-2470
✉: info@ncdsusa.org
www.ncdsusa.org
NCDS is a neutral administrator of disputes regarding auto warranties. NCDS facilitates the process under their rules, under the guidance of an independent arbitrator.

◆ Provided financial support for the publication of the Consumer Action Handbook.

Council

3033 Wilson Blvd., Suite 600
Arlington, VA 22201
703-276-0100

Alabama

Birmingham
2101 Highland Ave., Suite 410
Birmingham, AL 35205
205-558-2222

Boaz
100 Bartlett Ave.
Boaz, AL 35957
256-840-3888

Cullman
PO Box 189
Cullman, AL 35056
256-775-2917

Decatur
254 Moulton St., E
Decatur, AL 35601
256-355-2226

Dothan
1971 S. Brannon Stand Rd., Suite 3A
Dothan, AL 36305
334-794-0492

Florence
205 S. Seminary St., Suite 114
Florence, AL 35630
256-740-8224

Huntsville
210A Exchange Pl.
Huntsville, AL 35806
256-533-1640

Mobile
3 Dauphin St., Suite 2
Mobile, AL 36302
251-433-2227

Alaska

Anchorage
341 W. Tudor Rd., Suite 209
Anchorage, AK 99503
907-562-0704

Arizona

Lake Havasu
60 S. Acoma Blvd., Unit B102
Lake Havasu, AZ 86403
928-302-3701

Phoenix
4428 N. 12th St.
Phoenix, AZ 85014
602-264-1721

Contact Your Local Better Business Bureau

Better Business Bureaus (BBBs) are nonprofit organizations that encourage honest advertising and selling practices, and are supported primarily by local businesses. BBBs offer a variety of consumer services, including consumer education materials; business reports, researching unanswered consumer complaints or other problems; mediation and arbitration services; and information about charities and other organizations that are seeking public donations. They also provide ratings (A, B, C, D, or F) of local companies to express the BBB's confidence that the company operates in a trustworthy manner and demonstrates a willingness to resolve customer concerns.

Complaints should be submitted in writing so that an accurate record exists of the dispute. The BBB will then present the complaint to the company involved. If the complaint is not resolved, the BBB may offer an alternative dispute settlement process. BBBs do not judge or rate individual products or brands, handle employer/employee wage disputes, or give legal advice.

If you need help with a consumer question or complaint, contact your local BBB or visit its website.

BBBOnLine (www.bbb.org/online) provides Internet users an easy way to verify the legitimacy of online businesses. Companies carrying the BBBOnLine seal have been checked out by the BBB and agree to resolve customer concerns.

The Council of Better Business Bureaus, the umbrella organization for the BBBs, can assist with complaints about the truthfulness and accuracy of national advertising claims, including children's advertising; provide reports on national soliciting charities; and help to settle disputes with automobile manufacturers through the BBB Auto Line program (p. 62).

Prescott
213 Grove Ave.
Prescott, AZ 86301
928-772-3410

Tucson
5151 E. Broadway Blvd., Suite 100
Tucson, AZ 85711
520-888-5353

Yuma
350 W. 16th St., Suite 205
Yuma, AZ 85364
928-919-7940

Arkansas

Little Rock
12521 Kanis Rd.
Little Rock, AR 72211
501-664-7274

California

Bakersfield
1601 H St., Suite 101
Bakersfield, CA 93301
661-322-2074

Fresno
4201 W. Shaw Ave., Suite 107
Fresno, CA 93722
559-222-8111

Los Angeles
448 South Hill St., Suite 418
Los Angeles, CA 90013
213-631-3600

Oakland
1000 Broadway, Suite 625
Oakland, CA 94607
510-844-2000

San Diego
4747 Viewridge Ave., Suite 200
San Diego, CA 92123
858-496-2131

San Jose
1112 S. Bascom Ave.
San Jose, CA 95128
408-278-7400

Santa Barbara
PO Box 129
Santa Barbara, CA 93102
805-963-8657

Sacramento
3075 Beacon Blvd.
West Sacramento, CA 95691-3462
916-443-6843

Colorado

Colorado Springs
25 N. Wahsatch Ave.
Colorado Springs, CO 80903
719-636-1155

Denver
1020 Cherokee St.
Denver, CO 80204-4039
303-758-2100

Fort Collins
8020 S. County Rd. 5, Suite 100
Fort Collins, CO 80528
970-484-1348

Pueblo
131 S. Main St.
Pueblo, CO 81003
719-542-1605

Connecticut

Wallingford
94 S. Turnpike Rd.
Wallingford, CT 06492
203-269-2700

Delaware

New Castle
60 Reads Way
New Castle, DE 19720
302-221-5255

District Of Columbia

Washington
1411 K St., NW, Suite 1000
Washington, DC 20005
202-393-8000

Florida

Clearwater
2655 McCormick Dr.
Clearwater, FL 33759
727-535-5522

Jacksonville
4417 Beach Blvd., Suite 202
Jacksonville, FL 32207-4783
904-721-2288

Longwood
1600 S. Grant St.
Longwood, FL 32750
407-621-3300

Miami
14750 N.W. 77 Ct., Suite 317
Miami Lakes, FL 33016
305-827-5363

Pensacola
912 E. Gadsden St.
Pensacola, FL 32501
850-429-0002

Stuart
101 E. Ocean Blvd., Suite 202
Stuart, FL 34994
772-223-1492

West Palm Beach
4411 Beacon Circle, Suite 4
West Palm Beach, FL 33407
561-842-1918

Georgia

Atlanta
503 Oak Pl., Suite 590
Atlanta, GA 30349
404-766-0875

Augusta
1227 Augusta West Pkwy., Suite 15
Augusta, GA 30909
706-210-7676

Columbus
PO Box 2587
Columbus, GA 31902
706-324-0712

Macon
277 Martin Luther King Jr. Blvd.
Suite 102
Macon, GA 31201
478-742-7999

Savannah
6555 Abercorn St., Suite 120
Savannah, GA 31405-5817
912-354-7521

Hawaii

Honolulu
1132 Bishop St., Suite 615
Honolulu, HI 96813-2813
808-536-6956

Idaho

Boise
1200 N. Curtis Rd.
Boise, ID 83706
208-342-4649

Idaho Falls
420 Memorial Dr.
Idaho Falls, ID 83402
208-523-9754

Illinois

Chicago
330 N. Wabash Ave., Suite 3120
Chicago, IL 60611
312-832-0500

Peoria
112 Harrison St.
Peoria, IL 61602
309-688-5124

Rockford
401 W. State St., Suite 500
Rockford, IL 61101
815-963-2222

Indiana

Evansville
3101 N. Green River Rd., Suite 410
Evansville, IN 47715
812-473-0202

Fort Wayne
4011 Parnell Ave.
Fort Wayne, IN 46805
260-423-4433

Indianapolis
151 N. Delaware St., Suite 2020
Indianapolis, IN 46204-2599
317-488-2222

Osceola
10775 McKinley Hwy., Suite B
Osceola, IN 46561
574-675-9351

Schereville
222 Indianapolis Blvd., Suite 201-A
Schereville, IN 46375
219-227-8400

Iowa

Bettendorf
2435 Kimberly Rd., Suite 245 S
Bettendorf, IA 52722
515-243-8137

Cedar Rapids
1239 1st Ave., Suite A
Cedar Rapids, IA 52402
515-243-8137

Des Moines
505 5th Ave., Suite 950
Des Moines, IA 50309
515-243-8137

Kansas

Wichita
345 N. Riverview St., Suite 720
Wichita, KS 68137
316-263-3146

Kentucky

Lexington
1390 Olivia Ln., Suite 100
Lexington, KY 40511
859-259-1008

Louisville
844 S. Fourth St.
Louisville, KY 40203
502-583-6546

Louisiana

Alexandria
5220-C Rue Verdun
Alexandria, LA 71303
318-473-4494

Baton Rouge
748 Main St.
Baton Rouge, LA 70802-5526
225-346-5222

Houma
801 Barrow St., Suite 400
Houma, LA 70360
985-868-3456

Lafayette
4007 W. Congress St., Suite B
Lafayette, LA 70506
337-981-3497

Lake Charles
2309 E. Prien Lake Rd.
Lake Charles, LA 70601
337-478-6253

New Orleans
3421 N. Causeway Blvd., Suite 505
Metairie, LA 70002
504-581-6222

Monroe
1900 N. 18th St., Suite 411
Monroe, LA 71201
318-387-4600

Shreveport
2006 E. 70th St.
Shreveport, LA 71105
318-797-1330

Maryland

Baltimore
502 S. Sharp St., Suite 1200
Baltimore, MD 21201
410-347-3990

Massachusetts

Marlborough
290 Donald Lynch Blvd., Suite 102
Marlborough, MA 01752-4705
508-652-4800

Worcester
6 Park Ave., Suite 100
Worcester, MA 01605
Toll free: 1-866-566-9222

Michigan

Detroit
26777 Central Park Blvd., Suite 100
Southfield, MI 48076-4163
248-223-9400

Grand Rapids
2627 E. Beltline Ave., SE, Suite 320
Grand Rapids, MI 49546
616-774-8236

Minnesota

Minneapolis/St. Paul
220 S. River Ridge Circle
Burnsville, MN 55337
651-699-1111

Mississippi

Jackson
505 Avalon Way, Suite B
Brandon, MS 39047
601-398-1700

Missouri

Columbia
3610 Buttonwood Dr., Suite 200
Columbia, MO 65201
573-886-8965

Kansas City
8080 Ward Pkwy., Suite 401
Kansas City, MO 64114
816-421-7800

Springfield
2754 S. Campbell Ave.
Springfield, MO 65802
417-862-4222

St. Louis
211 N. Broadway, Suite 2060
St. Louis, MO 63102
314-645-3300

Nebraska

Lincoln
300 N. 44th St., Suite 100
Lincoln, NE 68503
402-436-2345

Omaha
11811 P St.
Omaha, NE 68137
402-391-7612

Nevada

Las Vegas
6040 S. Jones Blvd.
Las Vegas, NV 89118
702-320-4500

Reno
4834 Sparks Blvd., Suite 102
Sparks, NV 89436
775-322-0657

New Hampshire

Concord
48 Pleasant St.
Concord, NH 03301
603-224-1991

New Jersey

Hamilton
1262 Whitehorse Hamilton Square Rd.
Bldg. A, Suite 202
Hamilton, NJ 08690-3596
609-588-0808

New Mexico

Albuquerque
7007 Jefferson St., NE, Suite A
Albuquerque, NM 87109
505-346-0110

Farmington
308 N. Locke Ave.
Farmington, NM 87401
505-326-6501

New York

Amherst
100 Bryant Woods South
Amherst, NY 14228
716-881-5222

Farmingdale/Long Island
399 Conklin St., Suite 300
Farmingdale, NY 11735
516-420-0500

New York
30 E. 33rd St., 12th Floor
New York, NY 10016
212-533-6200

Tarrytown
150 White Plains Rd., Suite 107
Tarrytown, NY 10591
914-333-0550

North Carolina

Asheville
112 Executive Park
Asheville, NC 28801
828-253-2392

Charlotte
13860 Ballantyne Corporate Place
Suite 225
Charlotte, NC 28277
704-927-8611

Greensboro
529 College Rd., Suite G
Greensboro, NC 27410
336-852-4240

Raleigh
5540 Munford Rd., Suite 130
Raleigh, NC 27612-2655
919-277-4222

Winston-Salem
119 Brookstown Ave., Suite 304
Winston-Salem, NC 27101
336-725-8348

Ohio

Akron
222 W. Market St.
Akron, OH 44303
330-253-4590

Canton
1434 Cleveland Ave., NW
Canton, OH 44703
330-454-9401

Cincinnati
7 W. 7th St., Suite 1600
Cincinnati, OH 45202
513-421-3015

Cleveland
2800 Euclid Ave., 4th Floor
Cleveland, OH 44115
216-241-7678

Columbus
1169 Dublin Rd.
Columbus, OH 43215-1005
614-486-6336

Dayton
15 W. Fourth St., Suite 300
Dayton, OH 45402
937-222-5825

Lima
219 N. McDonel St.
Lima, OH 43617
419-223-7010

Toledo
Integrity Place
7668 King's Pointe Rd.
Toledo, OH 43617
419-531-3116

Youngstown
201 E. Commerce St.
Youngstown, OH 44503
330-744-3111

Oklahoma

Oklahoma City
17 S. Dewey St.
Oklahoma City, OK 73102-2400
405-239-6081

Tulsa
1722 S. Carson Ave., Suite 3200
Tulsa, OK 74119
918-492-1266

Oregon

Lake Oswego
4004 S.W. Kruse Way Pl., Suite 375
Lake Oswego, OR 97035
503-212-3022

Pennsylvania

Bethlehem
50 W. North St.
Bethlehem, PA 18018
610-866-8780

Erie
1001 State St.
Erie, PA 16501
Toll free: 1-877-267-5222

Harrisburg
1337 N. Front St.
Harrisburg, PA 17102
717-364-3250

Philadelphia
1880 John F. Kennedy Blvd., Suite 1330
Philadelphia, PA 19103
215-985-9313

Pittsburgh
400 Holiday Dr., Suite 220
Pittsburgh, PA 15220
Toll free: 1-877-267-5222

Scranton/Wilkes Barre
1054 Oak St.
Scranton, PA 18508
570-342-5100

South Carolina

Columbia
2442 Devine St.
Columbia, SC 29205
803-254-2525

Conway
1121 3rd Ave.
Conway, SC 29526
843-488-2227

Greenville
408 N. Church St., Suite C
Greenville, SC 29601
864-242-5052

South Dakota

Sioux Falls
300 N. Phillips Ave., Suite 202
Sioux Falls, SD 57104
605-271-2066

Tennessee

Chattanooga
508 N. Market St.
Chattanooga, TN 37405
423-266-6144

Clarksville
214 Main St.
Clarksville, TN 37040
931-503-2222

Columbia
502 N. Garden St., Suite 201
Columbia, TN 38401
931-388-9222

Cookeville
18 N. Jefferson St.
Cookeville, TN 38501
931-520-0000

Franklin
367 Riverside Dr., Suite 110
Franklin, TN 37064
615-250-7431

Knoxville
255 N. Peters Rd., Suite 102
Knoxville, TN 37923
865-692-1600

Memphis
3693 Tyndale Dr.
Memphis, TN 38125
901-759-1300

Murfreesboro
530 Uptown Square
Murfreesboro, TN 37129
615-242-4222

Nashville
201 4th Ave. N., Suite 100
Nashville, TN 37219
615-242-4222

Texas

Abilene
3300 S. 14th St., Suite 307
Abilene, TX 79605-5052
325-691-1533

Amarillo
600 S. Tyler St., Suite 1300
Amarillo, TX 79101
806-379-6222

Austin
1005 La Posada Dr.
Austin, TX 78752
512-445-2911

Beaumont
550 Fannin St., Suite 100
Beaumont, TX 77701
409-835-5348

College Station
418 Tarrow St.
College Station, TX 77840-1822
979-260-2222

Corpus Christi
719 S. Shoreline, Suite 304
Corpus Christi, TX 78401
361-852-4949

Dallas
1601 Elm St., Suite 3838
Dallas, TX 75201
214-220-2000

El Paso
550 E. Paisano
El Paso, TX 79901
915-577-0191

Fort Worth
1300 Summit Ave., Suite 700
Fort Worth, TX 76102
Toll free: 1-800-621-8566

Houston
1333 W. Loop South, Suite 1200
Houston, TX 77027
713-868-9500

Longview
102 Commander Dr., Suite 7
Longview, TX 75605
903-758-3222

Lubbock
3333 66th St.
Lubbock, TX 79413
806-763-0459

Midland
306 W. Wall St., Suite 1350
Midland, TX 79701
432-563-1880

San Angelo
3134 Executive Dr., Suite A
San Angelo, TX 76904
325-949-2989

San Antonio
425 Soledad St., Suite 500
San Antonio, TX 78205
210-828-9441

Tyler
3600 Old Bullard Rd.
Building 1, Suite 101
Tyler, TX 75701
903-581-5704

Waco
200 W. Hwy 6, Suite 225
Waco, TX 76712
254-755-7772

Weslaco
502 E. Expressway 83, Suite C
Weslaco, TX 78596
956-968-3678

Wichita Falls
2107 Kemp Blvd.
Wichita Falls, TX 76309
940-691-1172

Utah

Salt Lake City
5673 S. Redwood Rd., Suite 22
Salt Lake City, UT 84123
801-892-6009

Virginia

Norfolk
586 Virginian Dr.
Norfolk, VA 23505
757-531-1300

Richmond
720 Moorefield Park Dr., Suite 300
Richmond, VA 23236
804-648-0016

Roanoke
5115 Bernard Dr., Suite 202
Roanoke, VA 24018
540-342-3455

Washington

Seattle
1000 Station Dr., Suite 222
DuPont, WA 98327
206-431-2222

Spokane
152 S. Jefferson, Suite 200
Spokane, WA 99201
509-455-4200

West Virginia

Charleston
1018 Kanawha Blvd. E., Suite 301
Charleston, WV 25301
304-345-7502

Wisconsin

Appleton
1047 N. Lynndale Dr.
Appleton, WI 54914
920-734-4352

Madison
2702 International Ln.
Madison, WI 53704
608-268-2221

Milwaukee
10019 W. Greeenfield Ave.
Milwaukee, WI 53214
414-847-6000

Contact Corporate Consumer Affairs Departments

The following directory lists the addresses and phone numbers for hundreds of corporations. Many companies have a consumer affairs department that handles consumer questions and concerns. Consumer affairs offices are set up within companies because they want to hear from you. If you do not find the company you are looking for, try checking your public libraries for the following resources:

- The Standard & Poor's Register of Corporations, Directors and Executives
- Trade Names Directory
- Standard Directory of Advertisers
- Dun & Bradstreet Directory

Check the product label and other documents given to you at the time of your purchase to identify the name of a company that manufactures a specific product. ThomasNet, an online database of manufacturers, might also be helpful.

If you have a complaint about an item or service, it is usually best to go back to the seller BEFORE you contact the companies in this directory. Follow up with a letter, phone call, or email message to the consumer affairs department of the company to let it know about your complaint, and whether the seller was able to resolve your problem. You may express your complaint on a company's social media profile to get quick attention to your problem.

A

AAMCO Transmissions, Inc.
Consumer Affairs
201 Gibraltar Rd.
Horsham, PA 19044
Toll free: 1-800-523-0401
www.aamco.com

Abbott Nutrition Products Division
Public Affairs, Dept. 383
100 Abbott Park Rd.
Abbott Park, IL 60064-6048
Toll free: 1-800-227-5767
www.abbottnutrition.com

Abercrombie & Fitch
Customer Service
200 Abercrombie Way
New Albany, OH 43054
614-219-3026
Toll free: 1-866-681-3115
✉: abercrombie@abercrombie.com
www.abercrombie.com

Acer America
Customer Service
333 W. San Carlos St., Suite 1500
San Jose, CA 95110
408-533-7700
www.acer.com

Adidas America, Inc.
Customer Service
5055 N. Greeley Ave.
Portland, OR 97217
Toll free: 1-800-448-1796
Toll free: 1-800-982-9337 (Online)
✉: customerservice@us.adidas.com
www.adidas.com

Adobe Systems, Inc.
345 Park Ave.
San Jose, CA 95110-2704
408-536-6000
Toll free: 1-800-833-6687 (Customer Support))
www.adobe.com

Aetna, Inc.
151 Farmington Ave.
Hartford, CT 06156
Toll free: 1-800-872-3862
www.aetna.com

Aflac
1932 Wynnton Rd.
Columbus, GA 31999
Toll free: 1-800-992-3522
www.aflac.com

AirTran Airways, Inc.
See: Southwest Airlines
214-932-0333
Toll free: 1-800-435-9792
TTY: 1-800-533-1305
www.airtran.com

Alamo Rent A Car
Customer Care
600 Corporate Park Dr.
Saint Louis, MO 63105
Toll free: 1-888-233-8749
TTY: 1-800-522-9292
www.alamo.com

Alaska Airlines
Customer Care
PO Box 24948-SEAGT
Seattle, WA 98124-0948
Toll free: 1-800-654-5669
Toll free: 1-877-815-8253 (Baggage)
www.alaskaair.com

Albertsons, LLC
Customer Service
157 S. Howard St.
Spokane, WA 99201
Toll free: 1-877-932-7948
✉: albertsonscustomercare@albertsons.com
www.albertsons.com

Alcon Laboratories, Inc.
Customer Service
6201 South Freeway
Fort Worth, TX 76134-2001
Toll free: 1-800-862-5266
www.alcon.com

Allergan, Inc.
Customer Service
PO Box 19534
Irvine, CA 92623
714-246-4500
Toll free: 1-800-433-8871
www.allergan.com

Allied Van Lines, Inc.
Customer Service
One Parkview Plaza
Oakbrook Terrace, IL 60181
Toll free: 1-800-470-2851
✉: custsvc@alliedvan.com
www.allied.com

Allstate Insurance Company
PO Box 12055
1819 Electric Rd., SW
Roanoke, VA 24018
Toll free: 1-800-255-7828
TTY: 1-800-877-8973
www.allstate.com

Amana Appliances
Customer Service
553 Benson Rd.
Benton Harbor, MI 49022
Toll free: 1-866-616-2664
www.amana.com

Amazon.com, Inc.
Customer Service
PO Box 81226
Seattle, WA 98108-1226
Toll free: 1-866-216-1072
www.amazon.com

AMC Entertainment, Inc.
PO Box 725489
Atlanta, GA 31139-9923
www.amctheatres.com

American Airlines, Inc.
Customer Relations
PO Box 619612
Mail Drop 2400
Dallas/Fort Worth Airport, TX 75261-9612
817-967-2000
Toll free: 1-800-535-5225 (Baggage)
www.aa.com

American Eagle Outfitters
Customer Service
77 Hot Metal St.
Pittsburgh, PA 15203
Toll free: 1-888-232-4535
www.ae.com

American Express Company ○
Customer Service
PO Box 981540
El Paso, TX 79998-1540
Toll free: 1-800-528-4800
Toll free: 1-877-297-4438 (Gift Cards)
TTY: 1-800-221-9950
www.americanexpress.com

Amtrak
Customer Relations
60 Massachusetts Ave., NE
Washington, DC 20002
Toll free: 1-800-872-7245
TTY: 1-800-523-6590
www.amtrak.com

Andersen Windows, Inc. ○
Customer Service
100 4th Ave., N
Bayport, MN 55003-1096
Toll free: 1-888-888-7020
www.andersenwindows.com

Angie's List
1030 E. Washington St.
Indianapolis, IN 46202
Toll free: 1-888-944-5478
www.angieslist.com

Anheuser-Busch, Inc. ○
One Busch Pl.
St. Louis, MO 63118
Toll free: 1-800-342-5283
www.anheuser-busch.com

Anthem Blue Cross and Blue Shield
www.anthem.com

Anytime Fitness, LLC
Customer Service
12181 Margo Ave., S
Hastings, MN 55033
651-438-5000
www.anytimefitness.com

Apple Computer, Inc.
One Infinite Loop
Cupertino, CA 95014
Toll free: 1-800-275-2273 (iPod, iPad, and Mac Technical Support)
Toll free: 1-800-694-7466 (iPhone Technical Support)
TTY: 1-877-204-3930
www.apple.com

Applebee's
8140 Ward Pkwy.
Kansas City, MO 64114
Toll free: 1-888-592-7753
www.applebees.com

Arby's Restaurant Group, Inc.
1155 Perimeter Center W, 12th Floor
Atlanta, GA 30338
678-514-4100
✉: customerservice@arbys.com
www.arbys.com

Ariens Company ○
Customer Support
655 W. Ryan St.
Brillion, WI 54110-1098
920-756-4688
www.ariens.com

Ashley Furniture Industries, Inc.
Consumer Affairs
One Ashley Way
Arcadia, WI 54612
www.ashleyfurniture.com

Associated Bank ○
We Care Dept.
1305 Main St., Mail Stop 7722
Stevens Point, WI 54481
Toll free: 1-800-236-8866
✉: wecare@associatedbank.com
www.associatedbank.com

Asus Computer International
800 Corporate Way
Fremont, CA 94539
510-739-3777
Toll free: 1-888-678-3688
www.asus.com

Atlas World Group, Inc.
Customer Service
1212 Saint George Rd.
Evansville, IN 47711-2364
Toll free: 1-800-638-9797
www.atlasvanlines.com

AT&T, Inc.
Customer Service
208 S. Acard St.
Dallas, TX 75202
210-821-4105
Toll free: 1-800-331-0500 (Wireless Customer Service)
Toll free: 1-855-288-2727 (Home Security)
www.att.com

Avis Rent A Car System, LLC
Customer Service
PO Box 699000
Tulsa, OK 74169-9000
Toll free: 1-800-352-7900
TTY: 1-800-331-2323
✉: custserv@avis.com
www.avis.com

Avon Products, Inc.
Customer Service
777 Third Ave.
New York, NY 10017
212-282-7000
Toll free: 1-800-367-2866
✉: dearavon@avon.com
www.avon.com

B

Bacardi USA, Inc. ○
Consumer Affairs
2701 S. Le Jeune Rd.
Coral Gables, FL 33134
Toll free: 1-800-222-2734
www.bacardi.com

Bally Total Fitness Corporation
Member Services
PO Box 96241
Washington, DC 20090-6241
Toll free: 1-866-402-2559
www.ballyfitness.com

Banana Republic
Customer Service
5900 N. Meadows Dr.
Grove City, OH 43123
Toll free: 1-888-277-8953
TTY: 1-888-906-1345
✉: custserv@bananarepublic.com
www.bananarepublic.com

Bank of America Corporation
PO Box 25118
Tampa, FL 33622-5118
Toll free: 1-800-432-1000
TTY: 1-800-288-4408
www.bankofamerica.com

Barnes & Noble
PO Box 111
Lyndhurst, NJ 07071
Toll free: 1-800-962-6177
✉: customerservice@bn.com
www.bn.com

Baskin-Robbins
Customer Service
Dunkin Brands, Inc.
130 Royall St.
Canton, MA 02021
Toll free: 1-800-859-5339
www.baskinrobbins.com

Bassett Baby Furniture
3525 Fairystone Park Hwy.
PO Box 626
Bassett, VA 24055
Toll free: 1-877-525-7070 (Furniture)
Toll free: 1-800-308-7485 (Baby
Furniture)
Toll free: 1-800-697-3259 (Mattresses)
www.bassettfurniture.com

Bausch & Lomb
1400 N. Goodman St.
Rochester, NY 14609
Toll free: 1-800-553-5340
www.bausch.com

Bayer Consumer Care Products
Consumer Relations
100 Bayer Blvd.
Whippany, NJ 07981-0915
Toll free: (phone numbers appear on
all labels)
www.bayercare.com

BB&T
CEO Line
PO Box 632
Whiteville, NC 28472
Toll free: 1-888-628-3926
TTY: 1-888-833-4228
✉: ceoline@bbandt.com
www.bbt.com

Bed Bath and Beyond
Customer Service
650 Liberty Ave.
Union, NJ 07083
Toll free: 1-800-462-3966
✉: customer.service@bedbath.com
www.bedbathandbeyond.com

Beech-Nut Nutrition Corporation
Consumer Affairs
One Nutritious Pl.
Amsterdam, NY 12010
Toll free: 1-800-233-2468
www.beechnut.com

Beiersdorf, Inc.
Consumer Relations
45 Danbury Rd.
Wilton, CT 06897
Toll free: 1-800-227-4703
www.beiersdorfusa.com

Bellisio Foods, Inc.
Consumer Affairs
PO Box 16630
Duluth, MN 55816
Toll free: 1-800-446-5469
✉: info@bellisiofoods.com
www.bellisiofoods.com

Ben & Jerry's Homemade, Inc.
Consumer Services
30 Community Dr.
South Burlington, VT 05403-6828
802-846-1500
www.benjerry.com

Best Buy Company, Inc.
Customer Care
7601 Penn Ave., S
Richfield, MN 55423-3645
Toll free: 1-888-237-8289
✉: onlinestore@bestbuy.com
www.bestbuy.com

Best Western International, Inc.
Customer Care
PO Box 10203
Phoenix, AZ 85064
Toll free: 1-800-528-1238
TTY: 1-800-528-2222
✉: customercare@bestwestern.com
www.bestwestern.com

BIC Corporation
Consumer Affairs
One BIC Way, Suite 1
Shelton, CT 06484-6299
Toll free: 1-800-546-1111
www.bicworld.com

Big Lot Stores, Inc.
Customer Service
300 Phillipi Rd.
Columbus, OH 43228-5311
Toll free: 1-800-877-1253
✉: talk2us@biglots.com
www.biglots.com

Birds Eye Foods, Inc.
Pinnacle Consumer Relations
PO Box 971
Miami, FL 33152
Toll free: 1-800-432-3102
www.birdseye.com

Bissell Homecare, Inc.
Customer Service
PO Box 3606
Grand Rapids, MI 49501
Toll free: 1-800-237-7691
www.bissell.com

BJ's Wholesale Club, Inc.
Member Care
25 Research Dr.
Westborough, MA 01581
Toll free: 1-800-257-2582
Toll free: 1-866-425-7932 (Online
Inquiries)
www.bjs.com

Bloomingdales, Inc.
Customer Service
9111 Duke Blvd.
Mason, OH 45040
Toll free: 1-800-777-0000
www.bloomingdales.com

Bob Evans Farms, Inc.
Consumer Relations
8111 Smith's Mill Rd.
New Albany, OH 43054
Toll free: 1-800-939-2338
www.bobevans.com

The Breathe Right Company
Toll free: 1-800-858-6673
www.breatheright.com

Bridgestone Americas, Inc.
535 Marriott Dr.
PO Box 140990
Nashville, TN 37214-0990
615-937-1000
www.bridgestone-firestone.com

Brinker International
6820 LBJ Freeway
Dallas, TX 75240
972-980-9917
www.brinker.com

Brio Tuscan Grill
Guest Feedback
777 Goodale Blvd.
Suite 100
Columbus, OH 43212
Toll free: 1-888-452-7286
www.brioitalian.com

Bristol-Myers Squibb Company
Customer Relations
345 Park Ave.
New York, NY 10154
Toll free: 1-800-332-2056
www.bms.com

British Airways
Customer Relations
PO Box 300686
Jamaica, NY 11430-0686
Toll free: 1-800-247-9297
Toll free: 1-800-828-8144 (Baggage Claims)
Toll free: 1-800-403-0882 (Online)
TTY: 1-866-393-0961
www.britishairways.com

Brookstone
Customer Care Center
1655 Bassford Dr.
Mexico, MO 65265
Toll free: 1-800-846-3000
✉: customercare@brookstone.com
www.brookstone.com

Brown-Forman Beverages Worldwide
Consumer Support
850 Dixie Highway
Louisville, KY 40210
Toll free: 1-800-753-4567
✉: Brown-Forman@b-f.com
www.brown-forman.com

Brown Shoe Company, Inc.
Consumer Care
8300 Maryland Ave.
St. Louis, MO 63105
Toll free: 1-800-766-6465
www.brownshoe.com

Budget Rent A Car System, Inc.
Customer Service
PO Box 699000
Tulsa, OK 74169-9000
Toll free: 1-800-214-6094
TTY: 1-800-826-5510
✉: budgetcustomerservice@
budgetgroup.com
www.budget.com

Burger King Corporation
Guest Relations
5505 Blue Lagoon Dr.
Miami, FL 33126
Toll free: 1-866-394-2493
www.bk.com

Burlington Coat Factory
Customer Relations
1830 Route 130 N
Burlington, NJ 08016
Toll free: 1-855-355-2875
www.burlingtoncoatfactory.com

Bush Brothers Company ␥
Consumer Relations
PO Box 52330
Knoxville, TN 37950-2330
Toll free: 1-800-590-3797
www.bushbeans.com

C

Campbell Soup Company ␥
Consumer Affairs
One Campbell Place
Camden, NJ 08103-1701
Toll free: 1-800-257-8443
www.campbellsoup.com

Canon USA, Inc.
One Canon Park
Melville, NY 11747
Toll free: 1-800-652-2666
TTY: 1-866-251-3752
www.usa.canon.com

Capital One
General Correspondence
PO Box 30285
Salt Lake City, UT 84130-0285
1-800-227-4825
TTY: 1-800-206-7986
www.capitalone.com

Carfax, Inc.
Consumer Affairs
5860 Trinity Pkwy., Suite 600
Centerville, VA 20120
www.carfax.com/help

Carnival Cruise Lines
Guest Relations
3655 N.W. 87th Ave.
Miami, FL 33178-2428
Toll free: 1-888-227-6482
Toll free: 1-800-929-6400 (Baggage)
✉: guestcare@carnival.com
www.carnival.com

Carrier Air Conditioning Company
Customer Relations
PO Box 4808, Carrier Pkwy.
Syracuse, NY 13221-4808
Toll free: 1-800-227-7437
www.residential.carrier.com

Casio, Inc.
570 Mt. Pleasant Ave.
Dover, NJ 07801
973-361-5400
Toll free: 1-800-706-2534 (Repairs)
Toll free: 1-800-435-7732 (Technical Support)
www.casio.com

Chattem, Inc.
Consumer Affairs
PO Box 2219
Chattanooga, TN 37409-0219
Toll free: 1-888-442-4464
www.chattem.com

Check 'n Go
7755 Montgomery Rd., Suite 400
Cincinnati, OH 45236
Toll free: 1-800-561-2274
✉: customerservice@checkngo.com
www.checkngo.com

The Cheesecake Factory
26901 Malibu Hills Rd.
Calabasas Hills, CA 91301
818-871-3000
www.thecheesecakefactory.com

Chick-fil-A, Inc.
Customer Feedback
PO Box 725489
Atlanta, GA 31139-9923
Toll free: 1-866-232-2040
www.chick-fil-a.com

Children's Place
Customer Service
500 Plaza Dr.
Secaucus, NJ 07094
Toll free: 1-877-752-2387
www.childrensplace.com

Chili's
See: Brinker International
Toll free: 1-800-983-4637 (Guest Relations)
www.chilis.com

Chipotle Mexican Grill, Inc.
1401 Wynkoop St., Suite 500
Denver, CO 80202
303-595-4000
✉: customerservice@chipotle.com
www.chipotle.com

Choice Hotels ␥
Guest Relations
6811 E. Mayo Blvd., Suite 100
Phoenix, AZ 85054
Toll free: 1-800-300-8800
www.choicehotels.com

Church & Dwight Company, Inc. ␥
Consumer and Professional Relations
Princeton South Corporate Center
500 Charles Ewing Blvd.
Ewing, NJ 08628
Toll free: 1-800-833-9532
www.churchdwight.com

Citibank, Inc. ⟲
Client Services
100 Citibank Dr.
San Antonio, TX 78245-9004
Toll free: 1-800-374-9700 (Banking)
Toll free: 1-800-950-5114 (Credit cards)
TTY: 1-800-788-0002 (Banking)
TTY: 1-800-325-2865 (Credit cards)
www.citibank.com

The Clorox Company ⟲
Consumer Services
Mail Stop 2334
1221 Broadway
Oakland, CA 94612-1888
Toll free: (Phone numbers appear on all labels)
www.thecloroxcompany.com

The Coca-Cola Company ⟲
Industry and Consumer Affairs
PO Box 1734
Atlanta, GA 30301
Toll free: 1-800-438-2653
www.thecocacolacompany.com

The Colgate-Palmolive Company ⟲ ♦
Consumer Affairs
300 Park Ave.
New York, NY 10022
212-310-2000
Toll free: 1-800-468-6502
www.colgate.com

Colonial Penn Life Insurance
Customer Services
399 Market St.
Philadelphia, PA 19181-2150
Toll free: 1-800-523-9100
www.colonialpenn.com

Combe, Inc. ⟲
Consumer Resources
1101 Westchester Ave.
White Plains, NY 10604
Toll free: 1-800-431-2610
www.combe.com

Comcast Corporation
One Comcast Center
1701 JFK Blvd.
Philadelphia, PA 19103
Toll free: 1-800-266-2278
Toll free: 1-800-934-6489 (Xfinity)
www.comcast.com

ConAgra Foods ⟲
Consumer Affairs
One ConAgra Dr.
Omaha, NE 68102
Toll free: 1-877-266-2472
✉: consumeraffairs@conagrafoods.com
www.conagrafoods.com

Conair Cuisinart Corporation
Consumer Affairs
150 Milford Rd.
East Windsor, NJ 08520
Toll free: 1-800-326-6247 (Personal Care)
Toll free: 1-800-334-4031 (Oral Care)
✉: feedback@conair.com
www.conair.com

Costco Wholesale Corporation
Member Service
PO Box 34331
Seattle, WA 98124
Toll free: 1-800-774-2678
Toll free: 1-800-955-2292 (Online Members)
✉: customerservice@costco.com
www.costco.com

Coty Inc. ⟲
Consumer Affairs
500 American Rd.
Morris Plains, NJ 07950
Toll free: 1-800-715-4023
Toll free: 1-800-953-5080 (Sally Hansen and N.Y.C. New York Color)
www.coty.com

Cox Communications
1400 Lake Hearn Dr., NE
Atlanta, GA 30319
Toll free: 1-888-566-7751
✉: coxcorp.customerrelations@cox.com
www.cox.com

Cracker Barrel Old Country Store
PO Box 787
Lebanon, TN 37088-0787
Toll free: 1-800-333-9566
www.crackerbarrel.com

Crate and Barrel
Customer Service
1860 W. Jefferson Ave.
Naperville, IL 60540
Toll free: 1-800-967-6696
✉: customer_service@crateandbarrel.com
www.crateandbarrel.com

Crayola, LLC ⟲
Consumer Affairs
PO Box 431
Easton, PA 18044-0431
Toll free: 1-800-272-9652
www.crayola.com

Cricket Wireless
575 Morosgo Dr., NE
Alpharetta, GA 30324
Toll free: 1-855-924-6246 (Corporate)
Toll free: 1-800-274-2538 (Support)
www.mycricket.com

Crowne Plaza
See: InterContinental Hotels Group PLC
www.crowneplaza.com

Crunch Fitness
3595 Mt. Diablo Blvd., Suite 300
Lafayette, CA 94549
925-297-6360
✉: info@nev.com
www.crunch.com

Curves International
100 Ritchie Rd.
Woodway, TX 76712
Toll free: 1-877-673-3144
✉: membercomments@curves.com
www.curves.com

CVS Corporation
Customer Relations
One CVS Dr.
Woonsocket, RI 02895
401-765-1500
Toll free: 1-800-746-7287 (In-Store)
Toll free: 1-888-607-4287 (Online)
www.cvs.com

D

Dairy Queen Corporation ⟲
Customer Relations
7505 Metro Blvd.
Minneapolis, MN 55439-0286
952-830-0200
Toll free: 1-866-793-7582
www.dairyqueen.com

The Dannon Company, Inc. ⟲
Consumer Response Center
PO Box 90296
Allentown, PA 18109-0296
Toll free: 1-877-326-6668
www.dannon.com

Darden Restaurants ⟲
Guest Relations
PO Box 695011
Orlando, FL 32869-5011
407-245-4000
www.darden.com

Days Inn Worldwide, Inc.
Customer Service
PO Box 4090
Aberdeen, SD 57401
Toll free: 1-800-441-1618
www.daysinn.com

Dean Foods ⟲
PO Box 961447
El Paso, TX 79996
Toll free: 1-800-395-7004
✉: DeanFoods@CaSupport.com
www.deanfoods.com

♦ Provided financial support for the publication of the Consumer Action Handbook.

Dell, Inc.
Customer Service
One Dell Way
Round Rock, TX 78682
Toll free: 1-866-795-5597 (Customer Service)
Toll free: 1-800-624-9897 (Orders)
TTY: 1-877-335-5889
www.dell.com

Del Monte Foods, Inc.
Consumer Affairs
890 Mountain Ave, Suite 105
New Providence, NJ 07974
Toll free: 1-800-543-3090
www.delmonte.com

Delta Air Lines, Inc.
Customer Care
PO Box 20980
Department 980
Atlanta, GA 30320-2980
404-209-3434 (Disability Assistance)
Toll free: 1-800-455-2720
www.delta.com

Delta Faucets Company
55 E. 111th St.
Indianapolis, IN 46280
Toll free: 1-800-345-3358
✉: customerservice@deltafaucet.com
www.deltafaucet.com

Denny's Corporation
Call Center
203 E. Main St. P-7-3
Spartanburg, SC 29319
Toll free: 1-800-733-6697
www.dennys.com

Destination XL Group, Inc.
Customer Service
555 Turnpike St.
Canton, MA 02021
Toll free: 1-800-746-7395
www.destinationxl.com

Diageo North America, Inc.
Consumer Care
24460 W. 143 St.
Plainfield, IL 60544
www.diageo.com

Diamond Foods, Inc.
Consumer Affairs
1050 S. Diamond St.
Stockton, CA 95205
209-467-6000
www.diamondfoods.com

Dick's Sporting Goods
345 Court St.
Coraopolis, PA 15108
Toll free: 1-877-846-9997
www.dickssportinggoods.com

Dillard's, Inc.
Customer Service
PO Box 486
Little Rock, AR 72203
501-376-5200
Toll free: 1-800-345-5273
TTY: 1-800-444-1732
✉: questions@dillards.com
www.dillards.com

Diners Club International
Client Services
PO Box 6101
Carol Stream, IL 60197-6101
Toll free: 1-800-234-6377
www.dinersclubus.com

DIRECTV Enterprises, Inc.
PO Box 6550
Greenwood Village, CO 80155-6550
Toll free: 1-800-531-5000
TTY: 1-800-779-4388
www.DIRECTV.com

Discover Financial Services, Inc.
Customer Service
PO Box 30943
Salt Lake City, UT 84130-0943
801-902-3100
Toll free: 1-800-347-2683
TTY: 1-800-347-7449
www.discoverfinancial.com

Dish Network, LLC
9601 S. Meridian Blvd.
Englewood, CO 80112
Toll free: 1-855-318-0572
✉: tech@dish.com
www.dishnetwork.com

Dole Food Company, Inc.
Consumer Center
PO Box 5700
Thousand Oaks, CA 91359-5700
Toll free: 1-800-356-3111
www.dole.com

Dollar Rent A Car, Inc.
Customer Service 2W2
PO Box 33167
Tulsa, OK 74153-1167
Toll free: 1-800-800-5252
✉: internethelpdesk@dollar.com (for speech and hearing impaired)
www.dollar.com

Domino's Pizza, Inc.
Customer Service
30 Frank Lloyd Wright Dr.
PO Box 997
Ann Arbor, MI 48106
734-930-3030
www.dominos.com

Doubletree
See: Hilton Hospitality, Inc.
Toll free: 1-800-222-8733
TTY: 1-800-368-1133
www.doubletree.com

Dr. Pepper/Snapple Group, Inc.
Consumer Relations
PO Box 869077
Plano, TX 75086-9077
972-673-7000
Toll free: 1-800-696-5891
www.drpeppersnapplegroup.com

Dunkin Donuts
Consumer Care
130 Royall St.
Canton, MA 02021
Toll free: 1-800-859-5339
www.dunkindonuts.com

Dyson, Inc.
600 W. Chicago Ave., Suite 275
Chicago, IL 60654
Toll free: 1-844-679-1647
✉: questions@dyson.com
www.dyson.com

E

E*Trade Securities, LLC
PO Box 484
Jersey City, NJ 07303-0484
Toll free: 1-800-387-2331
www.etrade.com

eBay, Inc.
2065 Hamilton Ave.
San Jose, CA 95125
Toll free: 1-800-322-9266
www.eBay.com

Eddie Bauer, Inc.
Customer Service
PO Box 7001
Groveport, OH 43125
Toll free: 1-800-426-8020
TTY: 1-800-462-6757
✉: CustomerCare@csc.eddiebauer.com
www.eddiebauer.com

E. & J. Gallo Winery
Consumer Relations
1541 Cummins Dr.
Modesto, CA 95358
Toll free: 1-877-687-9463
www.gallo.com

The Electrolux Group
Kitchen and Laundry Consumer Assistance Center
PO Box 212237
Augusta, GA 30907
Toll free: 1-877-435-3287

Vacuums and Cleaners
PO Box 3900
Peoria, IL 61612
Toll free: 1-800-896-9756
www.electrolux.com

Eli Lilly Company ◊
Consumer Communications
Lilly Corporate Center
Indianapolis, IN 46285
317-276-2000
Toll free: 1-800-545-5979
www.lilly.com

Elizabeth Arden, Inc. ◊
Consumer Affairs
309 South St.
New Providence, NJ 07974
Toll free: 1-800-326-7337
✉: consumer@elizabetharden.com
www.elizabetharden.com

Embassy Suites
Hilton Hospitality, Inc.
Toll free: 1-800-362-2779
www.embassysuites.com

Energizer ◊
Customer Support
533 Maryville University Dr.
St. Louis, MO 63141
Toll free: 1-800-383-7323
www.energizer.com

Enterprise Rent-A-Car
600 Corporate Park Dr.
Saint Louis, MO 63105
Toll free: 1-800-264-6350
✉: customerservice@enterprise.com
www.enterprise.com

Equifax
PO Box 740241
Atlanta, GA 30374
Toll free: 1-800-685-1111
www.equifax.com

Equinox
Member Services
One Park Ave.
New York, NY 10016
212-774-6363
Toll free: 1-866-332-6549
www.equinox.com

The Estée Lauder ◊
Companies, Inc.
Consumer Care
767 5th Ave.
New York, NY 10153
212-572-4200
Toll free: 1-888-378-3359
✉: consumercare-us@gcc.
esteelauder.com
www.elcompanies.com

Ethan Allen, Inc.
PO Box 1966
Danbury, CT 06813
Toll free: 1-888-324-3571
✉: orders@ethanalleninc.com
www.ethanallen.com

Etsy
Support Team
55 Washington St., Suite 512
Brooklyn, NY 11201
718-855-7955
www.etsy.com

The Eureka Company
Customer Service
PO Box 3900
Peoria, IL 61612
Toll free: 1-800-282-2886
www.eureka.com

Eveready Battery Company, Inc.
533 Maryville University Dr.
St. Louis, MO 63141
Toll free: 1-800-383-7323
www.eveready.com

Expedia, Inc. ◊
Customer Support
333 108th Ave., NE
Bellevue, WA 98004
Toll free: 1-800-397-3342
www.expedia.com

Experian
National Consumer Assistance Center
PO Box 2002
Allen, TX 75013
Toll free: 1-888-397-3742
✉: support@experiandirect.com
www.experian.com

Express Scripts
One Express Way
St Louis, MO 63121
Toll free: 1-800-631-7780
www.express-scripts.com

F

Facebook, Inc.
1601 Willow Rd.
Menlo Park, CA 94025
650-543-4800
www.facebook.com

Fairfield Inn
Toll free: 1-800-721-7033
www.fairfieldinn.com

Farmers Insurance
4680 Wilshire Blvd.
Los Angeles, CA 90010
Toll free: 1-888-327-6335
TTY: 1-888-891-1660
www.farmers.com

FedEx Corporation ◊
Customer Relations
3875 Airways Blvd.
Module H3 Department 4634
Memphis, TN 38116
Toll free: 1-800-463-3339
TTY: 1-800-238-4461
www.fedex.com

Fidelity Investments, LLC
PO Box 770001
Cincinnati, OH 45277-0002
Toll free: 1-800-544-6666
www.fidelity.com

Fisher-Price
See: Mattel, Inc.
Toll free: 1-800-432-5437
www.fisher-price.com

Flowers Foods, Inc. ◊
1919 Flowers Circle
Thomasville, GA 31757
229-226-9110
www.flowersfoods.com

Food Lion, Inc.
Customer Relations
PO Box 1330
Salisbury, NC 28145-1330
Toll free: 1-800-210-9569
www.FoodLion.com

Frigidaire Home Products
PO Box 212378
Augusta, GA 30909
Toll free: 1-800-374-4432
www.frigidaire.com

Frito-Lay
Consumer Relations
PO Box 660634
Dallas, TX 75266-6234
Toll free: 1-800-352-4477
www.fritolay.com

Frontier Airlines, Inc.
Customer Relations
PO Box 492085
Denver, CO 80249
Toll free: 1-800-432-1359
www.flyfrontier.com

FTD, Inc.
Customer Service
3113 Woodcreek Dr.
Downers Grove, IL 60515
Toll free: 1-800-736-3383
www.ftd.com

Fujifilm Corporation
Consumer Information Service Center
1100 King Georges Post Rd.
Edison, NJ 08837
Toll free: 1-800-800-3854
www.fujifilm.com

G

Gap, Inc.
Customer Service
100 Gap Online Dr.
Grove City, OH 43123
Toll free: 1-800-427-7895
TTY: 1-888-906-1104
✉: custserv@gap.com
www.gap.com

Gateway, Inc.
Customer Service
PO Box 6137
Temple, TX 76503
www.gateway.com

GEICO
One GEICO Plaza
Washington, DC 20076
Toll free: 1-800-861-8380 (Car)
Toll free: 1-888-841-2964 (Home)
Toll free: 1-888-532-5433 (Life)
TTY: 1-800-833-8255
www.geico.com

General Electric Company
3135 Easton Turnpike
Fairfield, CT 06828
203-373-2211
Toll free: 1-800-626-2000 (Appliances and Lighting)
www.ge.com

General Mills, Inc. ᒃ
Consumer Services
PO Box 9452
Minneapolis, MN 55440
Toll free: 1-800-248-7310
www.generalmills.com

Georgia-Pacific Corporation ᒃ
Consumer Affairs
133 Peachtree St., NE
Atlanta, GA 30303
Toll free: 1-800-283-5547
www.gp.com

Gerber Products Company
Consumer Affairs
445 State St.
Fremont, MI 49413-0001
Toll free: 1-800-284-9488
www.gerber.com

GlaxoSmithKline Consumer Healthcare ᒃ
Consumer Information
5 Crescent Dr.
Philadelphia, PA 19112
Toll free: 1-888-825-5249 (Prescription Drugs)
Toll free: 1-800-245-1040 (Non-Prescription)
www.gsk.com

The Golden Grain Company
PO Box 049003
Chicago, IL 60604-9003
Toll free: 1-800-421-2444
Toll free: 1-800-570-8719 (in Spanish)
www.ricearoni.com

Goldman, Sachs & Company
Investor Relations
200 West St., 29th Floor
New York, NY 10282
212-902-0300
✉: gs-investor-relations@gs.com
www.goldmansachs.com

Gold's Gym International
Customer Support
4001 Maple Ave. Suite 200
Dallas, TX 75219
214-574-4653
www.goldsgym.com

Goodrich Corporation
Consumer Care
PO Box 19001
Greenville, SC 29602-9001
Toll free: 1-877-788-8899
www.bfgoodrichtires.com

The Goodyear Tire & Rubber Company
200 Innovation Way
Akron, OH 44316-0001
330-796-2121
Toll free: 1-800-321-2136
www.goodyear.com

Google.com
1600 Amphitheatre Pkwy.
Mountain View, CA 94043
650-253-0000
www.google.com

Graco Children's Products, Inc. ᒃ
Consumer Services
4410 Premer Dr.
High Point, NC 27265
Toll free: 1-800-345-4109
www.gracobaby.com

Greyhound Lines, Inc.
PO Box 660691
Mail Stop 470
Dallas, TX 75266-0691
214-849-8966
214-849-6246 (Baggage)
Toll free: 1-800-531-5332 (in Spanish)
TTY: 1-800- 345-3109
www.greyhound.com

Guess?, Inc.
Customer Care
1444 S. Alameda St.
Los Angeles, CA 90021
Toll free: 1-877-444-8377
www.guess.com

Guinness Company
203-229-2100
✉: guinness@consumer-care.net
www.guinness.com

Guthy|Renker ᒃ
3340 Ocean Park Blvd.
Santa Monica, CA 90405
Toll free: 1-888-651-6602
✉: customerservice@guthy-renker.com
www.guthyrenker.com

H

Häagen-Dazs
Consumer Services
PO Box 2178
Wilkes-Barre, PA 18703
Toll free: 1-800-767-0120
www.haagendazs.com

The Hain Celestial Group, Inc. ᒃ
Customer Care
4600 Sleepytime Dr.
Boulder, CO 80301
Toll free: 1-800-434-4246
www.hain-celestial.com

Hampton Inn & Suites
See: Hilton Hospitality, Inc.
Toll free: 1-800-426-7866
www.hamptoninn.com

H&R Block, Inc.
Customer Support
One H&R Block Way
Kansas City, MO 64105
Toll free: 1-800-472-5625
www.hrblock.com

Hanes Brands, Inc.
Consumer Services
PO Box 748
Rural Hall, NC 27098
Toll free: 1-800-832-0594 (Delivery questions)
Toll free: 1-800-994-4348 (Retail purchases)
www.hanes.com

Harris Teeter, Inc. ᒃ
Customer Relations
PO Box 10100
Matthews, NC 28106-0100
Toll free: 1-800-432-6111
✉: customerrelations@harristeeter.com
www.harristeeter.com

Harry & David
Customer Service
2500 S. Pacific Hwy.
Medford, OR 97501-2675
Toll free: 1-877-322-1200
✉: service@harryanddavid.com
www.harryanddavid.com

Hasbro, Inc.
Consumer Affairs
PO Box 200
Pawtucket, RI 02862
Toll free: 1-800-242-7276
✉: customersupport@hasbro.com
www.hasbro.com

Heinz North America
Consumer Resource Center
PO Box 57
Pittsburgh, PA 15230
Toll free: 1-800-255-5750
✉: heinzconsumeraffairs@
us.hjheinz.com
www.heinz.com

Henkel Consumer Goods
7201 E. Henkel Way
Scottsdale, AZ 85255
480-754-3425
www.henkelna.com

Hershey Company
Consumer Relations
100 Crystal A Dr.
Hershey, PA 17033
Toll free: 1-800-468-1714
www.hersheys.com

Hertz Corporation
Customer Service
PO Box 26120
Oklahoma City, OK 73126
Toll free: 1-800-654-4173
TTY: 1-800-654-2280
www.hertz.com

Hewlett-Packard Company
3000 Hanover St.
Bldg. 6A, Mail Stop 1247
Palo Alto, CA 94304
650-857-1501
Toll free: 1-800-474-6836
www.hp.com

Hillshire Brands
Consumer Affairs
PO Box 3901
Peoria, IL 61612
Toll free: 1-800-328-2426
Toll free: 1-800-323-7117 (Desserts)
www.hillshirebrands.com

Hilton Garden Inn
See: Hilton Hospitality, Inc.
Toll free: 1-877-782-9444
www.hiltongardeninn.com

Hilton Hospitality, Inc.
Guest Assistance
2050 Chenault Dr.
Carrollton, TX 75006
972-770-6100
Toll free: 1-800-445-8667
www.hilton.com

Hitachi America, Ltd.
Customer Service
PO Box 99652
Troy, MI 48099
Toll free: 1-800-448-2244
✉: 800Hitachi@hal.hitachi.com
www.hitachi-america.us

Holiday Inn/Holiday Inn Express
See: InterContinental Hotels Group, PLC
Toll free: 1-800-465-4329
www.holiday-inn.com

Home Depot, Inc.
Support Center
2455 Paces Ferry Rd.
Atlanta, GA 30339-4024
Toll free: 1-800-466-3337
Toll free: 1-800-430-3376 (Website
questions)
www.homedepot.com

Home Goods
See: TJX Companies, Inc.
Toll free: 1-800-888-0776
www.homegoods.com

Home Shopping Network
Customer Service
PO Box 9090
Clearwater, FL 33758
Toll free: 1-800-284-3900 (Phone)
Toll free: 1-800-933-2887 (Online)
www.hsn.com

Homewood Suites
See: Hilton Hospitality, Inc.
Toll free: 1-800-225-5466
www.homewoodsuites.com

Hoover Company
TTI Floor Care North America
7005 Cochran Rd.
Glenwillow, OH 44139
Toll free: 1-800-944-9200
www.hoover.com

Hormel Foods Corporation
Consumer Affairs
One Hormel Pl.
Austin, MN 55912
Toll free: 1-800-523-4635
www.hormel.com

Howard Johnson, Inc.
PO Box 4090
Aberdeen, SD 57401
Toll free: 1-800-544-9881
www.hojo.com

HTC America, Inc.
13920 S.E. Eastgate Way, Suite 400
Bellevue, WA 98005
Toll free: 1-866-449-8358
TTY: 1-855-580-2302
www.htc.com

Humana, Inc.
Correspondence Office
PO Box 14601
Lexington, KY 40512-4601
Toll free: 1-800-833-6917 (Individual and
family)
Toll free: 1-800-448-6262 (Employer
sponsored insurance)
www.humana.com

Hyatt Hotels & Resorts
Consumer Affairs
9805 Q St.
Omaha, NE 68127
Toll free: 1-800-323-7249
TTY: 1-800-228-9548
www.hyatt.com

I

Ikea
Customer Relations
420 Alan Wood Rd.
Conshohocken, PA 19428
Toll free: 1-888-888-4532 (In-Store
Questions)
Toll free: 1-888-434-4532 (Online Store
Questions)
✉: UScustomercare259@ikea.com
www.ikea.com

Innovis
250 E. Broad St.
Columbus, OH 43215
Toll free: 1-800-540-2505
✉: ica@innovis.com
www.innovis.com

Intel
2200 Mission College Blvd.
Santa Clara, CA 95054
408-765-8080
www.intel.com

InterContinental Hotels Group, PLC
Guest Relations
PO Box 30321
Salt Lake City, UT 84130-0321
Toll free: 1-800-621-0555
www.ihgplc.com

J

J.M. Smucker Company ꙮ
Consumer Response
One Strawberry Ln.
Orrville, OH 44667
Toll free: 1-888-550-9555
www.jmsmucker.com

J.P. Morgan Chase Bank
PO Box 36520
Louisville, KY 40233-6520
713-262-3300
Toll free: 1-877-242-7372
TTY: 1-800-242-7383
www.chase.com

Jack In The Box, Inc.
Guest Relations
9330 Balboa Ave.
San Diego, CA 92123-1516
858-522-4716
Toll free: 1-800-955-5225
www.jackinthebox.com

Jackson Hewitt Tax Service, Inc.
Three Sylvan Way, Suite 301
Parsippany, NJ 07054
Toll free: 1-800-234-1040
www.jacksonhewitt.com

Jarden Consumer Solutions, Inc. ꙮ
Consumer Affairs
2381 N.W. Executive Center Dr.
Boca Raton, FL 33431
Toll free: 1-800-777-5452
www.jardencs.com

JCPenney Company, Inc.
Corporate Customer Relations
PO Box 10001
Dallas, TX 75301
Toll free: 1-800-322-1189
www.jcpenney.com

J. Crew
Customer Relations
One Ivy Crescent
Lynchburg, VA 24513-1001
Toll free: 1-800-562-0258
✉: contactus@jcrew.com
www.jcrew.com

Jenny Craig, Inc.
Customer Care
5770 Fleet St.
Carlsbad, CA 92008
760-696-4000
Toll free: 1-800-536-6922
✉: WebCustomerService@jennycraig.com
www.jennycraig.com

JetBlue Airways Corporation
Customer Relations
PO Box 17435
Salt Lake City, UT 84117-7435
Toll free: 1-800-538-2583
www.jetblue.com

Jiffy Lube International, Inc.
Customer Service
PO Box 4427
Houston, TX 77210-4458
Toll free: 1-800-344-6933
www.jiffylube.com

John Deere
Customer Assistance
One John Deere Pl.
Moline, IL 61265
Toll free: 1-800-537-8233
www.deere.com

John Hancock Financial Services, Inc.
197 Clarendon St.
Boston, MA 02116
Toll free: 1-800-732-5543
www.johnhancock.com

Johnson & Johnson Consumer Products, Inc. ꙮ
One Johnson & Johnson Plaza
New Brunswick, NJ 08933
732-524-0400
www.jnj.com

Just Born, Inc ꙮ
Consumer Relations
1300 Stefko Blvd.
Bethlehem, PA 18017
610-867-7568
Toll free: 1-888-645-3453
www.justborn.com

JVC Company of America
Customer Care
1700 Valley Rd.
Wayne, NJ 07470
Toll free: 1-800-252-5722
www.jvc.com

K

Kao Brands Company ꙮ
Consumer Relations
2535 Spring Grove Ave.
Cincinnati, OH 45214
www.kaobrands.com

KAYAK.com
Seven Market St.
Stamford, CT 06902
Toll free: 1-855-529-2501
www.kayak.com

Kellogg Company ꙮ♦
Consumer Affairs
PO Box CAMB
Battle Creek, MI 49016
Toll free: 1-800-962-1413
www.kelloggs.com

KFC
See: YUM! Brands, Inc.
Toll free: 1-800-225-5532
www.kfc.com

Kimberly-Clark Corporation ꙮ
Consumer Services
Dept. INT
PO Box 2020
Neenah, WI 54957-2020
Toll free: 1-888-525-8388
www.kimberly-clark.com

The Kirby Company
Customer Relations
1920 W. 114th St.
Cleveland, OH 44102
Toll free: 1-800-494-8586
www.kirby.com

KitchenAid
Customer Experience Center
PO Box 218
St. Joseph, MI 49085
Toll free: 1-800-541-6390 (Small Appliances)
www.kitchenaid.com

Kmart Corporation
See: Sears
Toll free: 1-866-562-7848
www.kmart.com

Kohl's Corporation
Customer Service
PO Box 3120
Milwaukee, WI 53201
Toll free: 1-855-564-5705
Toll free: 1-855-564-5748 (Credit)
www.kohls.com

Kraft Foods Group, Inc. ꙮ
Consumer Relations
Three Lakes Dr.
Northfield, IL 60093
Toll free: 1-877-535-5666
www.kraftfoods.com

Kroger Company
Customer Service
1014 Vine St.
Cincinnati, OH 45202-1100
Toll free: 1-800-576-4377
www.kroger.com

L

LA Fitness International, LLC
Member Services
PO Box 54170
Irvine, CA 92619
✉: contact@fitnessintl.com
www.lafitness.com

Lancôme
Customer Care
PO Box 2007
Westfield, NJ 07091
Toll free: 1-800-526-2663
www.lancome-usa.com

Land O'Lakes, Inc. ⟲
Consumer Affairs
PO Box 64050
St. Paul, MN 55164-9784
Toll free: 1-800-328-4155 (Consumer Affairs)
Toll free: 1-800-328-9680 (Corporate)
www.landolakes.com

Lands' End, Inc.
Customer Service
One Lands' End Ln.
Dodgeville, WI 53595
Toll free: 1-800-963-4816
TTY: 1-800-541-3459
www.landsend.com

Lane Furniture
Consumer Services
14250A Manchester Rd.
Ballwin, MO 63011
Toll free: 1-800-327-6944
✉: service@lanefurniture.com
www.lanefurniture.com

La-Z-Boy, Inc.
Consumer Services
1284 N. Telegraph Rd.
Monroe, MI 48162-3390
Toll free: 1-855-802-6636
www.la-z-boy.com

LeapFrog Enterprises, Inc.
Customer Support
6401 Hollis St., Suite 100
Emeryville, CA 94608-1071
Toll free: 1-800-701-5327
Toll free: 1-866-334-5327 (Online Store)
✉: support@leapfrog.com
www.leapfrog.com

Lee Jeans
Consumer Services
9001 W. 67th St.
Merriam, KS 66202
Toll free: 1-800-453-3348
www.lee.com

LEGO Systems, Inc.
Consumer Affairs
555 Taylor Rd.
PO Box 1138
Enfield, CT 06083-1138
Toll free: 1-800-453-4652
Toll free: 1-800-835-4386 (Online Store)
www.lego.com

Lennox Industries, Inc.
Consumer Affairs
PO Box 799900
Dallas, TX 75379
Toll free: 1-800-953-6669
www.lennox.com

Lenovo
Customer Service
1009 Think Pl.
Morrisville, NC 27560
Toll free: 1-855-253-6686
www.lenovo.com

LensCrafters
4000 Luxottica Pl.
Mason, OH 45040
Toll free: 1-877-753-6727
TTY: 1-855-589-8891
www.lenscrafters.com

Levi Strauss Company ⟲
1155 Battery St.
San Francisco, CA 94111
Toll free: 1-866-860-8907
www.levi.com

LG Electronics, Inc ⟲
Customer Service
1000 Sylvan Ave.
Englewood Cliffs, NJ 07632
Toll free: 1-800-243-0000
www.lge.com

Liberty Mutual Insurance Group ⟲
Customer Service
100 Liberty Way
Dover, NH 03820
Toll free: 1-800-398-8924
Toll free: 1-800-225-2467 (Claim Status)
www.libertymutual.com

The Limited
Customer Service
PO Box 182651
Columbus, OH 43218-2651
Toll free: 1-877-583-1963
Toll free: 1-800-888-3257 (Credit Services)
www.thelimited.com

LinkedIn Corporation
2029 Stierlin Ct.
Mountain View, CA 94043
www.linkedin.com

Little Tikes
Consumer Services
2180 Barlow Rd.
Hudson, OH 44236
Toll free: 1-800-321-0183
www.littletikes.com

L.L. Bean, Inc.
Dept. CFM
Freeport, ME 04033-0001
207-552-3028
Toll free: 1-800-441-5713
TTY: 1-800-545-0090
www.llbean.com

L'Oréal USA ⟲
Consumer Care Center
575 Fifth Ave.
New York, NY 10017
212-818-1500 (Headquarters)
Toll free: 1-800-322-2036
www.lorealusa.com

Lowe's
Customer Care
PO Box 1111
North Wilkesboro, NC 28656
Toll free: 1-800-445-6937
✉: customercare@lowes.com
www.lowes.com

Lyft, Inc.
548 Market St. #68514
San Francisco, CA 94104
✉: support@lyft.com
www.lyft.com

M

MAACO Enterprises, Inc.
440 S. Church St., Suite 700
Charlotte, NC 28202
704-377-8855
Toll free: 1-800-523-1180
✉: customerfirst@maaco.com
www.maaco.com

Macy's
Credit and Customer Service
PO Box 8113
Mason, OH 45040
Toll free: 1-877-876-2297 (Customer Service)
Toll free: 1-877-493-9207 (Credit)
www.macys.com

Magnavox
Toll free: 1-800-605-8610 (TV, DVD Player, Blu-ray Disc Player)
✉: magnavox@funaisupport.com
www.magnavox.com

Marc Jacobs
Customer Service
Toll free: 1-877-707-6272
✉: customerservice@marcjacobs.com
www.marcjacobs.com

Marriott International, Inc.
Customer Support
310 Bearcat Drive
Salt Lake City, UT 84115-2544
Toll free: 1-800-721-7033
www.marriott.com

Mars Chocolate North America ⑤
800 High St.
Hackettstown, NJ 07840
www.mars.com

Marshalls, Inc.
See: TJX Companies, Inc.
Toll free: 1-888-627-7425
www.marshallsonline.com

Mary Kay, Inc. ⑤
PO Box 799045
Dallas, TX 75379-9045
Toll free: 1-800-627-9529
www.marykay.com

Massachusetts Mutual Insurance Company (Mass Mutual)
Customer Relations
1295 State St.
Springfield, MA 01111-0001
Toll free: 1-800-272-2216 (Life Insurance)
Toll free: 1-800-505-8952 (Long-Term Care Insurance)
www.massmutual.com

MasterCard Worldwide
Consumer Inquiries
(Contact your issuing bank first)
2000 Purchase St.
Purchase, NY 10577
1-636-722-7111
Toll free: 1-800-627-8372
✉: consumer_inquiries@mastercard.com
www.mastercard.com

Mattel, Inc.
Customer Service
333 Continental Blvd.
El Segundo, CA 90245-5012
Toll free: 1-800-524-8697
TTY: 1-800-382-7470
www.mattel.com

Maybelline, Inc.
Customer Care
PO Box 1010
Clark, NJ 07066
Toll free: 1-800-944-0730
www.maybelline.com

Mayflower Transit, LLC
One Mayflower Dr.
St. Louis, MO 63026
Toll free: 1-800-241-1321
Toll free: 1-800-325-9970 (Claims)
www.mayflower.com

Maytag
Customer Service
553 Benson Rd.
Benton Harbor, MI 49022
Toll free: 1-800-344-1274
www.maytag.com

McCain Foods USA, Inc. ⑤
2275 Cabot Dr.
Lisle, IL 60532-3653
Toll free: 1-800-938-7799
✉: contactus@mccain.com
www.mccainfoods.com

McCormick & Company, Inc. ⑤
Consumer Affairs
211 Schilling Circle
Hunt Valley, MD 21031
410-527-6000
Toll free: 1-800-632-5847
✉: consumer_affairs@mccormick.com
www.mccormick.com

McDonald's Corporation ⑤
2111 McDonald's Dr.
Oak Brook, IL 60523
Toll free: 1-800-244-6227
www.mcdonalds.com

McKee Foods Corporation ⑤
Consumer Services
PO Box 750
Collegedale, TN 37315
Toll free: 1-800-522-4499
www.mckeefoods.com

Mead Johnson
2701 Patriot Blvd., 4th Floor
Glenview, IL 60026
847-832-2420
www.meadjohnson.com

Meijer, Inc. ⑤
2929 Walker Ave., NW
Grand Rapids, MI 49544-9424
Toll free: 1-877-363-4537
www.meijer.com

Meineke Car Care Centers, Inc.
Toll free: 1-800-447-3070
www.meineke.com

Men's Warehouse
Customer Relations
6380 Rogerdale Rd.
Houston, TX 77072
Toll free: 1-800-851-6744
www.menswarehouse.com

The Mentholatum Company, Inc.
Consumer Affairs
707 Sterling Dr.
Orchard Park, NY 14127
716-677-2500
Toll free: 1-877-636-2677
www.mentholatum.com

Merck & Co., Inc.
One Merck Dr.
PO Box 100
Whitehouse Station, NJ 08889
908-423-1000
Toll free: 1-800-444-2080
Toll free: 1-800-727-5400 (Patient Assistance)
www.merck.com

Merrill Lynch Company, Inc.
(Contact local branch manager first)
4 World Financial Center
250 Vesey St.
New York, NY 10080
Toll free: 1-800-637-7455
TTY: 1-866-657-3323
✉: general_askml@ml.com
www.merrilllynch.com

Merry Maids
PO Box 751017
Memphis, TN 38175-1017
Toll free: 1-800-798-8000
www.merrymaids.com

MetLife, Inc.
200 Park Ave.
New York, NY 10166
Toll free: 1-800-638-5000 (Life Insurance)
Toll free: 1-800-422-4272 (Auto and Home Insurance)
Toll free: 1-800-308-0179 (Long-Term Care Insurance)
www.metlife.com

Michael Kors ⑤
11 W. 42 St.
New York, NY 10036
Toll free: 1-866-709-5677
TTY: 1-855-889-5677
✉: customerservice@michaelkors.com
www.michaelkors.com

Michelina's
See: Bellisio Foods, Inc.
Toll free: 1-800-446-5469
✉: michelinas@bellisiofoods.com
www.michelinas.com

Michelin North America, Inc. ⑤
Consumer Care
PO Box 19001
Greenville, SC 29602-9001
Toll free: 1-866-866-6605
www.michelinman.com

Micro Center
Customer Service
4119 Leap Rd.
Hilliard, OH 43026
614-850-3675
www.microcenter.com

Microsoft Corporation
Customer Service
One Microsoft Way
Redmond, WA 98052-6399
425-882-8080
Toll free: 1-800-642-7676
TTY: 1-800-892-5234
www.microsoft.com

Midas, Inc.
Consumer Relations
823 Donald Ross Rd.
Juno Beach, FL 33408
Toll free: 1-800-621-8545
www.midas.com

MillerCoors
Consumer Affairs
250 S. Wacker Dr.
Chicago, IL 60606
Toll free: 1-800-645-5376
www.millercoors.com

Mitsubishi Digital Electronics America, Inc.
Consumer Relations
10833 Valley View St., Suite 300
Cypress, CA 90630
Toll free: 1-800-332-2119
www.mitsubishi-tv.com

Mondelez International
Consumer Relations
100 Deforest Ave.
East Hanover, NJ 07936
Toll free: 1-855-535-5648
www.nabiscoworld.com

Morgan Stanley
Client Advocate
PO Box 95002
South Jordan, UT 84095
Toll free: 1-866-227-2256
✉: ClientAdvocate@morganstanley.com
www.morganstanley.com

Motel 6
Guest Relations
PO Box 326
Worthington, OH 43085
Toll free: 1-800-557-3435
www.motel6.com

Motorola, Inc.
222 W. Merchandise Mart Plaza, Suite 1800
Chicago, IL 60654
Toll free: 1-800-734-5870
TTY: 1-888-390-6456
www.motorola.com

Mott's LLP
Consumer Relations
PO Box 869077
Plano, TX 75086-9077
Toll free: 1-800-426-4891
www.motts.com

Mutual of Omaha Insurance Company
Customer Service
Mutual of Omaha Plaza
Omaha, NE 68175
Toll free: 1-800-228-7104
Toll free: 1-800-775-1000 (Claims)
www.mutualofomaha.com

N

National Car Rental System, Inc.
Customer Services
8420 St. John Industrial Dr.
St. Louis, MO 63114
Toll free: 1-800-468-3334
TTY: 1-800-328-6323
✉: customerservice@nationalcar.com
www.nationalcar.com

Nationwide Mutual Insurance Company
Customer Advocacy
One Nationwide Plaza
Columbus, OH 43215-2220
Toll free: 1-800-882-2822 ext. 9-6985 (Customer Advocacy)
Toll free: 1-877-669-6877 (Auto and Property Insurance)
Toll free: 1-800-848-6331 (Investments)
www.nationwide.com

Nautica Apparel, Inc.
Consumer Relations
40 West 57th St.
New York, NY 10019
Toll free: 1-866-376-4184
www.nautica.com

The Neiman-Marcus Group, Inc.
Customer Care
PO Box 650589
Dallas, TX 75265-0589
Toll free: 1-888-888-4757
www.neimanmarcus.com

Nestlé Purina PetCare Company
Office of Consumer Affairs
PO Box 1326
Wilkes-Barre, PA 18703
Toll free: 1-800-778-7462
www.purina.com

Nestlé USA
Office of Consumer Services
800 N. Brand Blvd.
Glendale, CA 91203
Toll free: 1-800-225-2270
✉: nestleconsumerservice@casupport.com
www.nestleusa.com

Nestlé Waters North America, Inc.
900 Long Ridge Rd.
Building 2
Stamford, CT 06902-1138
Toll free: 1-888-747-7437
www.nestle-watersna.com

Netflix
Customer Service
100 Winchester Circle
Los Gatos, CA 95032
Toll free: 1-866-579-7172
www.netflix.com

Neutrogena Corporation
Consumer Affairs
199 Grandview Rd.
Skillman, NJ 08558
Toll free: 1-800-582-4048
www.neutrogena.com

Newell Rubbermaid, Inc.
Consumer Services
4110 Premier Dr.
High Point, NC 27265
Toll free: 1-888-895-2110
www.rubbermaid.com

New York & Company
Customer Service
450 W. 33rd St., Fifth Floor
New York, NY 10001
Toll free: 1-800-324-1952 (In-Store)
Toll free: 1-800-961-9906 (Online)
✉: service@nyandcompany.com
www.nyandcompany.com

New York Life Insurance Company
51 Madison Ave.
New York, NY 10010
Toll free: 1-800-710-7945
www.newyorklife.com

Nike, Inc.
Consumer Services
One Bowerman Dr.
Beaverton, OR 97005-6453
Toll free: 1-800-344-6453
www.nike.com

Nikon, Inc.
Consumer Affairs
1300 Walt Whitman Rd.
Melville, NY 11747-3064
631-547-4200 (Corporate)
Toll free: 1-800-645-6687 (Technical and Service Support)
www.nikonusa.com

Nine West Group, Inc.
Customer Service
1129 Westchester Ave.
White Plains, NY 10604
Toll free: 1-800-999-1877
✉: customer_relations@ninewest.com
www.ninewest.com

Nintendo
4600 150th Ave., NE
Redmond, WA 98052
Toll free: 1-800-255-3700
www.nintendo.com

Nokia USA
See: Microsoft Corporation
Toll free: 1-888-665-4228
TTY: 1-800-246-6542
www.nokia.com

Nordstrom, Inc.
Customer Service
1600 7th Ave., Suite 2600
Seattle, WA 98101
Toll free: 1-888-282-6060
TTY: 1-800-685-2100
www.nordstrom.com

North American Van Lines
North American Claims Department
PO Box 988
Ft. Wayne, IN 46801-0988
Toll free: 1-800-348-2111
✉: claims@navl.com
www.northamerican.com

The North Face, Inc.
Customer Service
14450 Doolittle Dr.
San Leandro, CA 94577
Toll free: 1-888-863-1968
Toll free: 1-855-500-8639 (Warranties)
✉: tnfsupport@vfc.com
www.thenorthface.com

Northwestern Mutual Life Insurance Company
Corporate Relations
720 E. Wisconsin Ave.
Milwaukee, WI 53202-4797
414-271-1444
www.northwesternmutual.com

Norwegian Cruise Lines
Guest Relations
7665 Corporate Center Dr.
Miami, FL 33126
Toll free: 1-866-625-1164
Toll free: 1-866-584-9756 (Special Needs)
www.ncl.com

Novartis Pharmaceuticals Corporation
Customer Interaction Center
One Health Plaza
East Hanover, NJ 07936-1080
Toll free: 1-888-669-6682
www.pharma.us.novartis.com

Nutrisystem, Inc.
Customer Service
600 Office Center Dr.
Fort Washington, PA 19034
Toll free: 1-800-585-5483
✉: customerservice@nutrisystem.com
www.nutrisystem.com

O

Ocean Spray Cranberries, Inc.
Consumer Affairs
One Ocean Spray Dr.
Lakeville-Middleboro, MA 02349
Toll free: 1-800-662-3263
www.oceanspray.com

Office Depot, Inc.
6600 N. Military Trail
Boca Raton, FL 33496
Toll free: 1-800-463-3768
www.officedepot.com

OfficeMax, Inc.
See: Office Depot, Inc.
Toll free: 1-800-463-3768
www.officemax.com

Old Navy
Customer Relations
200 Old Navy Ln.
Grove City, OH 43123-8605
Toll free: 1-800-653-6289
TTY: 1-800-449-4253
✉: custserv@oldnavy.com
www.oldnavy.com

Olive Garden
See: Darden Restaurants
Toll free: 1-800-331-2729
www.olivegarden.com

Olympus America
3500 Corporate Pkwy.
PO Box 610
Center Valley, PA 18034-0610
Toll free: 1-800-622-6372
Toll free: 1-888-553-4448 (Digital Cameras)
www.olympusamerica.com

Omni Hotels
Guest Relations
4001 Maple Ave.
Dallas, TX 75219
Toll free: 1-800-809-6664
www.omnihotels.com

1-800-FLOWERS
Customer Satisfaction Department
One Old Country Rd., Suite 500
Carle Place, NY 11514
Toll free: 1-800-356-9377
Toll free: 1-800-716-4851 (Customer Service)
www.1800flowers.com

Orbitz, LLC
Customer Service
500 W. Madison St., Suite 1000
Chicago, IL 60661
Toll free: 1-888-656-4546
www.orbitz.com

Orkin
Customer Care Center
2170 Piedmont Rd., NE
Atlanta, GA 30324
Toll free: 1-888-675-4662
www.orkin.com

Oster
See: Jarden Consumer Solutions, Inc.
Toll free: 1-800-334-0759
www.oster.com

Outback Steakhouse
2202 N. West Shore Blvd., Suite 500
Tampa, FL 33607
813-282-1225
✉: news@outback.com
www.outback.com

Overstock.com
Customer Service
6350 S. 3000 East
Salt Lake City, UT 84121
Toll free: 1-800-843-2446
✉: customercare@overstock.com
www.overstock.com

P

Panasonic Corporation of North America
Customer Experience Department
661 Independence Pkwy.
Chesapeake, VA 23320
Toll free: 1-800-211-7262
Toll free: 1-800-405-0652 (Online store)
www.panasonic.com

Panera Bread
Customer Service
3630 S. Geyer Rd.
St. Louis, MO 63127
www.panerabread.com

Papa John's International, Inc.
PO Box 99900
Louisville, KY 40269-9990
Toll free: 1-877-547-7272
✉: consumer_services@papajohns.com
www.papajohns.com

PayPal.com
2211 N. First St.
San Jose, CA 95131
Toll free: 1-888-221-1161
www.paypal.com

PearleVision
Customer Service
4000 Luxottica Pl.
Mason, OH 45040
Toll free: 1-800-937-3937
www.pearlevision.com

Pella Corporation
Customer Service
102 Main St.
Pella, IA 50219
Toll free: 1-877-473-5527
www.pella.com

Pep Boys Auto
Customer Relations
3111 W. Allegheny Ave.
Philadelphia, PA 19132
Toll free: 1-800-737-2697
✉: contactus@pepboys.com
www.pepboys.com

Pepperidge Farm, Inc. ⟳
Consumer Affairs
595 Westport Ave.
Norwalk, CT 06851
Toll free: 1-888-737-7374
www.pepperidgefarm.com

PepsiCo., Inc. ⟳
700 Anderson Hill Rd.
Purchase, NY 10577
Toll free: 1-800-433-2652
www.pepsico.com

Pepsi-Cola Company
See: PepsiCo., Inc.
Toll free: 1-800-433-2652
www.pepsi.com

Perdue Farms, Inc. ⟳
Consumer Relations
PO Box 788
Kings Mountain, NC 28086
Toll free: 1-800-473-7383
www.perdue.com

Perrigo ⟳
515 Eastern Ave.
Allegan, MI 49010
269-673-8451
Toll free: 1-866-703-4222 (Vitamins)
Toll free: 1-800-719-9260 (Over the Counter)
Toll free: 1-866-634-9120 (Prescription Drugs)
Toll free: 1-800-272-5095 (Infant Products)
www.perrigo.com

Petco
9125 Rehco Rd.
San Diego, CA 92121
Toll free: 1-888-824-7257
www.petco.com

PetSmart, Inc.
Customer Service
19601 N. 27th Ave.
Phoenix, AZ 85027
Toll free: 1-888-839-9638
✉: customercare@petsmart.com
www.petsmart.com

P.F. Changs China Bistro, Inc.
7676 E. Pinnacle Peak Rd.
Scottsdale, AZ 85255
Toll free: 1-866-732-4264
www.pfchangs.com

Pfizer, Inc.
Consumer Affairs
235 E. 42nd St.
New York, NY 10017
212-733-2323
Toll free: 1-800-879-3477 (Customer Response)
www.pfizer.com

Pharmavite Corporation ⟳
Consumer Affairs
PO Box 9606
Mission Hills, CA 91346-9606
818-221-6200
Toll free: 1-800-276-2878 (Nature Made)
Toll free: 1-888-676-9569 (SoyJoy)
www.pharmavite.com

Philips Consumer Electronics North America
Customer Service
3000 Minuteman Rd., Mail Stop 109
Andover, MA 01810
Toll free: 1-888-744-5477
www.philips.com

Pier 1 Imports ⟳
Customer Service
100 Pier 1 Pl.
Ft. Worth, TX 76102
Toll free: 1-800-245-4595
✉: CustomerService@pier1.com
www.pier1.com

Pioneer Electronics Service, Inc.
Customer Service
1925 E. Dominguez St.
Long Beach, CA 90810
Toll free: 1-800-421-1404
www.pioneerelectronics.com

Pirelli Tire Corporation
100 Pirelli Dr.
Rome, GA 30161
Toll free: 1-800-747-3554
www.us.pirelli.com

Pizza Hut ⟳
7100 Corporate Dr.
Plano, TX 75024
972-338-7700
Toll free: 1-800-948-8488
www.pizzahut.com

Planet Fitness
Member Support
26 Fox Run Rd.
Newington, NH 03801
Toll free: 1-844-880-7180
✉: info@planetfitness.com
www.planetfitness.com

Playskool
See: Hasbro, Inc.
Toll free: 1-800-752-9755
www.hasbro.com/playskool

Playstation
See: Sony Corporation of America
Toll free: 1-800-345-7669
www.us.playstation.com

Playtex Products, Inc.
Consumer Affairs
890 Mountain Ave.
New Providence, NJ 07974
Toll free: 1-888-310-4290
www.playtexproductsinc.com

PNC Bank
249 5th Ave.
One PNC Plaza
Pittsburgh, PA 15222
Toll free: 1-888-762-2265
www.pnc.com

♦ Provided financial support for the publication of the Consumer Action Handbook.

Polaroid Corporation
Customer Care Center
Toll free: 1-800-765-2764
www.polaroid.com

Polo/Ralph Lauren Corporation
Customer Assistance
625 Madison Ave.
New York, NY 10022
Toll free: 1-888-475-7674
✉: customerassistance@ralphlauren.com
www.polo.com

Popeyes Louisiana Kitchen
Guest Hospitality
400 Perimeter Center Terrace, Suite 1000
Atlanta, GA 30346
Toll free: 1-877-767-3937
www.popeyes.com

Post Holdings, Inc.
Consumer Affairs
275 Cliff St.
Battle Creek, MI 49014
Toll free: 1-800-431-7678
www.postfoods.com

Prestige Brands
Consumer Affairs
660 White Plains Rd., Suite 205
Tarrytown, NY 10591
Toll free: 1-800-443-4908
www.prestigebrandsinc.com

Price Chopper Supermarket/ Market 32 ⟲
Consumer Services
461 Nott St.
Schenectady, NY 12308
Toll free: 1-800-666-7667
www.pricechopper.com

Priceline.com, LLC
800 Connecticut Ave.
Norwalk, CT 06854
Toll free: 1-877-477-5807
www.priceline.com

Princess Cruise Lines
Customer Relations
24305 Town Center Dr.
Santa Clarita, CA 91355
Toll free: 1-800-774-6237
✉: customerrelations@
princesscruises.com
www.princess.com

The Procter & Gamble ⟲ ♦
Company
Consumer Relations
PO Box 599
Cincinnati, OH 45201
513-983-1100
Toll free: (Phone numbers appear on all labels)
www.pg.com

The Progressive Corporation
Customer Service
6300 Wilson Mills Rd.
Mayfield Village, OH 44143
440-461-5000 (Corporate)
Toll free: 1-800-776-4737
www.progressive.com

Prudential Financial, Inc.
Policyowner Relations Department
One Corporate Dr.
Shelton, CT 06484
Toll free: 1-800-778-2255 (Insurance)
Toll free: 1-888-778-2888 (Annuities)
Toll free: 1-800-732-0416 (Long-Term Care)
TTY: 1-800-526-8061
www.prudential.com

Public Storage
Customer Service
PO Box 25050
Glendale, CA 91221-5050
Toll free: 1-800-567-0759
www.publicstorage.com

Publishers Clearing House ⟲
Consumer Affairs
101 Winners Circle
Port Washington, NY 11050
Toll free: 1-800-459-4724
Toll free: 1-800-392-4190 (Sweepstakes scams using PCH name)
www.pch.com

Publix Super Markets ⟲
Customer Care
PO Box 407
Lakeland, FL 33802-0407
Toll free: 1-800-242-1227
www.publix.com

Purex
See: Henkel Consumer Goods
Toll free: 1-800-457-8739
www.purex.com

PVH Corporation
Customer Services
1001 Frontier Rd., Mail Stop 44
Bridgewater, NJ 08807
Toll free: 1-800-388-9122 (Van Heusen)
Toll free: 1-800-866-7292 (Izod)
Toll free: 1-866-214-6694 (Calvin Klein)
www.pvh.com

Q

The Quaker Oats Company
PO Box 049003
Chicago, IL 60604-9003
Toll free: 1-800-367-6287
www.quakeroats.com

QuikTrip Corporation
PO Box 3475
Tulsa, OK 74101
918-615-7700
Toll free: 1-800-848-1966
www.quiktrip.com

Quizno's
7595 Technology Way, Suite 200
Denver, CO 80237
720-359-3300 (Headquarters)
Toll free: 1-866-486-2783 (Customer Comments)
www.quiznos.com

QVC, Inc.
Customer Service
1200 Wilson Dr.
West Chester, PA 19380
Toll free: 1-888-345-5788
www.qvc.com

R

Radisson Hotels
11340 Blondo St., Suite 100
Omaha, NE 68164
Toll free: 1-800-615-7253
www.radisson.com

Ramada Inn
PO Box 4090
Aberdeen, SD 57401
Toll free: 1-800-828-6644
www.ramada.com

Rayovac Corporation
Consumer Service
PO Box 620992
Middleton, WI 53562-0992
Toll free: 1-800-237-7000
www.rayovac.com

Reckitt Benckiser Group PLC ⟲
Consumer Relations
PO Box 224
Parsippany, NJ 07054-0224
Toll free: 1-800-228-4722
✉: corpcomms@reckittbenckiser.com
www.reckittbenckiser.com

Red Lobster
Guest Relations
450 S. Orange Ave.
Orlando, FL 32801
Toll free: 1-800-562-7837
www.redlobster.com

CORPORATE CONSUMER CONTACTS

Reebok, Inc.
See: Adidas America, Inc.
Toll free: 1-866-870-1743
www.reebok.com

Regent Seven Seas Cruises
8300 N.W. 33rd St., Suite 100
Miami, FL 33122
Toll free: 1-844-473-4368
www.rssc.com

Remington Products Company
Consumer Services
507 Stokely Dr.
PO Box 1
DeForest, WI 53532
Toll free: 1-800-392-6544
✉: ContactUs@remingtonproducts.com
www.remington-products.com

Rent-A-Center
Customer Care
5501 Headquarters Dr.
Plano, TX 75024
Toll free: 1-800-422-8186
www.rentacenter.com

Residence Inn
See: Marriott International, Inc.
Toll free: 1-800-228-2800
www.residenceinn.com

Revlon, Inc. ⟲
Consumer Affairs
1501 Williamsboro St.
Oxford, NC 27565
Toll free: 1-800-473-8566
www.revlon.com

Rich Products ⟲
Consumer Relations
PO Box 20670
127 Airport Rd.
St. Simons Island, GA 31522
912-638-5000
Toll free: 1-800-828-2021
✉: rsp-consumer.relations@rich.com

Rite Aid Corporation
Customer Support
30 Hunter Ln.
Camp Hill, PA 17011
717-761-2633
Toll free: 1-800-748-3243
TTY: 1-800-821-1833
www.riteaid.com

Royal Caribbean International
Corporate Guest Relations
1050 Caribbean Way
Miami, FL 33132
Toll free: 1-800-256-6649
Toll free: 1-800-398-9819 (Website)
www.royalcaribbean.com

S

SafeAuto Insurance
Customer Service
PO Box 182109
Columbus, OH 43218-2109
Toll free: 1-800-723-3288
✉: CSD@safeauto.com
www.safeauto.com

Safeway, Inc.
Customer Service Center
MS 10501
PO Box 29093
Phoenix, AZ 85038-9093
Toll free: 1-877-723-3929
www.safeway.com

Saks Fifth Avenue
Customer Relations
PO Box 10327
Jackson, MS 39289
Toll free: 1-877-551-7257
✉: service@saks.com
www.saks.com

Sam's Club
Member Service
2101 S.E. Simple Savings Dr.
Bentonville, AR 72716-0745
Toll free: 1-888-746-7726
www.samsclub.com

Samsonite Corporation
Customer Service
575 West St., Suite 110
Mansfield, MA 02048
Toll free: 1-800-765-2247
Toll free: 1-800-262-8282 (Warranty)
www.samsonite.com

Samsung Electronics America
Customer Service and Technical
Support
85 Challenger Rd.
Ridgefield Park, NJ 07660
Toll free: 1-800-726-7864
Toll free: 1-888-987-4357 (Mobile
Phones)
TTY: 1-888-899-7608
www.samsung.com

Sargento Foods, Inc. ⟲
Consumer Affairs
One Persnickety Place
Plymouth, WI 53073
Toll free: 1-800-243-3737
www.sargento.com

SC Johnson and Son, Inc. ⟲
1525 Howe St.
Racine, WI 53403
Toll free: 1-800-494-4855
www.scjohnson.com

Schwan Food Company ⟲
Customer Service
115 W. College Dr.
Marshall, MN 56258
Toll free: 1-800-533-5290
www.theschwanfoodcompany.com

The Scotts Company ⟲
Help Center
14111 Scottslawn Rd.
Marysville, OH 43041
Toll free: 1-888-270-3714
✉: private@scotts.com
www.scotts.com

Seabourn Cruise Line
Guest Relations
300 Elliott Ave. W
Seattle, WA 98119
Toll free: 1-866-755-5619
✉: guestrelations@seabourn.com
www.seabourn.com

Sealy Corporation
Consumer Support
One Office Parkway at Sealy Dr.
Trinity, NC 27370
Toll free: 1-800-697-3259
✉: ConsumerSupport@sealy.com
www.sealy.com

Sears
Executive Customer Relations
3333 Beverly Rd.
Hoffman Estates, IL 60179
847-286-2500
Toll free: 1-800-549-4505 (Retail)
Toll free: 1-800-697-3277 (Online)
www.sears.com

Seneca Foods Corporation
Consumer Affairs
100 Gambee Rd.
Geneva, NY 14456
315-926-8100
Toll free: 1-800-872-1110
✉: customer_service@senecafoods.com
www.senecafoods.com

Serta, Inc. ⟲
Customer Service
3 Golf Center #392
Hoffman Estates, IL 60169
Toll free: 1-888-557-3782
www.serta.com

Service Master Company
860 Ridge Lake Blvd.
Memphis, TN 38120
www.servicemaster.com

7-Eleven, Inc
Customer Relations
PO Box 711
Dallas, TX 75221-0711
972-828-7011
Toll free: 1-800-255-0711
www.7-eleven.com

Sharp Electronics Corporation
Customer Service
Sharp Plaza
Mahwah, NJ 07495-1163
Toll free: 1-800-237-4277
www.sharpusa.com

Sheraton Hotels
See: Starwood Hotels & Resorts
Worldwide, Inc.
Toll free: 1-800-325-3535
www.sheraton.com

Shiseido
900 Third Ave.
New York, NY 10022-4795
Toll free: 1-866-758-5966
✉: customerservice@shiseidousa.com
www.shiseido.com

Simmons Bedding Company
Consumer Services
One Concourse Pkwy., Suite 800
Atlanta, GA 30328
Toll free: 1-877-399-9397
✉: customerassistance@simmons.com
www.simmons.com

Slim-Fast Foods Company
See: Unilever
Toll free: 1-800-754-6327
www.slimfast.com

Smithfield Foods
111 Commerce St.
Smithfield, VA 23430
Toll free: 1-855-411-7675
www.smithfield.com

Snackworks
See: Mondelez International
www.snackworks.com

Sonesta International Hotels Corporation
255 Washington St.
Newton, MA 02458
Toll free: 1-800-766-3782
www.sonesta.com

Sony Corporation of America
550 Madison Ave.
New York, NY 10022
239-768-7547 (Consumer Eletronics)
Toll free: 1-800-345-7669 (Playstation)
www.sony.com

Southwest Airlines
Customer Relations
PO Box 36647-1CR
Dallas, TX 75235
214-932-0333
Toll free: 1-800-435-9792
TTY: 1-800-533-1305
www.southwest.com

Spirit Airlines
2800 Executive Way
Miramar, FL 33025
801-401-2222
TTY: 1-800-955-8771
✉: support@spirit.com
www.spiritair.com

The Sports Authority, Inc.
Customer Service
1050 W. Hampden Ave.
Englewood, CO 80110
Toll free: 1-800-360-8721
✉: customerservice@
thesportsauthority.com
www.sportsauthority.com

Sprint
KSOPHT0101-Z4300
6391 Sprint Pkwy.
Overland Park, KS 66251-4300
Toll free: 1-844-665-6327 (Mobile Phones)
Toll free: 1-877-877-8748 (Wireline Service)
www.sprint.com/consumerinfo

Stanley Black & Decker, Inc.
1000 Stanley Dr.
New Britain, CT 06053
Toll free: 1-800-544-6986
www.stanleyblackanddecker.com

Staples, Inc.
Consumer Affairs
500 Staples Dr.
Framingham, MA 01702
Toll free: 1-800-333-3330
www.staples.com

Starbucks
Customer Service
PO Box 6363
Dover, DE 19905-6363
Toll free: 1-800-782-7282
www.starbucks.com

Starwood Hotels & Resorts Worldwide, Inc.
Consumer Affairs
PO Box 6020
Lancaster, CA 93539-6020
Toll free: 1-800-328-6242
✉: customercare@starwoodhotels.com
www.starwoodhotels.com

State Farm
Customer Service
One State Farm Plaza
Bloomington, IL 61710
309-766-2311
Toll free: 1-800-782-8332
www.statefarm.com

SteinMart
1200 Riverplace Blvd., 5th Floor
Jacksonville, FL 32207
Toll free: 1-888-783-4662
www.steinmart.com

Stop & Shop Supermarket Company, Inc.
Customer Service
1385 Hancock St.
Quincy, MA 02169
Toll free: 1-800-767-7772
www.stopandshop.com

StubHub, Inc.
199 Fremont St., Floor 4
San Francisco, CA 94105
Toll free: 1-866-788-2482
✉: customerservice@stubhub.com
www.stubhub.com

Subway
325 Bic Dr.
Milford, CT 06461
Toll free: 1-800-888-4848
www.subway.com

Suntrust
PO Box 85024
Richmond, VA 23285-5024
Toll free: 1-800-786-8787
TTY: 1-800-854-8965
www.suntrust.com

T

Taco Bell
Customer Relations
1 Glen Bell Way
Irvine, CA 92618
Toll free: 1-800-822-6235
www.tacobell.com

Talbots
Customer Service
One Talbots Dr.
Hingham, MA 02043
781-741-4028
Toll free: 1-800-992-9010
TTY: 1-800-624-9179
www.talbots.com

Target Stores
Guest Relations and Quality Assurance
PO Box 9350
Minneapolis, MN 55440
Toll free: 1-800-440-0680
✉: guest.relations@target.com
www.target.com

TD Bank, N.A.
PO Box 219
Lewiston, ME 04243-0219
Toll free: 1-888-937-1050
www.tdbank.com

TEAC America, Inc.
Customer Service
1834 Gage Rd.
Montebello, CA 90640
323-726-0303
✉: custser@teac.com
✉: dsvce@teac.com (Service and Repair)
www.teac.com

Teleflora
PO Box 60910
Los Angeles, CA 90060-0910
Toll free: 1-800-835-3356
✉: service@teleflora.com
www.teleflora.com

Terminix
See: Service Master Company
Toll free: 1-866-399-0453
✉: terminixcares@terminix.com
www.terminix.com

TGI Friday's
Guest Relations
4201 Marsh Ln.
Carrollton, TX 75007
Toll free: 1-800-374-3297
www.tgifridays.com

3M
Customer Relations
3M Center
St. Paul, MN 55144-1000
Toll free: 1-800-364-3577
www.3m.com

Thrifty Car Rental
Customer Service 2W2
PO Box 33167
Tulsa, OK 74153-1167
Toll free: 1-800-334-1705
www.thrifty.com

TicketMaster
Attn: Fan Support
1000 Corporate Landing
Charleston, WV 25311
Toll free: 1-800-653-8000
www.ticketmaster.com

Time Warner, Inc.
One Time Warner Center
New York, NY 10019
212-484-8000
www.timewarner.com

TJ Maxx
See: TJX Companies, Inc.
508-390-3000
Toll free: 1-800-926-6299
www.tjmaxx.com

TJX Companies, Inc.
770 Cochituate Rd.
Framingham, MA 01701
508-390-1000
Toll free: 1-800-926-6299 (TJ Maxx)
Toll free: 1-800-888-0776 (Home Goods)
Toll free: 1-888-627-7425 (Marshalls)
www.tjx.com

T-Mobile Wireless
Customer Relations
PO Box 37380
Albuquerque, NM 87176-7380
Toll free: 1-877-453-1304 (Customer Care)
Toll free: 1-800-866-2453 (Product Questions)
TTY: 1-877-296-1018
www.tmobile.com

The Toro Company
Customer Care
8111 Lyndale Ave., S
Bloomington, MN 55420
Toll free: 1-888-384-9939
www.toro.com

Toshiba America
Digital Products Division
9740 Irvine Blvd.
Irvine, CA 92618-1697
949-461-4510
Toll free: 1-800-618-4444 (Customer Support)
Toll free: 1-800-631-3811 (TVs)
Toll free: 1-800-457-7777 (Computers)
✉: customerservice@ToshibaDirect.com
www.toshiba.com/us

Toys 'R Us
Guest Relations
One Geoffrey Way
Wayne, NJ 07470
973-617-3500
Toll free: 1-800-869-7787
✉: contactus@toysrus.com
www.toysrus.com

Trader Joe's
PO Box 5049
Monrovia, CA 91016
626-599-3817
www.traderjoes.com

Trane
Consumer Relations
20 Corporate Woods Dr.
Bridgeton, MO 63044
Toll free: 1-800-945-5884
www.trane.com

TransUnion, LLC
Consumer Solutions
PO Box 2000
Chester, PA 19022
Toll free: 1-800-888-4213 (Obtain a Report)
Toll free: 1-800-916-8800 (Disputes)
Toll free: 1-800-680-7289 (Frauds)
www.transunion.com

Travelers Companies, Inc.
Consumer Affairs
One Tower Square 8MS
Hartford, CT 06183
Toll free: 1-866-336-2077 (Customer Advocacy)
Toll free: 1-800-252-4633 (Claim Inquiry)
www.travelers.com

Travelocity.com LP
Customer Care
11603 Crosswinds Way, Suite 125
San Antonio, TX 78233
Toll free: 1-855-201-7800
Toll free: 1-877-815-5446 (Cruises)
TTY: 1-800-555-7585
www.travelocity.com

Travelodge
PO Box 4090
Aberdeen, SD 57401
Toll free: 1-800-835-2424
www.travelodge.com

Travel Zoo
590 Madison Ave.
New York, NY 10022
Toll free: 1-877-665-0000
www.travelzoo.com

True Value Company
Customer Service
8600 W. Bryn Mawr Ave.
Chicago, IL 60631
Toll free: 1-877-502-4641
www.truevalue.com

TruGreen Lawn Care
See: Service Master Company
860 Ridge Lake Blvd.
Memphis, TN 38120
Toll free: 1-877-905-5147
✉: customercare@trugreenmail.com
www.trugreen.com

24 Hour Fitness
Member Services
PO Box 2689
Carlsbad, CA 92018
www.24hourfitness.com

Twitter.com
1355 Market St., Suite 900
San Francisco, CA 94103
www.twitter.com

Tyson Foods
Consumer Relations CP631
PO Box 2020
Springdale, AR 72765-2020
Toll free: 1-800-233-6332
✉: comments@tyson.com
www.tyson.com

U

Uber
Customer Support
1455 Market St.
San Francisco, CA 94103
✉: support@uber.com
www.uber.com

U-Haul International
Customer Service
2727 N. Central Ave.
Phoenix, AZ 85004
Toll free: 1-800-789-3638
www.uhaul.com

Under Armour, Inc.
Customer Service
1020 Hull St.
Baltimore, MD 21230
Toll free: 1-888-727-6687
www.underarmour.com

Uniden America Corporation
Customer Service
3001 Gateway Dr., Suite 130
Irving, TX 75038
817-858-3300
Toll free: 1-800-297-1023
TTY: 1-800-874-9214
www.uniden.com

Unilever
Consumer Services
920 Sylvan Ave.
Englewood Cliffs, NJ 07632
Toll free: 1-800-298-5018
www.unilever.com

Uniroyal Tires
Consumer Care Department
PO Box 19001
Greenville, SC 29602-9001
Toll free: 1-877-458-5878
www.uniroyal.com

United Airlines
Customer Care
900 Grand Plaza NHCCR
Houston, TX 77067-4323
Toll free: 1-800-864-8331
Toll free: 1-800-335-2247 (Baggage)
Toll free: 1-877-624-2660 (Post-travel Feedback)
TTY: 1-800-323-0170
www.ual.com

United Healthcare
Customer Service
PO Box 29675
Hot Springs, AR 71903-9802
Toll free: 1-866-633-2446
www.uhc.com

United Parcel Service (UPS)
Customer Service
55 Glenlake Pkwy., NE
Atlanta, GA 30328
Toll free: 1-800-742-5877
TTY: 1-800-833-0056
www.ups.com

United Van Lines, Inc.
Claims Department
One United Dr.
Fenton, MO 63026
Toll free: 1-800-948-4885
Toll free: 1-800-325-9970 (Claims)
www.unitedvanlines.com

Uno Chicago Grill
100 Charles Park Rd.
Boston, MA 02132
617-323-9200
✉: mail@unos.com
www.unos.com

USAA Federal Savings Bank
10750 McDermott Fwy.
San Antonio, TX 78288-9876
210-531-8722
Toll free: 1-800-531-8722
www.usaa.com

US Airways
Customer Relations
4000 E. Sky Harbor Blvd.
Phoenix, AZ 85034
480-693-0800
Toll free: 1-800-428-4322
TTY: 1-800-245-2966
www.usairways.com

US Bancorp
US Bancorp Center
800 Nicollet Mall
Minneapolis, MN 55402
Toll free: 1-800-872-2657
TTY: 1-800-685-5065
www.usbank.com

V

Vera Bradley
Customer Service
11222 Stonebridge Rd.
Roanoke, IN 46783
Toll free: 1-888-855-8372
✉: customercare@verabradley.com
www.verabradley.com

Verizon Communications, Inc.
PO Box 11328
St. Petersburg, FL 33733
Toll free: 1-800-837-4966
TTY: 1-800-974-6006
www.verizon.com

Viking Cruises
Customer Service
5700 Canoga Ave.
Woodland Hills, CA 91367
Toll free: 1-855-338-4546
www.vikingcruises.com

Virgin Atlantic Airways, Ltd.
PO Box 570
Canton, MA 02021
Toll free: 1-888-747-7474
✉: customer.relations.us@fly.virgin.com
www.virgin-atlantic.com

Virgin Mobile USA, LLP
Customer Resolutions
PO Box 4600
Reston, VA 20195
Toll free: 1-888-322-1122
www.virginmobileusa.com

Visa USA, Inc.
(Contact your issuing bank first)
PO Box 194607
San Francisco, CA 94119-4607
Toll free: 1-800-847-2911
✉: AskVisaUSA@visa.com
www.visa.com

Vonage
Customer Care
23 Main St.
Holmdel, NJ 07733
Toll free: 1-866-243-4357
www.vonage.com

The Vons Companies, Inc.
See: Safeway, Inc.
Toll free: 1-877-723-3929
www.vons.com

Voya Financial, Inc.
230 Park Ave.
New York, NY 10169
Toll free: 1-800-262-3862 (Retirement Plans)
Toll free: 1-877-886-5050 (Life Insurance)
www.voya.com

W

Wakefern Food Corporation ○
Customer Service
PO Box 7812
Edison, NJ 08818
908-527-3300
www.wakefern.com

Walgreens ○
Consumer Relations
200 Wilmot Rd.
Deerfield, IL 60015
Toll free: 1-800-925-4733 (In-Store)
Toll free: 1-877-250-5823 (Online)
www.walgreens.com

Wal-Mart Stores, Inc.
Customer Service
850 Cherry Ave.
San Bruno, CA 94066
Toll free: 1-800-925-6278
Toll free: 1-800-966-6546 (Website Questions)
www.wal-mart.com

Wegman's Food Markets
Consumer Affairs
1500 Brooks Ave.
PO Box 30844
Rochester, NY 14603-0844
Toll free: 1-800-934-6267
www.wegmans.com

Weight Watchers International
Corporate Affairs
675 Sixth Ave., 6th Floor
New York, NY 10010
Toll free: 1-800-651-6000
www.weightwatchers.com

Wells Fargo Company ○
Customer Service
PO Box 560948
Charlotte, NC 28256
Toll free: 1-800-869-3557 (General)
TTY: 1-800-877-4833
www.wellsfargo.com

Wendy's Group
One Dave Thomas Blvd.
Dublin, OH 43017
Toll free: 1-888-624-8140
✉: Consumer.Relations@wendys.com
www.wendys.com

Western Union Financial Services, Inc.
Customer Advocate Department
PO Box 6036
Englewood, CO 80112
Toll free: 1-800-325-6000
TTY: 1-800-877-8973
✉: customeradvocatedept@westernunion.com
www.westernunion.com

Westin
See: Starwood Hotels & Resorts Worldwide, Inc.
Toll free: 1-800-937-8461
www.westin.com

Whirlpool Corporation
Customer Service
553 Benson Rd.
Benton Harbor, MI 49022
Toll free: 1-866-698-2538
Toll free: 1-800-344-1274 (Maytag)
Toll free: 1-800-422-1230 (KitchenAid)
www.whirlpool.com

Whitewave Foods ○
Consumer Affairs
12002 Airport Way
Broomfield, CO 80021
Toll free: 1-800-878-9762 (Land O' Lakes)
Toll free: 1-888-820-9283 (Silk)
www.whitewave.com

Whole Foods Markets, Inc.
Customer Service
550 Bowie St.
Austin, TX 78703-4644
512-542-0878
www.wholefoods.com

W Hotels
See: Starwood Hotels & Resorts Worldwide, Inc.
www.whotels.com

Williams-Sonoma, Inc.
Customer Service
3250 Van Ness Ave.
San Francisco, CA 94109
Toll free: 1-877-812-6235
✉: customerservice@williams-sonoma.com
www.williams-sonoma.com

Wrangler
Consumer Relations
105 Corporate Center Blvd.
Greensboro, NC 27408
Toll free: 1-888-784-8571
www.wrangler.com

Wyndham Hotel Group
Customer Service
1910 8th Ave. NE
Aberdeen, SD 57401
Toll free: 1-800-347-7559
www.wyndhamworldwide.com

X

Xbox
See: Microsoft Corporation
Toll free: 1-800-469-9269
TTY: 1-866-740-9269
www.xbox.com

Y

Yahoo! Online
Customer Care
701 First Ave.
Sunnyvale, CA 94089
408-349-5070
www.yahoo.com

Yokohama Tire USA ○
Consumer Affairs
1 MacArthur Pl., Suite 800
Santa Ana, CA 92707
Toll free: 1-800-722-9888
www.yokohamatire.com

YUM! Brands, Inc.
Customer Relations
1441 Gardiner Ln.
Louisville, KY 40213
Toll free: 1-800-225-5532 (KFC)
Toll free: 1-800-948-8488 (Pizza Hut)
Toll free: 1-800-822-6235 (Taco Bell)
www.yum.com

Z

Zappos.com
Customer Loyalty
400 E. Stewart Ave.
Las Vegas, NV 89101
Toll free: 1-800-927-7671
✉: cs@zappos.com
www.zappos.com

Zipcar
35 Thomson Pl.
Boston, MA 02210
Toll free: 1-866-494-7227
✉: info@zipcar.com
www.zipcar.com

Contact Federal Agencies

Many federal agencies have enforcement and/or complaint-handling duties for products and services used by the general public. Others act for the benefit of the public, but do not resolve individual consumer problems. Agencies also create printed publications, and websites that may be helpful when making purchase decisions or dealing with consumer problems. Some agencies provide timely information to citizens through profile pages and videos on social media outlets, blogs, text messages, and news feeds. Call toll free 1-844-872-4681 to get help determining the right agency to contact.

Commission on Civil Rights

Public Affairs Unit
1331 Pennsylvania Ave., NW, Suite 1150
Washington, DC 20425
202-376-8591
202-376-8128 (Publications)
Toll free: 1-800-552-6843 (Complaint Referrals)
TTY: 1-800-877-8339 (Nationwide Complaint Referral)
✉: referrals@usccr.gov
www.usccr.gov
The U.S. Commission on Civil Rights is an independent, bipartisan agency charged with monitoring federal civil rights enforcement. The agency's complaint referral services help to place you in contact with an office that can help you file a discrimination complaint.

Consumer Financial Protection Bureau (CFPB)

Consumer Help
PO Box 4503
Iowa City, IA 52244
Toll free: 1-855-411-2372
TTY: 1-855-729-2372
✉: info@consumerfinance.gov
www.consumerfinance.gov
The CFPB ensures that financial products and services work for consumers. The Bureau provides educational materials and accepts complaints. It also supervises banks, lenders, credit unions, as well as non bank entities and products, such as credit reporting agencies, debt collection companies, prepaid cards, credit and debt repair services, pawn shops, and title loan companies. The CFPB also makes loan disclosures clearer so consumers can understand their rights and responsibilities.

Consumer Product Safety Commission (CPSC)

4330 East West Hwy.
Bethesda, MD 20814
301-504-7923
Toll free: 1-800-638-2772 (8:00 am - 5:30 pm, ET)
TTY: 301-595-7054
www.cpsc.gov
www.recalls.gov (Government Recalls)
www.saferproducts.gov (Report incidents, injuries or safety concerns)
www.cpsc.gov/es/SeguridadConsumidor (in Spanish)
The CPSC protects the public from unreasonable risks of serious injury or death from thousands of types of consumer products under its jurisdiction, including products that pose a fire, electrical, chemical, or mechanical hazard.

Department of Agriculture (USDA)

Center for Nutrition Policy and Promotion (CNPP)
3101 Park Center Dr., 10th Floor
Alexandria, VA 22302-1594
703-305-7600
www.cnpp.usda.gov
www.choosemyplate.gov (Dietary Guidelines)
www.nutrition.gov (Nutrition information)
The CNPP develops and promotes dietary guidance to improve the health and well-being of consumers.

Food and Nutrition Service (FNS)
3101 Park Center Dr.
Alexandria, VA 22302
www.fns.usda.gov
www.fns.usda.gov/forms (Library of forms for food assistance programs)
FNS provides children and low-income people access to food, a healthful diet, and nutrition education. The agency manages several programs, including Supplemental Nutrition Assistance Program (SNAP), school meals, and Women, Infants and Children (WIC).

Meat and Poultry Hotline
Food Safety and Inspection Service
1400 Independence Ave., SW
Washington, DC, DC 20250-3700
Toll free: 1-888-674-6854 (10:00 am - 4:00 pm, ET)
✉: mphotline.fsis@usda.gov
www.fsis.usda.gov
This hotline prevents foodborne illness by answering questions about the safe storage, handling, and preparation of meat, poultry, and egg products.

National Institute of Food and Agriculture (NIFA)
1400 Independence Ave., SW
Mail Stop 2201
Washington, DC 20250-2201
202-720-4423
www.nifa.usda.gov/Extension/index.html (Find local Cooperative Extension offices)
www.nifa.usda.gov
www.extension.org (Information from extension educators).
NIFA shares research-based information on health, nutrition, and personal finance topics through a network of county extension offices. The educators in extension offices conduct workshops, create, and distribute publications. Check the county government listings in your local telephone directory to find your local Cooperative Extension office.

FEDERAL AGENCIES

Department of Commerce (DOC)

Seafood Inspection Program
1315 East West Hwy.
Silver Spring, MD 20910
301-427-8300
Toll free: 1-800-422-2750
✉: NMFS.Seafood.Services@noaa.gov
www.seafood.nmfs.noaa.gov
www.fishwatch.gov (Choosing seafood)
NOAA oversees fisheries management in the United States and provides a voluntary inspection service to the industry. The Seafood Inspection Program offers consumer tips on purchasing, storing, and preparing seafood (fish and shellfish).

United States Patent and Trademark Office (USPTO)
PO Box 1450
Alexandria, VA 22313-1450
Toll free: 1-800-786-9199 (8:30 am - 8:00 pm, ET)
TTY: 1-800-877-8339
✉: usptoinfo@uspto.gov
www.uspto.gov
The USPTO grants patents for intellectual property and trademarks for brand names symbols, protecting the rights of inventors and designers.

Department of Education (ED)

The Education Publications Center (EDPUBS)
PO Box 22207
Alexandria, VA 22304
Toll free: 1-877-433-7827 (9:00 am - 6:00 pm, ET, English and Spanish)
TTY: 1-877-576-7734
✉: edpubs@edpubs.ed.gov
www.edpubs.gov
EDPUBS helps consumers order free publications and resources from the U.S. Department of Education.

Federal Student Aid Information Center
PO Box 84
Washington, DC 20044-0084
319-337-5665
Toll free: 1-800-433-3243 (English and Spanish)
Toll free: 1-800-621-3115 (Defaulted Loans)
Toll free: 1-800-557-7392 (Loan Consolidation)
TTY: 1-800-730-8913 (English and Spanish)
TTY: 1-877-825-9923 (Defaulted Loans)
TTY: 1-800-557-7395 (Loan consolidation)
✉: FederalStudentAidCustomerService@ed.gov
www.studentaid.ed.gov
Federal Student Aid provides grants, work-study, and federal loans for students attending career schools, colleges, and universities. Visit the website to learn how to plan and pay for postsecondary education, apply for federal student aid, and repay student loans.

Office for Civil Rights (OCR)
400 Maryland Ave., SW
Washington, DC 20202-1100
202-245-6100
Toll free: 1-800-421-3481
✉: ocr@ed.gov
www.ed.gov/ocr
The OCR ensures equal access to education and resolves complaints of discrimination.

Office of Career, Technical, and Adult Education (OCTAE)
400 Maryland Ave., SW
Washington, DC 20202-7100
202-245-7700
Toll free: 1-800-872-5327 (Multiple languages)
✉: octae@ed.gov
www2.ed.gov/about/offices/list/ovae/index.html
OCTAE administers and coordinates programs that are related to adult education and literacy, career and technical education, and community colleges.

Office of Postsecondary Education (OPE)
1990 K St., NW
Washington, DC 20006
202-502-7750
www2.ed.gov/about/offices/list/ope/index.html
www.ope.ed.gov/accreditation
OPE develops programs to increase access to postsecondary education. This office works with state accreditation agencies to recognize institutions of higher learning that provide quality education, and provides a searchable database of accredited postsecondary institutions and programs.

Office of Special Education and Rehabilitative Services (OSERS)
400 Maryland Ave., SW
Washington, DC 20202-7100
202-245-7468
Toll free: 1-800-872-5327 (Multiple languages)
www2.ed.gov/about/offices/list/osers/index.html
OSERS provides resources to parents and individuals, school districts and states in three main areas: special education, vocational rehabilitation, and research.

Department of Energy (DOE)

Public Affairs
1000 Independence Ave., SW
Washington, DC 20585
202-586-5575
Toll free: 1-800-342-5363
TTY: 1-800-877-8339
www.energy.gov/public-services

Energy Efficiency and Renewable Energy (EERE)
Department of Energy, Office of the Assistant Secretary
1000 Independence Ave., SW, Mail Stop EE-1
Washington, DC 20585
202-586-9220
✉: eereic@ee.doe.gov
energy.gov/eere/office-energy-efficiency-renewable-energy

♦ Provided financial support for the publication of the Consumer Action Handbook.

EERE provides tips and information on products, services, rebates, and tax credits on ways to save money and energy.

Department of Health and Human Services (HHS)

AIDS.gov
200 Independence Ave., SW
Room 443H
Washington, DC 20201
✉: contact@aids.gov
www.aids.gov
AIDS.gov works to increase knowledge about HIV/AIDs and access to services for people at-risk for or living with HIV.

Centers for Disease Control and Prevention (CDC)
1600 Clifton Rd.
Atlanta, GA 30329-4027
Toll free: 1-800-232-4636 (24 hrs./7 days a week, in English and Spanish)
TTY: 1-888-232-6348
✉: cdcinfo@cdc.gov
www.cdc.gov
www.cdc.gov/spanish (in Spanish)
www.cdc.gov/std (Sexually transmitted disease resources)
www.cdc.gov/std/Spanish (Sexually transmitted disease resources, in Spanish)
www.cdc.gov/hiv (HIV and AIDs research and resources)
www.cdc.gov/hiv/spanish (HIV and AIDs research and resources, in Spanish)
As the nation's health protection agency, CDC protects the country from health, safety, and security threats. The CDC also promotes healthy behaviors and communities. The CDC conducts research and provides resources for people that live with HIV, AIDS, and sexually transmitted diseases.

Flu.gov
www.flu.gov
Flu.gov provides information about the flu, symptoms and treament, and where to get vaccinations.

Health Resources and Services Administration (HRSA)
5600 Fishers Ln.
Rockville, MD 20857
Toll free: 1-888-275-4772 (8:00 am - 8:00 pm, ET)
TTY: 1-877-489-4772
✉: ask@hrsa.gov
www.hrsa.gov
findahealthcenter.hrsa.gov/Search_HCC.aspx (Find a local health center)
HRSA improves access to health care services for people that are geographically isolated, or economically and medically vulnerable.

HHS-TIPS Fraud Hotline
Office of Inspector General
Attn: OIG Hotline Operations
PO Box 23489
Washington, DC 20026
Toll free: 1-800-447-8477
TTY: 1-800-377-4950
www.oig.hhs.gov
www.stopmedicarefraud.gov (Report Medicare Fraud)

The Office of Inspector General (OIG) protects the integrity of HHS programs, as well as the health and welfare of those programs' beneficiaries.

National Health Information Center (NHIC)
1101 Wootton Pkwy., Suite LL100
Rockville, MD 20852
240-453-8280
✉: nhic@hhs.gov
www.health.gov/nhic
www.healthfinder.gov (Tools for healthy living)
www.healthfinder.gov/espanol (in Spanish)
NHIC is a health information referral service that links consumers and health professionals with organizations that are best able to provide answers to their health-related questions.

Office for Civil Rights (OCR)
200 Independence Ave., SW
Room 509F, HHH Building
Washington, DC 20201
Toll free: 1-800-368-1019
TTY: 1-800-537-7697
✉: OCRMail@hhs.gov
www.hhs.gov/ocr
OCR helps to protect you from discrimination in certain health care and social service programs, as well as protects the privacy of your health information.

Substance Abuse and Mental Health Services Administration (SAMHSA)
1 Choke Cherry Rd.
Rockville, MD 20857
Toll free: 1-877-726-4727
TTY: 1-800-487-4889
✉: SAMHSAInfo@samhsa.hhs.gov
www.samhsa.gov
SAMHSA helps people that live with mental illness or are dealing with substance abuse. The agency works to connect mental health professionals and treatment centers with people that need their services through a referral hotline and an online treatment center locator.

Vaccines.gov
www.vacines.gov
Vaccines.gov provides information about vaccines, vaccinations, and immunizations through each stage of life.

Administration for Children & Families (ACF)

370 L'Enfant Promenade, SW
Washington, DC 20447
www.acf.hhs.gov
The ACF funds state, territory, local, and tribal organizations to provide family assistance (welfare), child support, child care, Head Start, child welfare, and other programs relating to children and families.

Child Welfare Information Gateway
Administration for Children & Families (ACF)
Children's Bureau / ACYF
1250 Maryland Ave., SW, 8th Floor
Washington, DC 20024
Toll free: 1-800-394-3366 (9:30 am - 5:30 pm, ET)

✉: info@childwelfare.gov
www.childwelfare.gov
Child Welfare Information Gateway connects child welfare and related professionals to comprehensive information and resources to help protect children and strengthen families.

National Runaway Safeline (NRS)
3080 N. Lincoln Ave.
Chicago, IL 60657
773-880-9860
Toll free: 1-800-786-2929 (24 hrs./7 days a week)
www.1800runaway.org
NRS helps keep America's runaway and at-risk youth safe and off the streets. The organization serves as the federally designated national communication system for runaway and homeless youth.

Office of Child Support Enforcement (OCSE)
Administration for Children & Families (ACF)
370 L'Enfant Promenade, SW
Washington, DC 20447
202-401-9373
✉: ocsehotline@acf.hhs.gov
www.acf.hhs.gov/programs/css
The OCSE assures that assistance in obtaining support (both financial and medical) is available to children by locating parents, establishing paternity and support obligations, and enforcing those obligations.

Administration for Community Living (ACL)

Administration on Aging (AoA)
1 Massachusetts Ave., NW
Washington, DC 20001
202-619-0724
✉: aclinfo@acl.hhs.gov
www.aoa.gov
The Administration on Aging promotes the well-being of older individuals by providing services and programs designed to help them live independently in their homes and communities.

Eldercare Locator
Toll free: 1-800-677-1116 (M-F, 9:00 am - 8:00 pm, ET)
TTY: 1-800-677-1116
✉: eldercarelocator@n4a.org
www.eldercare.gov
The Eldercare Locator is the first step to finding resources for older adults in any U.S. community. It is a free national service of the Administration on Aging that provides an instant connection to resources that enable older persons to live independently in their communities and offers support for caregivers. The Eldercare Locator is administered by The National Association of Area Agencies on Aging (n4a).

Centers for Medicare & Medicaid Services (CMS)

Office of External Affairs
7500 Security Blvd.
Baltimore, MD 21244
www.cms.gov

Health Insurance Marketplace
Toll free: 1-800-318-2596 (24 hrs./7 days a week)
TTY: 1-855-889-4325
www.healthcare.gov
www.cuidadodesalud.gov (in Spanish)
The Health Insurance Marketplace helps uninsured people enroll in a health insurance plan. Use this office's website to understand how the marketplace works, criteria for applying for insurance, and how to lower your costs and to apply for insurance coverage.

Center for Medicaid and CHIP Services (CMCS)
Toll free: 1-877-267-2323
www.medicaid.gov
www.insurekidsnow.gov (Health insurance for children)
Medicaid and Child Health Insurance Programs (CHIP) provide health insurance for people with lower incomes, children, pregnant women, the elderly, and people with disabilities. Eligibility is determined by each state.

Medicare Service Center
Toll free: 1-800-633-4227
TTY: 1-877-486-2048
www.medicare.gov
www.mymedicare.gov (Personalized Medicare benefits)
Medicare is a government sponsored health care program for people that are 65 years old, some younger people with disabilities, and those with permanent kidney failure. The Medicare Service Center answers your questions about Medicare topics, manages your orders of Medicare publications, provides detailed information about the Medicare managed care plans in your area, and helps locate health care providers that participate in Medicare.

Food and Drug Administration (FDA)

10903 New Hampshire Ave.
Silver Spring, MD 20993-0002
Toll free: 1-888-463-6332
www.fda.gov/forconsumers
www.fda.gov
The FDA is responsible for protecting the public health by assuring the safety, efficacy, and security of human and veterinary drugs, biological products, medical devices, our nation's food supply, cosmetics, and products that emit radiation. The FDA also provides accurate, science-based health information to the public.

Center for Food Safety and Applied Nutrition (CFSAN)
Food and Drug Administration (FDA)
Outreach and Information Center
5100 Paint Branch Pkwy.
HFS 009
College Park, MD 20740
Toll free: 1-888-723-3366 (M-F, 10:00 am - 4:00 pm, ET)
✉: consumer@fda.gov
www.fda.gov/Food
The CFSAN Information Line is a general information line for questions pertaining to food safety and applied nutrition.

Center for Tobacco Products (CTP)

Food and Drug Administration (FDA)
10903 New Hampshire Ave.
Silver Spring, MD 20993-0002
Toll free: 1-877-287-1373 (9:00 am - 4:00 pm, ET)
www.fda.gov/tobaccoproducts
The CTP sets standards for tobacco products and label requirements, and enforces advertising restrictions.

National Institutes of Health (NIH)

9000 Rockville Pike
Bethesda, MD 20892
301-496-4000
TTY: 301-402-9612
✉: NIHinfo@od.nih.gov
www.nih.gov
www.salud.nih.gov (in Spanish)
NIH is the primary federal agency for conducting and supporting medical research and its application to enhance health, lengthen life, and reduce illness and disability.

AIDSinfo

National Institutes of Health (NIH)
PO Box 4780
Rockville, MD 20849-6303
301-315-2816
Toll free: 1-800-448-0440 (1:00 pm - 4:00 pm, ET, English and Spanish)
TTY: 1-888-480-3739
✉: contactus@aidsinfo.nih.gov
aidsinfo.nih.gov
infosida.nih.gov (in Spanish)
AIDSinfo offers the latest federally approved information on HIV/AIDS clinical research, treatment and prevention, and medical practice guidelines for people living with HIV/AIDS, their families, health care providers, scientists, and researchers.

National Institute of Allergy and Infectious Diseases (NIAID)

National Institutes of Health (NIH)
5601 Fishers Ln., MSC 9806
Bethesda, MD 20892-9806
301-496-5717
Toll free: 1-866-284-4107
TTY: 1-800-877-8339
✉: ocpostoffice@niaid.nih.gov
www.niaid.nih.gov
NIAID provides health information on allergic, infectious, and immunologic diseases. Diseases include food allergy, sinusitis, and genital herpes. Call or write the institute with questions, and order publications by phone or on the website.

National Cancer Institute (NCI)

National Institutes of Health (NIH)
BG 9609 MSC 9760
9609 Medical Center Dr.
Bethesda, MD 20892-9760
Toll free: 1-800-422-6237 (M-F, 8:00 am - 8:00 pm, ET, English and Spanish)
✉: cancergovstaff@mail.nih.gov
www.cancer.gov
www.cancer.gov/espanol (in Spanish)
NCI's National Cancer Program conducts and supports research, training, health information dissemination. It also provides programs that address the cause, diagnosis, prevention, treatment, and rehabilitation from cancer. The NCI also focuses on the continuing care of cancer patients and their families.

National Institute of Mental Health (NIMH)

National Institutes of Health (NIH)
6001 Executive Blvd.
Room 6200, MSC 9663
Bethesda, MD 20892-9663
301-443-4513
Toll free: 1-866-615-6464 (8:30 am - 5:00 pm, ET)
TTY: 301-443-8431, 1-866-415-8051
✉: nimhinfo@nih.gov
www.nimh.nih.gov
NIMH is the federal agency that conducts and supports research that seeks to understand, treat, and prevent mental illness. Contact NIMH for information on the symptoms, diagnosis and treatment of mental disorders, clinical trials and research. A publication ordering system is available on the NIMH website.

Department of Homeland Security (DHS)

245 Murray Ln., SW
Washington, DC 20528-0075
202-282-8000
202-282-8495 (Comment Line)
www.dhs.gov
www.dhs.gov/en-espanol (in Spanish)
The Department's missions include preventing terrorism and enhancing security; managing our borders, administering immigration laws, securing cyberspace, and ensuring disaster resilience.

Transportation Security Administration (TSA)

601 S. 12th St.
TSA-9
Arlington, VA 20598-6009
Toll free: 1-866-289-9673 (M-F, 8:00 am - 11:00 pm, ET, Sat-Sun/holidays 9:00 am - 8:00 pm, ET)
✉: TSA-ContactCenter@dhs.gov
www.tsa.gov
The TSA can assist you with questions or concerns about travel tips, permitted and prohibited items, and information on filing a claim for items that were damaged or lost during a TSA screening.

U.S. Citizenship and Immigration Services (USCIS)

Information and Customer Service Division
111 Massachusetts Ave., NW
MS 2260
Washington, DC 20529-2260
Toll free: 1-800-375-5283 (M-F, 8:00 am - 8:00 pm, ET)
TTY: 1-800-767-1833
www.uscis.gov
www.uscis.gov/es (in Spanish)
The USCIS is responsible for processing immigration and naturalization applications, and establishing policies regarding immigration services.

U.S. Computer Emergency Readiness Team (US-CERT)
Attn: NPPD/CS&C/NCCIC/US-CERT
Mail Stop 0635
245 Murray Ln., SW Bldg. 410
Washington, DC 20598
Toll free: 1-888-282-0870
TTY: 1-888-232-6348
✉: info@us-cert.gov
www.us-cert.gov
US-CERT strives for a safer Internet by responding to major incidents and analyzing threats.

U.S. Customs and Border Protection (CBP)
1300 Pennsylvania Ave., NW
Washington, DC 20229
202-325-8000 (International callers)
Toll free: 1-877-227-5511 (General inquiries, M-F, 9:00 am - 4:00 pm, ET)
TTY: 1-866-880-6582
www.cbp.gov
CBP prevents individuals from entering the country illegally or bringing harmful and illegal substances into the U.S. They also protect agricultural products from pests, and American businesses from theft of their intellectual property.

Federal Emergency Management Agency (FEMA)

500 C St., SW
Washington, DC 20472
Toll free: 1-800-621-3362
TTY: 1-800-462-7585
www.fema.gov
www.fema.gov/es (in Spanish)
www.ready.gov (Disaster Preparedness)
www.ready.gov/es (Disaster Preparedness, in Spanish)
FEMA supports citizens and emergency personnel to build, sustain, and improve the nation's capability to prepare for, protect against, respond to, recover from, and mitigate all hazards.

FEMA Disaster Assistance
PO Box 10055
Hyattsville, MD 20782-8055
Toll free: 1-800-621-3362 (M-F, 7:00 am - 11:00 pm)
TTY: 1-800-462-7585
www.disasterassistance.gov
www.disasterassistance.gov/es (Disaster Assistance, in Spanish)
FEMA Disaster Assistance provides information about how you can get help before, during, or after a disaster and apply for assistance from the federal government. This office also provides information to help you prepare for, respond to, and recover from disasters.

National Flood Insurance Program (NFIP)
Federal Emergency Management Agency
500 C St., SW
Washington, DC 20472
Toll free: 1-888-379-9531
TTY: 1-800-720-1090
✉: FloodSmart@dhs.gov
www.floodsmart.gov

The NFIP offers flood insurance to homeowners, renters, and business owners if their community participates in the NFIP.

Department of Housing and Urban Development (HUD)

Office of Fair Housing and Equal Opportunity (FHEO)
451 7th St., SW Room 5204
Washington, DC 20410-2000
Toll free: 1-800-669-9777 (Complaints hotline, English and Spanish)
TTY: 1-800-927-9275
www.hud.gov/offices/fheo
www.hud.gov/complaints/housediscrim.cfm (File a complaint)
FHEO enforces federal laws and establishes policies that make sure all Americans have equal access to the housing of their choice. File a complaint with this office if you believe that you have been the victim of housing discrimination.

Department of Housing

451 7th St., SW
Washington, DC 20410
TTY: 202-708-1455
portal.hud.gov/portal/page/portal/HUD/program_offices/housing
The Department of Housing provides public services through its nationally administered programs. It oversees the Federal Housing Administration mortgage insurance program and regulates the housing industry business.

Federal Housing Administration (FHA)
451 7th St., SW
Washington, DC 20410
Toll free: 1-800-225-5342 (English and Spanish)
TTY: 1-877-833-2483
✉: answers@hud.gov
portal.hud.gov/hudportal/HUD?src=/federal_housing_administration
FHA provides mortgage insurance on single family, multifamily, and manufactured homes made by FHA-approved lenders.

Interstate Land Sales Division
451 7th St., SW, Room 9146
Washington, DC 20410
www.hud.gov/complaints/landsales.cfm
The Interstate Land Sales program protects consumers from fraud and abuse when buying or selling land from developers.

Office of Manufactured Housing Programs
Office of Regulatory Affairs and Manufactured Housing
451 7th St., SW, Room 9164
Washington, DC 20410-8000
202-708-6423
Toll free: 1-800-927-2891 (English and Spanish)
TTY: 202-708-1455
✉: mhs@hud.gov
www.hud.gov/mhs

The Manufactured Housing Program is a consumer protection program that regulates the construction of factory-built or manufactured homes. HUD works with many states to respond to consumer complaints.

Department of the Interior (DOI)

Fish and Wildlife Service
1849 C St., NW
Washington, DC 20240
Toll free: 1-800-344-9453
www.fws.gov
The Fish and Wildlife Service works to conserve, protect and enhance fish, wildlife, and plants and their habitats.

National Park Service (NPS)
1849 C St., NW
Washington, DC 20240
202-208-6843 (Public Affairs routes all calls from here)
www.nps.gov
www.recreation.gov (Federal recreational activities and reservations)
NPS preserves the nation's national parks and historic landmarks so that individuals may enjoy the natural environment for years to come.

Department of Justice (DOJ)

Americans with Disabilities Act (ADA) Information Line
950 Pennsylvania Ave., NW
Disability Rights Section–NYAV
Washington, DC 20530
Toll free: 1-800-514-0301 (M-W, and F, 9:30 am - 5:30 pm, ET, Th 12:30 pm - 5:30 pm, ET)
TTY: 1-800-514-0383
www.ada.gov
This service permits businesses, state and local governments, or others, to call and ask questions about general or specific ADA requirements including questions about the ADA Standards for Accessible Design.

U.S. Trustee Program
Executive Offices for U.S. Trustees
441 G St., NW, Suite 6150
Washington, DC 20530
202-307-1391
✉: ustrustee.program@usdoj.gov
www.justice.gov/ust
The Trustee Program protects the integrity of the Federal bankruptcy system. The program monitors the conduct of bankruptcy parties and private estate trustees. It also identifies and helps investigate bankruptcy fraud and abuse. This office also approves credit counseling agencies and debtor education providers, both of which are required for bankruptcy filers.

Department of Labor (DOL)

Employee Benefits Security Administration (EBSA)
Office of Participant Assistance
200 Constitution Ave., NW
Washington, DC 20210
Toll free: 1-866-444-3272

TTY: 1-877-889-5627
www.dol.gov/ebsa
EBSA provides information and assistance on private sector, employer-sponsored retirement and health benefit plans. The agency educates plan participants, beneficiaries, and sponsors to ensure that they have access to documents and to help them understand their rights and responsibilities.

Job Corps
200 Constitution Ave., NW, Suite N4463
Washington, DC 20210
202-693-3000
Toll free: 1-800-733-5627
TTY: 1-877-889-5627
✉: national_office@jobcorps.gov
www.jobcorps.gov
Job Corps is a no-cost education and vocational training program that helps young people learn a career, earn a high school diploma or GED, and find employment.

National Contact Center
Toll free: 1-866-487-2365
TTY: 1-877-889-5627
www.dol.gov
The Department of Labor National Contact Center provides employees and employers with a reliable resource to receive consistent, accurate, and current information assistance for all DOL programs.

Office of Disability Employment Policy (ODEP)
200 Constitution Ave., NW, Room S1303
Washington, DC 20210
202-693-7880
Toll free: 1-866-633-7365
TTY: 1-877-889-5627
✉: odep@dol.gov
www.dol.gov/odep
ODEP creates policies to ensure that people with disabilities are fully integrated into the workforce.

Occupational Safety and Health Administration (OSHA)
200 Constitution Ave., NW
Washington, DC 20210
Toll free: 1-800-321-6742
TTY: 1-877-889-5627
www.osha.gov
OSHA ensures safe and healthful working conditions by setting and enforcing standards and by providing training, outreach, education, and assistance.

Veterans' Employment and Training Service (VETS)
200 Constitution Ave., NW, Room S1325
Washington, DC 20210
Toll free: 1-866-487-2365
TTY: 1-877-889-5627
www.dol.gov/vets
VETS provides resources to prepare and assist veterans and separating service members obtain meaningful careers and maximize their employment opportunities.

Department of State (DOS)

National Passport Information Center (NPIC)
Toll free: 1-877-487-2778 (M-F, 8:00 am - 10:00 pm, ET)
TTY: 1-888-874-7793
✉: NPIC@state.gov
www.travel.state.gov
Contact the NPIC for information on U.S. passports, the status of pending applications, and the locations of the passport application acceptance facilities.

Overseas Citizens Services
Bureau of Consular Affairs
202-501-4444 (From overseas, M-F, 8:00 am - 8:00 pm, ET, except federal holidays).
202-647-4000 (After hours emergencies, Sundays, and holidays ask for the duty officer).
Toll free: 1-888-407-4747 (Emergencies and non-emergencies, M-F, 8:00 am - 8:00 pm, ET, except federal holidays).
www.travel.state.gov
Contact the State Department for help with emergencies and non-emergencies affecting private Americans abroad.

Visa Services
202-485-7600 (M-F, 8:30 am - 5:00 pm, ET)
✉: usvisa@state.gov
usvisas.state.gov
Contact Visa Services for information on U.S. visas for foreigners.

Department of Transportation (DOT)

Aviation Consumer Protection Division (ACPD)
1200 New Jersey Ave., SE
Washington, DC 20590
202-366-2220 (Airline Service Complaints)
Toll free: 1-800-778-4838 (Air Travelers with Disabilities Hotline)
TTY: 202-366-0511, 1-800-455-9880 (Air Travelers with Disabilities Hotline)
www.dot.gov/airconsumer/file-consumer-complaint
airconsumer.ost.dot.gov/spanish (in Spanish)
The ACPD receives complaints from members of the public regarding air travel consumer issues. It verifies compliance with the Department's aviation consumer protection requirements and provides guidance to the industry and members of the public on consumer protection matters, like lost baggage, ticketing, or boarding.

Federal Aviation Administration (FAA)
800 Independence Ave., SW
Washington, DC 20591
Toll free: 1-866-835-5322
www.faa.gov
The FAA works to ensure that all air travel is safe.

Federal Motor Carrier Safety Administration (FMCSA)
1200 New Jersey Ave., SE
Suite W60-300
Washington, DC 20590
202-366-2519
Toll free: 1-800-832-5660 (Information Line)
www.fmcsa.dot.gov

www.protectyourmove.gov (Interstate moving information)
The FMCSA provides information about your rights when moving across state lines (interstate moves). Submit household goods commercial complaints, or dangerous safety violations involving a commercial truck or passenger bus, to this agency.

National Highway Traffic Safety Administration (NHTSA)
1200 New Jersey Ave., SE
West Building
Washington, DC 20590
Toll free: 1-888-327-4236 (Vehicle Safety Hotline)
TTY: 1-800-424-9153
www.nhtsa.dot.gov
NHTSA wants to hear from consumers regarding potential defects in their cars. NHTSA's hotline has information on safety recalls, crash test ratings, child safety seats, bicycles, air bags, and impaired driving prevention.

Department of the Treasury

Bureau of the Fiscal Service
1-800-304-3107 (Questions about debt owed to the U.S.)
1-800-826-9434 (Questions about payments)
www.fiscal.treasury.gov
www.treasurydirect.gov (Treasury Bonds)
This bureau operates the government's collection and deposit systems, and borrows money through Treasury Direct. Contact them to purchase bonds or to check on the maturity of your bonds.

Internal Revenue Service (IRS)
Toll free: 1-800-829-1040 (Help for Individuals)
Toll free: 1-800-829-4933 (Help for Businesses)
TTY: 1-800-829-4059
www.irs.gov
www.irs.gov/uac/Contact-Your-Local-IRS-Office-1
(Find a local taxpayer assistance center)
The IRS is responsible for collecting taxes for the federal government and enforcing tax laws. Use their website to access resources and taxpayer assistance services, print tax forms and instructions, and check the status of your refund. Visit the Taxpayer Assistance Centers closest to you if your personal tax questions require face-to-face assistance.

MyRA
Toll free: 1-855-406-6972
TTY: 1-855-408-6972
✉: myra@treasury.gov
myRA.treasury.gov
MyRA is a savings account to help you save money for retirement., without fees or minimum deposit requirements.

Office of the Comptroller of the Currency (OCC)
Customer Assistance Group
1301 McKinney St., Suite 3450
Houston, TX 77010
Toll free: 1-800-613-6743 (M-F, 8:00 am - 8:00 pm, ET)
TTY: 713-658-0340
www.helpwithmybank.gov
The OCC charters, regulates, and supervises all national banks and federal savings associations. It also supervises the

federal branches and agencies of foreign banks. OCC ensures that financial institutions operate in a safe and sound manner and in compliance with the laws requiring that consumers receive fair treatment and access to financial products.

United States Mint

Customer Service Center
1201 Elm St., Suite 400
Dallas, TX 75270
1-800-872-6468
TTY: 1-888-321-6468 (M-F, 8:30 am - 5:00 pm, ET)
www.usmint.gov
The Mint produces the coins that circulate throughout the U.S. They also produce special edition coinage that can be purchased for coin collections.

Department of Veterans Affairs (VA) ♦

810 Vermont Ave., NW
Washington, DC 20420
Toll free: 1-800-827-1000
TTY: 1-800-829-4833
www.va.gov
www.va.gov/directory (Find the VA facility in your area)
www.cem.va.gov (National Cemetery Administration)
www.benefits.va.gov/benefits (Veterans Benefits Administration)
www.va.gov/health (Veterans Health Administration)
The VA oversees and administers benefits for veterans and their families. Some programs include home loans, life insurance policies, financing education through the GI Bill, job training, health resources, and burials at veterans' cemeteries. For information about VA benefits, write, call or visit your nearest VA facility.

Environmental Protection Agency (EPA)

Energy Star Program

1200 Pennsylvania Ave., NW, Room 6202J
Washington, DC 20460
703-412-3086
Toll free: 1-888-782-7937 (M-F, 9:00 am - 5:00 pm, ET)
www.energystar.gov
The ENERGY STAR label is awarded to products for the home and office that are highly energy efficient. The program encourages the use of energy efficient products that both protect the environment and save consumers money.

Indoor Environments Division

1200 Pennsylvania Ave., NW
Mail Code 6609J
Washington, DC 20460
202-343-9370
www.epa.gov/iaq/index.html
This agency is a central source of information on indoor air quality. It is responsible for implementing the Indoor Environments Program, a voluntary (non-regulatory) program to address indoor air pollution.

National Pesticide Information Center (NPIC)

Oregon State University
310 Weniger Hall
Corvallis, OR 97331-6502

Toll free: 1-800-858-7378 (11:00 am - 3:00 pm, ET, Multiple languages)
✉: npic@ace.orst.edu
www.npic.orst.edu
NPIC is a service that provides objective, science-based information about a wide variety of pesticide-related subjects, including pesticide products, pesticide poisonings, toxicology, and environmental chemistry.

National Service Center for Environmental Publications (NSCEP)

PO Box 42419
Cincinnati, OH 45242-0419
Toll free: 1-800-490-9198
✉: nscep@bps-lmit.com
www.epa.gov/nscep
NSCEP distributes EPA's publications to the public. Consumers can order copies by phone and mail or download digital versions of the publications.

Office of Pollution Prevention and Toxics (OPPT)

1200 Pennsylvania Ave., NW
Mail Code 7401-M
Washington, DC 20460
202-564-3810
✉: oppt.homepage@epa.gov
www.epa.gov/oppt
www.epa.gov/dfe (Design for the Environment Safer Product Labeling Program)
OPPT manages the risk of chemicals in the marketplace to keep pollutants out of the environment and promotes environmental stewardship. OPPT creates tools and provides information to the public so they can properly store and dispose of chemical products.

Safe Drinking Water Hotline

1200 Pennsylvania Ave., NW
4606M
Washington, DC 20460
Toll free: 1-800-426-4791 (10:00 am - 4:00 pm, ET, English and Spanish)
www.epa.gov/safewater/hotline
The Office of Ground Water and Drinking Water helps protect public health by ensuring safe drinking water and protecting ground water.

Equal Employment Opportunity Commission (EEOC)

131 M St., NE
Washington, DC 20507
202-663-4900
Toll free: 1-800-669-4000
TTY: 202-663-4494
✉: info@eeoc.gov
www.eeoc.gov
The EEOC enforces laws that make discrimination illegal in the workplace. The commission oversees all types of work situations including hiring, firing, promotions, harassment, training, wages, and benefits.

Federal Communications Commission (FCC)

Consumer and Governmental Affairs Bureau (CGB)
445 12th St., SW
Washington, DC 20554
Toll free: 1-888-225-5322 (English and Spanish)
TTY: 1-888-835-5322
✉: fccinfo@fcc.gov
www.fcc.gov/consumer-governmental-affairs-bureau
CGB serves as the public face of the commission through outreach and education, as well as through the Consumer Center, which is responsible for responding to consumer inquiries and complaints. FCC accepts public inquiries, informal complaints, and questions regarding cable, radio, satellite, telephone, television, and wireless services.

Federal Deposit Insurance Corporation (FDIC) ♦

Division of Depositor and Consumer Protection
Consumer Response Center
1100 Walnut St., Box 11
Kansas City, MO 64106
Toll free: 1-877-275-3342 (M-F, 8:00 am - 8:00 pm, ET)
TTY: 1-800-925-4618
www.fdic.gov
FDIC responds to questions about federal deposit insurance coverage and handles complaints and inquiries about FDIC insured state banks which are not members of the Federal Reserve System.

Federal Maritime Commission

800 N. Capitol St., NW
Washington, DC 20573
202-523-5807
Toll free: 1-866-448-9586
✉: complaints@fmc.gov
www.fmc.gov
FMC assists consumers engaged in disputes with transporting carriers, ocean transportation intermediaries, and cruise operators.

Federal Reserve System

Federal Reserve Consumer Help
PO Box 1200
Minneapolis, MN 55480
Toll free: 1-888-851-1920 (9:00 am - 7:00 pm, ET)
TTY: 1-877-766-8533 (9:00 am - 7:00 pm, ET)
✉: consumerhelp@federalreserve.gov
www.federalreserveconsumerhelp.gov
This division receives and tracks consumer complaints and questions regarding practices by banks and other financial institutions supervised by the Board of Governors of the Federal Reserve System.

Federal Trade Commission (FTC) ♦

Consumer Response Center
600 Pennsylvania Ave., NW
Washington, DC 20580
Toll free: 1-877-382-4357
TTY: 1-866-653-4261
www.ftc.gov
www.consumer.ftc.gov (Consumer information)
www.consumer.gov (Consumer basics)
www.consumidor.gov (Consumer basics, in Spanish)
www.OnGuardOnline.gov (Online security tips)
www.alertaenlinea.gov (OnGuard Online in Spanish)
www.ftccomplaintassistant.gov (File a complaint)
The FTC works to prevent fraudulent, deceptive, and unfair business practices in the marketplace and to provide information to help consumers spot, stop, and avoid them. To file a complaint or to get free information on consumer issues, visit the website or call the toll free number. The FTC records consumer complaints (Internet, telemarketing, identity theft, and other fraud-related complaints) into the Consumer Sentinel database, a secure investigative tool available to hundreds of civil and criminal law enforcement agencies.

General Services Administration (GSA) ♦

Fleet Vehicle Sales
1800 F St., NW
Suite 3400
Washington, DC 20405
✉: autoauctions@gsa.gov
www.autoauctions.gsa.gov
GSA Fleet sells previously government-owned cars, trucks and other vehicles to consumers. These vehicles are sold at a discount through regional auctions.

Federal Citizen Information Center (FCIC)
Office of Citizen Services, Innovative Technologies, and 18F
1800 F St., NW, 2nd Floor, Wing 1
Washington, DC 20405
For Catalog Orders: Send your name and address to Catalog, Pueblo, CO 81009
202-501-0705
Toll free: 1-844-872-4681 (8:00 am - 8:00 pm, ET, English and Spanish)
www.USA.gov (U.S. government's official web portal)
www.Publications.USA.gov (View and order publications)
www.Kids.gov (Government websites for kids)
www.GobiernoUSA.gov (USA.gov in Spanish)
FCIC helps the public access government information, online, in print, and by phone. This office publishes the free *Consumer Information Catalog*, which lists free and low-cost federal booklets on consumer topics. FCIC also maintains a family of websites to help provide free, timely and useful information. Speak to a person by calling 1-844-USA-GOV1 (872-4681). You can also follow FCIC on social media at www.facebook.com/USAgov, Twitter: @USAgov and plus.google.com/+usagov.

Surplus Federal Property Sales
1800 F St., NW
Washington, DC 20405
Toll free: 1-866-333-7472
✉: gsaauctionshelp@gsa.gov
www.gsa.gov
www.gsaauctions.gov (GSA online auctions)

GSA helps federal agencies dispose of unneeded property by selling directly to the public. It sells personal property, real estate, and vehicles to the public through online auctions.

National Credit Union Administration (NCUA)

1775 Duke St.
Alexandria, VA 22314-3428
703-518-1140 (Office of Consumer Protection)
✉: consumerassistance@ncua.gov
www.ncua.gov
www.mycreditunion.gov (Consumer resources)
NCUA is the federal agency that charters and supervises federal credit unions and insures savings in federal and most state-chartered credit unions across the country through the National Credit Union Share Insurance Fund.

Office of Personnel Management (OPM)

1900 E St., NW
Washington, DC 20415
202-606-1800
TTY: 202-606-2532
✉: general@opm.gov
www.opm.gov
www.usajobs.gov (Federal employment opportunities)
OPM manages the civil service of the federal government, coordinates recruiting of new government employees, and manages their health insurance and retirement benefits programs. OPM also provides resources for locating student jobs, summer jobs, scholarships, and internships.

Pension Benefit Guaranty Corporation (PBGC)

PO Box 151750
Alexandria, VA 22315-1750
Toll free: 1-800-400-7242 (M-F, 8:00 am - 7:00 pm, ET)
✉: mypension@pbgc.gov
www.pbgc.gov
The PBGC protects the retirement incomes of workers in private sector defined pension benefit plans. Have your social security number and your plan's name or number when you call.

Securities and Exchange Commission (SEC) ♦

Office of Investor Education and Advocacy (OIEA)
100 F St., NE
Washington, DC 20549-0213
Toll free: 1-800-732-0330
✉: help@sec.gov
www.sec.gov
www.investor.gov (Investor information)
OIEA serves individual investors and is ready to help resolve investor complaints and answer questions.

Small Business Administration (SBA)

409 3rd St., SW, Suite 7600
Washington, DC 20416
202-205-6740
Toll free: 1-800-827-5722 (Information)
✉: answerdesk@sba.gov
www.sba.gov
www.business.usa.gov (Small business resources)
The SBA helps Americans start, build and grow businesses. Through an extensive network of field offices and partnerships the SBA aids, counsels, assists, and protects the interests of small business concerns.

Social Security Administration (SSA)

Office of Public Inquiries
6401 Security Blvd.
1100 West High Rise
Baltimore, MD 21235
Toll free: 1-800-772-1213
TTY: 1-800-325-0778 (M-F, 7:00 am - 7:00 pm ET)
www.socialsecurity.gov
www.socialsecurity.gov/espanol (in Spanish)
www.socialsecurity.gov/myaccount (Account Management)
The Social Security Administration provides retirement, survivors and disability benefits, and administers Supplemental Security Income (SSI) payments.

U.S. Commodity Futures Trading Commission (CFTC)

Office of External Affairs
Three Lafayette Center
1155 21st St., NW
Washington, DC 20581
202-418-5000
Toll free: 1-866-366-2382 (Consumer Assistance and Complaints)
TTY: 202-418-5514
✉: questions@cftc.gov
www.cftc.gov/consumerprotection
www.cftc.gov
www.smartcheck.cftc.gov (Research financial professionals)
CFTC protects market users and the public from fraud, manipulation, and abusive practices related to the sale of commodity and financial futures and options. It fosters open, competitive, and financially sound futures and option markets. CFTC investigates and prosecutes commodities fraud, including foreign currency schemes, energy manipulation and hedge fund fraud, and works with other government agencies to bring criminal and other actions.

U.S. Postal Service (USPS)

United States Postal Inspection Service (USPIS)
Attn: Mail Fraud
433 W. Harrison St., Room 3255
Chicago, IL 60699-3255
Toll free: 1-877-876-2455
www.postalinspectors.uspis.gov
The USPIS investigates criminals who misuse the postal system to defraud or endanger the public. Contact your nearest USPIS office to report a mail related crime.

AARP
601 E St., NW
Washington, DC 20049
Toll free: 1-888-687-2277
Toll free: 1-877-342-2277 (in Spanish)
TTY: 1-877-434-7598
✉: member@aarp.org
www.aarp.org
AARP addresses the consumer problems and issues that especially impact the financial security of people 50 years and older. Through advocacy, AARP works to make the marketplace safer for all consumers, and empowers members to protect themselves from fraud and deceptive practices.

American Council on Science and Health (ACSH)
1995 Broadway, Suite 202
New York, NY 10023-5882
212-362-7044
Toll free: 1-866-905-2694
✉: acsh@acsh.org
www.acsh.org
ACSH provides consumers with up-to-date scientifically sound information on the relationship between human health and chemicals, foods, lifestyles, and the environment. Booklets and special reports on a variety of topics are available.

Call for Action
11820 Parklawn Dr., Suite 340
Rockville, MD 20852
240-747-0229
www.callforaction.org
Call for Action is a nonprofit network of consumer hotlines. Their trained volunteers assist consumers to resolve problems with businesses, government agencies and other organizations.

Center for Auto Safety (CAS)
1825 Connecticut Ave., NW, Suite 330
Washington, DC 20009-5708
202-328-7700
www.autosafety.org
CAS advocates for auto safety and quality, fuel efficiency, emissions, and other related consumer issues.

Center for Science in the Public Interest (CSPI)
1220 L St., NW, Suite 300
Washington, DC 20005
202-332-9110
✉: cspi@cspinet.org
www.cspinet.org
CSPI conducts research on nutrition, health, food safety, and related issues. It also provides consumers with current information about their health and well being via their monthly *Nutrition Action* Health Letter.

Center for the Study of Services (CSS)
1625 K St., NW, 8th Floor
Washington, DC 20006
Toll free: 1-800-213-7283
www.checkbook.org
CSS publishes Consumers' *CHECKBOOK* so that consumers can evaluate the quality and prices of service firms and stores in their local area.

Contact National Consumer Organizations
National Consumer Organizations are committed to assisting consumers and protecting their rights via advocacy, research, and outreach efforts. Some organizations assist individuals with problems, while others collect consumer complaints and statistics to better understand consumer trends and direct their advocacy efforts.

Coalition Against Insurance Fraud
1012 14th St., NW, Suite 200
Washington, DC 20005
202-393-7330
✉: info@insurancefraud.org
www.InsuranceFraud.org
The Coaltion is an alliance of consumer groups, government agencies, and insurance companies dedicated to combating insurance fraud through research and public information.

Consumer Action
221 Main St., Suite 480
San Francisco, CA 94105
415-777-9635
✉: hotline@consumer-action.org
www.consumer-action.org
Consumer Action is an education and advocacy organization specializing in finance, privacy, insurance, and healthcare issues. Consumer Action offers a multi-lingual consumer complaint hotline, and consumer education materials in several languages. Community-based organizations can receive these free publications in bulk quantities.

Consumer Federation of America (CFA)
1620 I St., NW, Suite 200
Washington, DC 20006
202-387-6121
✉: cfa@consumerfed.org
www.consumerfed.org
CFA is a consumer advocacy and education organization. It represents consumer interests on issues such as telephone service, insurance and financial services, product safety, health care, product liability, and utilities. It develops and distributes studies of various consumer issues, as well as printed consumer guides.

Consumers Reports
101 Truman Ave.
Yonkers, NY 10703
914-378-2000
Toll free: 1-800-666-5261 (*Consumer Reports* magazine)
Toll free: 1-800-333-0663 (ConsumerReports.org)
✉: customerservice@cr.consumer.org
www.consumerreports.org
www.consumersunion.org
Consumer Reports publishes a magazine of the same name. It is an independent, nonprofit testing and information organization serving only consumers. Consumer Reports is a comprehensive source for unbiased advice about products and services, personal finance, health and nutrition, and other categories based on their independent tests.

◆ Provided financial support for the publication of the Consumer Action Handbook.

Families USA

1201 New York Ave. NW, Suite 1100
Washington, DC 20005
202-628-3030
✉: info@familiesusa.org
www.familiesusa.org
A national, nonprofit membership organization committed to comprehensive reform of health and long-term care, Families USA works to create materials to educate and mobilize consumers on health care issues.

The Federation of American Consumers and Travelers (FACT)

318 Hillsboro Ave.
PO Box 104
Edwardsville, IL 62025
Toll free: 1-800-872-3228
✉: cservice@usafact.org
www.usafact.org
FACT is a national not-for-profit consumer group that provides help to individuals and small associations. FACT provides disaster aid, assistance for small business owners, travel discounts, and a Consumer Hotline and library.

Funeral Consumers Alliance (FCA)

33 Patchen Rd.
South Burlington, VT 05403
802-865-8300
www.funerals.org
FCA protects a consumers right to choose a dignified and affordable funeral. Local affiliates of FCA provide funeral planning information and some conduct funeral price surveys.

The Medicare Rights Center

520 Eighth Ave.
North Wing, 3rd Floor
New York City, NY 10018
Toll free: 1-800-333-4114 (Helpline)
✉: info@medicarerights.org
www.medicarerights.org
The Medicare Rights Center helps people with Medicare get the health care and medications they need, and make the most of their Medicare rights and options.

Senior Medicare Patrol National Resource Center (SMP)

2101 Kimball Ave., Suite 320
PO Box 388
Waterloo, IA 50704-0388
Toll free: 1-877-808-2468
✉: info@smpresource.org
www.smpresource.org
The SMP program empowers and assists Medicare beneficiaries, their families, and caregivers to prevent, detect, and report health care fraud, errors, and abuse through outreach, counseling, and education. The SMP National Resource Center increases public awareness about the problem of health care fraud, how their SMP can help, and how to access local SMP services.

National Consumers League (NCL)

1701 K St., NW, Suite 1200
Washington, DC 20006
202-835-3323
www.nclnet.org
www.fakechecks.org
www.fraud.org
www.lifesmarts.org
The NCL provides government and businesses with the consumer's perspective on consumer issues and workplace concerns. The League sponsors the LifeSmarts competition, which is designed to develop the consumer and marketplace knowledge of teenagers. NCL also provides consumers with information to avoid becoming victims of fraud and to convey their complaints to law enforcement.

National Council on Aging

1901 L St., 4th Floor
Washington, DC 20036
202-479-1200
www.ncoa.org
NCOA is a national voice for older adults, especially those who are vulnerable and disadvantage, and the community organizations that serve them.

Alabama

State Offices

Alabama Office of the Attorney General
Consumer Protection Section
501 Washington Ave.
Montgomery, AL 36104
334-242-7335
Toll free: 1-800-392-5658
www.ago.state.al.us

Alaska

State Offices

Alaska Office of the Attorney General
Consumer Protection Unit
1031 W. 4th Ave., Suite 200
Anchorage, AK 99501-5903
907-269-5200
Toll free: 1-888-576-2529
✉: consumerprotection@alaska.gov
www.law.alaska.gov

Arizona

State Offices

Arizona Office of the Attorney General - Phoenix
Consumer Information and Complaints
1275 W. Washington St.
Phoenix, AZ 85007
602-542-5763
✉: consumerinfo@azag.gov
www.azag.gov

Arizona Office of the Attorney General - Prescott
Consumer Information and Complaints
1000 Ainsworth Dr., Suite A-210
Prescott, AZ 86305
928-778-1265
Toll free: 1-800-352-8431
✉: consumerinfo@azag.gov
www.azag.gov

Arizona Office of the Attorney General - Tucson
Consumer Information and Complaints
400 W. Congress St.
South Bldg., Suite 315
Tucson, AZ 85701-1367
520-628-6504
Toll free: 1-800-352-8431 (except in Phoenix)
✉: consumerinfo@azag.gov
www.azag.gov

Contact Your Local Consumer Protection Offices

State, county, and city consumer protection offices offer a variety of important services. They might mediate complaints, conduct investigations, prosecute offenders of consumer laws, license and regulate professionals, provide educational materials, and advocate in the consumer interest.

An advantage of contacting a city or county government office is that it is familiar with local businesses, ordinances, and state laws.

You can also contact your state consumer protection office to get more information about other local resources or nonprofit organizations that help consumers.

Before sending a written complaint, call the office to confirm that it handles the type of complaint you have. Many offices distribute consumer materials specifically geared to state laws and local issues. Ask whether any information is available regarding your problem.

Note: Toll free phone numbers may be restricted to use only within the state listed.

Arkansas

State Offices

Arkansas Office of the Attorney General
Consumer Protection Division
323 Center St., Suite 200
Little Rock, AR 72201
501-682-2341
Toll free: 1-800-482-8982
✉: gotyourback@arkansasag.gov
www.arkansasag.gov
www.gotyourbackarkansas.org

California

State Offices

California Bureau of Automotive Repair
Department of Consumer Affairs
10949 N. Mather Blvd.
Rancho Cordova, CA 95670
Toll free: 1-800-952-5210 (Consumer Questions)
Toll free: 1-866-799-3811 (Auto Body Program)
✉: BAREditor@dca.ca.gov
www.autorepair.ca.gov

California Department of Consumer Affairs
Consumer Information Division
1625 N. Market Blvd., Suite N 112
Sacramento, CA 95834
916-445-1254
Toll free: 1-800-952-5210
TTY: 916-928-1227; 1-800-326-2297
✉: dca@dca.ca.gov
www.dca.ca.gov

California Office of the Attorney General
Public Inquiry Unit
PO Box 944255
Sacramento, CA 94244-2550
916-322-3360
Toll free: 1-800-952-5225
TTY: 1-800-735-2929
www.oag.ca.gov

Contractors State License Board
9821 Business Park Dr.
Sacramento, CA 95827
916-255-3900 (Headquarters)
916-255-2924 (Northern CA.)
562-345-7600 (Southern CA.)
Toll free: 1-800-321-2752
www.cslb.ca.gov

County Offices

Contra Costa County District Attorney's Office
Special Operations Division
Consumer Division
900 Ward St., 4th Floor
Martinez, CA 94553
925-957-8604
www.contracosta.ca.gov

Fresno County District Attorney's Office
Consumer Protection Division
929 L St.
Fresno, CA 93721
559-600-3156
✉: damail@co.fresno.ca.us
www.co.fresno.ca.us

Kern County District Attorney's Office
Consumer Protection Unit
Justice Building
1215 Truxtun Ave., 4th Floor
Bakersfield, CA 93301
661-868-2340
✉: investigation@co.kern.ca.us
www.co.kern.ca.us/da

Los Angeles County Department of Consumer and Business Affairs
500 W. Temple St., Room B96
Los Angeles, CA 90012
213-974-1452
Toll free: 1-800-593-8222 (L.A. County)
TTY: 213-626-0913
✉: info@dca.lacounty.gov
dcba.lacounty.gov

Marin County District Attorney's Office
Consumer Protection Unit
Hall of Justice, Room 130
3501 Civic Center Dr.
San Rafael, CA 94903
415-473-6450
415-473-6495 (Mediation)
TTY: 415-473-3232
www.marincounty.org/depts/da

Monterey County District Attorney's Office
Consumer Protection Division
1200 Aguajito Rd., Room 301
Monterey, CA 93940
831-385-8325 (King City)
831-647-7770 (Monterey)
831-755-5073 (Salinas)
www.co.monterey.ca.us

Napa County District Attorney's Office
Consumer Affairs
931 Parkway Mall
Napa, CA 94559
707-253-4059 (Hotline)
✉: daconsumer@countyofnapa.org
www.countyofnapa.org

Orange County District Attorney's Office
Consumer Protection Unit
401 Civic Center Dr., W
Santa Ana, CA 92701
714-834-6553
✉: consumercomplaint@da.ocgov.com
orangecountyda.org

San Diego County District Attorney's Office
Consumer Protection Unit
330 W. Broadway
San Diego, CA 92101
619-531-4040
619-531-3507 (Consumer Fraud Hotline)
www.sdcda.org

San Francisco County District Attorney's Office
Consumer Protection Unit
732 Brannan St.
San Francisco, CA 94102
415-551-9595
415-553-9535 (Fraud Hotline)
www.sfdistrictattorney.org

San Luis Obispo County District Attorney's Office
Economic Crime Unit
County Courthouse Annex
1050 Monterey St., Room 223
San Luis Obispo, CA 93408
805-781-5856
www.slocounty.ca.gov

San Mateo County District Attorney's Office
Consumer and Environmental Protection
Hall of Justice and Records
400 County Center, 3rd Floor
Redwood City, CA 94063
650-363-4651
da.smcgov.org

Santa Barbara County District Attorney's Office
Consumer Protection Unit
1112 Santa Barbara St.
Santa Barbara, CA 93101
805-568-2300
www.countyofsb.org/da

Santa Clara County District Attorney's Office
Consumer Protection Unit
70 W. Hedding St., West Wing
San Jose, CA 95110
408-792-2880
✉: consumer@da.sccgov.org
www.sccgov.org

Santa Cruz County District Attorney's Office
Consumer Protection
701 Ocean St., Room 200
Santa Cruz, CA 95060
831-454-2050
TTY: 831-454-2123
✉: dao@co.santa-cruz.ca.us
www.co.santa-cruz.ca.us

Solano County District Attorney's Office
Consumer and Environmental Crimes
675 Texas St., Suite 4500
Fairfield, CA 94533
707-784-6859
✉: dacepu@solanocounty.com
www.co.solano.ca.us/depts/da

Stanislaus County District Attorney's Office
Consumer Protection Unit
832 12th St., Suite 300
Modesto, CA 95354
209-525-5550
www.stanislaus-da.org

Ventura County District Attorney's Office
Consumer Mediation Section
800 S. Victoria Ave., Suite 314
Ventura, CA 93009
805-662-1750 (Consumer Fraud)
805-654-3110 (Mediation)
www.vcdistrictattorney.com

City Offices

Los Angeles City Attorney's Office
Consumer Protection
200 N. Main St.
800 City Hall East
Los Angeles, CA 90012
213-978-8040
TTY: 213-978-8310
www.atty.lacity.org

San Diego City Attorney's Office
Consumer and Environmental Protection Unit
1200 3rd Ave., Suite 700
San Diego, CA 92101
619-533-5500
619-533-5600 (Recorded Information)
TTY: 619-702-7198
✉: cityattorney@sandiego.gov
www.sandiego.gov/cityattorney

Santa Monica City Attorney's Office
Consumer Protection Division
1685 Main St., 3rd Floor
Santa Monica, CA 90401
310-458-8336
TTY: 310-458-8696
✉: consumer.mailbox@smgov.net
www.smgov.net/atty

Colorado

State Offices

Colorado Office of the Attorney General
Consumer Protection Section
1300 Broadway, 7th Floor
Denver, CO 80203
720-508-6006
303-222-4444 (Denver)
Toll free: 1-800-222-4444
www.coloradoattorneygeneral.gov

County Offices

Fourth Judicial District Attorney's Office
Economic Crimes Division - El Paso and Teller Counties
105 E. Vermijo Ave.
Colorado Springs, CO 80903
719-520-6000
719-520-6002 (Fraud Hotline)
www.4thjudicialda.com

Pueblo County District Attorney's Office
Economic Crimes Unit
701 Court St.
Pueblo, CO 81003
719-583-6030
county.pueblo.org

Weld County District Attorney's Office
PO Box 758
Greeley, CO 80632
970-336-7235
www.co.weld.co.us

City Offices

Denver District Attorney's Office
Economic Crimes Unit
201 W. Colfax Ave.
Denver, CO 80202
720-913-9179
✉: info@denverda.org
www.denverda.org

Connecticut

State Offices

Connecticut Office of the Attorney General
Consumer Assistance Unit
55 Elm St.
Hartford, CT 06106
860-808-5420
www.ct.gov/ag

Department of Consumer Protection
165 Capitol Ave.
Hartford, CT 06106-1630
860-713-6300
Toll free: 1-800-842-2649
TTY: 860-713-7240
✉: dcp.frauds@ct.gov
www.ct.gov/dcp

Delaware

State Offices

Delaware Department of Justice
Consumer Protection Division
Carvel State Office Building
820 N. French St., 5th Floor
Wilmington, DE 19801
302-577-8600
Toll free: 1-800-220-5424
✉: consumer.protection@state.de.us
www.attorneygeneral.delaware.gov

District Of Columbia

City Offices

Department of Consumer and Regulatory Affairs
1100 4th St., SW
Washington, DC 20024
202-442-4400
TTY: 202-123-4567
✉: dcra@dc.gov
www.dcra.dc.gov

District of Columbia Office of the Attorney General
Consumer Protection
441 4th St., NW
Washington, DC 20001
202-442-9828 (Hotline)
✉: consumer.protection@dc.gov
www.consumer.dc.gov
www.oag.dc.gov

Florida

State Offices

Florida Department of Agriculture and Consumer Services
Division of Consumer Services
PO Box 6700
Tallahassee, FL 32399-6700
850-410-3800
Toll free: 1-800-435-7352
Toll free: 1-800-352-9832 (in Spanish)
www.freshfromflorida.com

Florida Department of Financial Services
Division of Consumer Services
200 E. Gaines St.
Tallahassee, FL 32399
850-413-3089
Toll free: 1-877-693-5236
✉: consumer.services@myfloridacfo.com
www.myfloridacfo.com/Division/Consumers

Florida Office of the Attorney General
PL-01 The Capitol
Tallahassee, FL 32399-1050
850-414-3990
Toll free: 1-866-966-7226 (Fraud)
Toll free: 1-800-321-5366 (Lemon Law)
TTY: 1-800-955-8771
myfloridalegal.com
www.seniorsvscrime.com

Regional Offices

Ft. Lauderdale Branch - Office of the Attorney General
Consumer Protection Division
110 S.E. 6th St., 9th Floor
Fort Lauderdale, FL 33301-5000
954-712-4600
Toll free: 1-866-966-7226 (Fraud Hotline)
www.myfloridalegal.com

Jacksonville Branch - Office of the Attorney General
Consumer Protection Division
1300 Riverplace Blvd., Suite 405
Jacksonville, FL 32207
904-348-2720
Toll free: 1-866-966-7226 (Fraud Hotline)
www.myfloridalegal.com

Miami Branch - Office of the Attorney General
Consumer Protection Division
444 Brickell Ave.
Rivergate Plaza, 5th Floor
Miami, FL 33131
305-377-5835
Toll free: 1-866-966-7226 (Fraud Hotline)
www.myfloridalegal.com

Orlando Branch - Office of the Attorney General
Consumer Protection Division
135 W. Central Blvd., Suite 1000
Orlando, FL 32801
407-999-5588
Toll free: 1-866-966-7226 (Fraud Hotline)
www.myfloridalegal.com

Tampa Branch - Office of the Attorney General
Consumer Protection Division
Concourse Center 4
3507 E. Frontage Rd., Suite 325
Tampa, FL 33607-1795
813-287-7950
Toll free: 1-866-966-7226 (Fraud Hotline)
www.myfloridalegal.com

West Palm Beach Branch - Office of the Attorney General
Consumer Protection Division
1515 N. Flagler Dr., Suite 900
West Palm Beach, FL 33401
561-837-5007
Toll free: 1-866-966-7226 (Fraud Hotline)
myfloridalegal.com

County Offices

Broward County Permitting, Licensing, and Consumer Protection Division
1 N. University Dr., Box 302
Plantation, FL 33324
954-357-5350
www.broward.org/
permittingandlicensing

Hillsborough County Consumer Protection Agency
1101 E. 139th Ave.
Tampa, FL 33613
813-903-3430
www.hillsboroughcounty.org/
consumerprotection

Miami-Dade County Consumer Services Department
Consumer Protection Section
140 W. Flagler St., Suite 902
Miami, FL 33130
305-375-3677
www.miamidade.gov/economy

Office of the State Attorney for Miami-Dade County
Economic Crime Division
1350 N.W. 12th Ave.
Miami, FL 33136-2111
305-547-0671
www.miamisao.com

Orange County Consumer Fraud Unit
415 N. Orange Ave.
Orlando, FL 32801
407-836-2490
✉: fraudhelp@sao9.org
www.orangecountyfl.net

Palm Beach County Consumer Affairs Division
50 S. Military Tr., Suite 201
West Palm Beach, FL 33415
561-712-6600
Toll free: 1-888-852-7362 (Boca Raton/Delray/Glades)
www.pbcgov.com/consumer

Pinellas County Office of Consumer Services
631 Chestnut St.
Clearwater, FL 33756
727-464-6200
✉: consumer@pinellascounty.org
www.pinellascounty.org/consumer

Georgia

State Offices

Georgia Governor's Office of Consumer Protection
2 Martin Luther King, Jr. Dr., SE
Suite 356
Atlanta, GA 30334-9077
404-651-8600
Toll free: 1-800-869-1123
consumer.georgia.gov

Georgia Office of the Attorney General
40 Capitol Square, SW
Atlanta, GA 30334
404-656-3300
✉: AGOlens@law.ga.gov
www.law.ga.gov

Hawaii

State Offices

Hawaii Department of Commerce and Consumer Affairs - Hilo
Office of Consumer Protection
120 Pauahi St., Suite 212
Hilo, HI 96720
808-933-0910
✉: ocp@dcca.hawaii.gov
cca.hawaii.gov/ocp

Hawaii Department of Commerce and Consumer Affairs - Honolulu
Office of Consumer Protection
Leiopapa A Kamehameha Building
235 S. Beretania St., Suite 801
Honolulu, HI 96813
808-586-2630
808-587-4272 (Consumer Resource Center)
✉: ocp@dcca.hawaii.gov
cca.hawaii.gov/ocp

Hawaii Department of Commerce and Consumer Affairs - Wailuku
Office of Consumer Protection
1063 Lower Main St., Suite C-216
Wailuku, HI 96793
808-243-4648
808-984-2400 (Consumer Resource Center)
✉: ocp@dcca.hawaii.gov
cca.hawaii.gov/ocp

Hawaii Office of the Attorney General
Commerce and Economic Development
425 Queen St.
Honolulu, HI 96813
808-586-1500
www.ag.hawaii.gov

Idaho

State Offices

Idaho Office of the Attorney General
Consumer Protection Division
954 W. Jefferson, 2nd Floor
Boise, ID 83720
208-334-2424
Toll free: 1-800-432-3545
www.ag.idaho.gov

Illinois

State Offices

Illinois Office of the Attorney General - Carbondale
Consumer Fraud Bureau
601 S. University Ave.
Carbondale, IL 62901
618-529-6400
Toll free: 1-800-243-0607 (Fraud Hotline)
Toll free: 1-866-310-8398 (in Spanish)
TTY: 1-877-675-9339
www.illinoisattorneygeneral.gov

Illinois Office of the Attorney General - Chicago
Consumer Fraud Bureau
100 W. Randolph St.
Chicago, IL 60601
312-814-3000
Toll free: 1-800-386-5438 (Fraud Hotline)
Toll free: 1-866-310-8398 (in Spanish)
TTY: 1-800-964-3013
www.illinoisattorneygeneral.gov

Illinois Office of the Attorney General - Springfield
Consumer Fraud Bureau
500 S. 2nd St.
Springfield, IL 62706
217-782-1090
Toll free: 1-800-243-0618 (Fraud Hotline)
Toll free: 1-866-310-8398 (in Spanish)
TTY: 1-877-844-5461
www.illinoisattorneygeneral.gov

Regional Offices

Chicago South Regional Office of the Attorney General
7906 S. Cottage Grove Ave.
Chicago, IL 60619
773-488-2600
TTY: 1-866-717-8798
www.illinoisattorneygeneral.gov

Chicago West Regional Office of the Attorney General
306 N. Pulaski Rd.
Chicago, IL 60624
773-265-8808
TTY: 1-866-717-8804
www.illinoisattorneygeneral.gov

East Central Illinois Regional Office of the Attorney General
1776 E. Washington St.
Urbana, IL 61802
217-278-3366
TTY: 217-278-3371
www.illinoisattorneygeneral.gov

Metro East Illinois Regional Office of the Attorney General
201 W. Pointe Dr., Suite 7
Belleville, IL 62226
618-236-8616
TTY: 618-236-8619
www.illinoisattorneygeneral.gov

Northern Illinois Regional Office of the Attorney General
Zeke Giorgi Center
200 S. Wyman St., Suite 307
Rockford, IL 61101
815-967-3883
TTY: 815-967-3891
www.illinoisattorneygeneral.gov

West Central Illinois Regional Office of the Attorney General
628 Maine St.
Quincy, IL 62301
217-223-2221
TTY: 217-223-2254
www.illinoisattorneygeneral.gov

County Offices

Cook County State Attorney's Office
Consumer Fraud Unit
69 W. Washington St., Suite 3130
Chicago, IL 60602
312-603-8600
312-603-8700 (Consumer Line)
✉: consumer@cookcountygov.com.
www.statesattorney.org/index2/
consumer_fraud.html

City Offices

Des Plaines Consumer Protection Commission
City Hall
1420 Miner St., 6th Floor
Des Plaines, IL 60016
847-391-5006
✉: consumerprotection@desplaines.org
www.desplaines.org

Chicago Division of Business Affairs and Consumer Protection
121 N. LaSalle St., 8th Floor
Chicago, IL 60602
312-744-6060
TTY: 312-744-1944
www.cityofchicago.org/
ConsumerServices

Indiana

State Offices

Indiana Office of the Attorney General
Consumer Protection Division
302 W. Washington St., 5th Floor
Indianapolis, IN 46204
317-232-6330
Toll free: 1-800-382-5516
www.in.gov/attorneygeneral

Iowa

State Offices

Iowa Office of the Attorney General
Consumer Protection Division
1305 E. Walnut St.
Des Moines, IA 50319
515-281-5926
Toll free: 1-888-777-4590
✉: consumer@ag.state.ia.us
www.IowaAttorneyGeneral.org

Kansas

State Offices

Kansas Office of the Attorney General
Consumer Protection Division
120 S.W. 10th Ave., 2nd Floor
Topeka, KS 66612-1597
785-296-3751
Toll free: 1-800-432-2310
www.ag.ks.gov

County Offices

Douglas County District Attorney's Office
Consumer Protection Division
111 E. 11th St.
Lawrence, KS 66044
785-330-2849 (Consumer Hotline)
785-841-0211 (Main)
✉: districtattorney@douglas-county.com
www.douglascountyks.org/depts/
distrtict-attorney

Johnson County District Attorney's Office
Consumer Protection Division
PO Box 728
Olathe, KS 66051
913-715-3003 (Consumer Hotline)
da.jocogov.org

Sedgwick County District Attorney's Office
Consumer Division
535 N. Main St.
Wichita, KS 67203
316-660-3600
Toll free: 1-800-432-6878
✉: consumer@sedgwick.gov
www.sedgwickcounty.org/da

Kentucky

State Offices

Kentucky Office of the Attorney General
Consumer Protection Division
1024 Capital Center Dr., Suite 200
Frankfort, KY 40601
502-696-5389
Toll free: 1-888-432-9257
www.ag.ky.gov/cp

Kentucky Office of the Attorney General - Louisville
Consumer Protection Division
310 Whittington Pkwy., Suite 101
Louisville, KY 40222
502-429-7134
Toll free: 1-888-432-9257

www.ag.ky.gov/cp

Kentucky Office of the Attorney General - Prestonsburg
361 N. Lake Dr.
Prestonsburg, KY 41653
606-889-1821
Toll free: 1-888-432-9257 (Consumer Hotline)
www.ag.ky.gov/cp

Louisiana

State Offices

Louisiana Office of the Attorney General
Consumer Protection Section
PO Box 94005
Baton Rouge, LA 70804-9005
225-326-6465
Toll free: 1-800-351-4889
✉: consumerinfo@ag.state.la.us
www.ag.state.la.us

Parish Offices

Jefferson Parish District Attorney's Office
Economic Crime Unit
200 Derbigny St.
Gretna, LA 70053
504-361-2920
www.jpda.us

Maine

State Offices

Maine Office of the Attorney General
Consumer Information and Mediation Service
Six State House Station
Augusta, ME 04333
207-626-8849
Toll free: 1-800-436-2131
✉: consumer.mediation@maine.gov
www.maine.gov/ag

Bureau of Consumer Credit Protection
35 State House Station
Augusta, ME 04333
207-624-8527
Toll free: 1-800-332-8529
www.credit.maine.gov

Maryland

State Offices

Maryland Office of the Attorney General
Consumer Protection Division
200 Saint Paul Pl.
Baltimore, MD 21202
410-528-8662 (Consumer Mediation)

410-576-6550 (Consumer Information)
410-528-1840 (Medical billing complaints)
Toll free: 1-888-743-0023 (Switchboard)
Toll free: 1-877-261-8807 (Health plan decision appeals)
TTY: 410-576-6372
✉: consumer@oag.state.md.us
www.oag.state.md.us/consumer

Regional Offices

Maryland Attorney General's Office - Eastern Shore
Consumer Protection Division
201 Baptist St.
Salisbury, MD 21801
410-713-3620
TTY: 410-576-6372 (Baltimore office)
✉: consumer@oag.state.md.us
www.oag.state.md.us/consumer

Maryland Attorney General's Office - Southern Maryland
15045 Burnt Store Rd.
Hughesville, MD 20637
301-274-4620
Toll free: 1-866-366-8343
TTY: 410-576-6372 (Baltimore office)
✉: consumer@oag.state.md.us
www.oag.state.md.us/consumer

Maryland Attorney General's Office - Western Maryland
Consumer Protection Division
44 N. Potomac St., Suite 104
Hagerstown, MD 21740
301-791-4780
TTY: 410-576-6372 (Baltimore office)
✉: consumer@oag.state.md.us
www.oag.state.md.us/consumer

County Offices

Howard County Office of Consumer Affairs
6751 Columbia Gateway Dr.
Columbia, MD 21046
410-313-6420
✉: consumer@howardcountymd.gov
www.howardcountymd.gov

Montgomery County Office of Consumer Protection
100 Maryland Ave., Suite 330
Rockville, MD 20850
240-777-3636
240-777-3681 (Consumer Tip Line)
TTY: 240-773-3556
✉: ConsumerProtection@montgomerycountymd.gov
montgomerycountymd.gov/ocp

Massachusetts

State Offices

Massachusetts Office of the Attorney General
Public Inquiry and Assistance Center
One Ashburton Pl., 18th Floor
Boston, MA 02108-1518
617-727-8400 (Consumer Hotline)
TTY: 617-727-4765
✉: ago@state.ma.us
www.mass.gov/ago

Office of Consumer Affairs and Business Regulation
10 Park Plaza, Suite 5170
Boston, MA 02116
617-973-8787
Toll free: 1-888-283-3757 (Consumer Hotline)
TTY: 1-800-720-3480
www.mass.gov/ocabr

Regional Offices

Massachusetts Office of the Attorney General - New Bedford
Public Inquiry and Assistance Center
105 William St., 1st Floor
New Bedford, MA 02740-6257
508-990-9700
617-727-8400 (Assistance Center Hotline)
TTY: 617-727-4765
✉: ago@state.ma.us
www.mass.gov/ago

Massachusetts Office of the Attorney General - Springfield
Public Inquiry and Assistance Center
1350 Main St., 4th Floor
Springfield, MA 01103-1629
413-784-1240
617-727-8400 (Assistance Center Hotline)
TTY: 617-727-4765
✉: ago@state.ma.us
www.mass.gov/ago

Massachusetts Office of the Attorney General - Worcester
Public Inquiry and Assistance Center
10 Mechanic St., Suite 301
Worcester, MA 01608-2417
508-792-7600
617-727-8400 (Hotline)
TTY: 617-727-4765
✉: ago@state.ma.us
www.mass.gov/ago

County Offices

Norfolk District Attorney's Office
Consumer Protection Division
45 Shawmut Rd.
Canton, MA 02021
781-830-4800 ext. 279
www.norfolkda.com

Northwestern District Attorney's Office - Franklin County
Consumer Protection Division
13 Conway St.
Greenfield, MA 01301
413-774-3186
www.
northwesterndistrictattorney.org

Northwestern District Attorney's Office - Hampshire County
Consumer Protection Division
One Gleason Plaza
Northampton, MA 01060
413-586-9225
www.
northwesterndistrictattorney.org

Springfield Mayor's Office of Consumer Information
City Hall, Room 315
36 Court St.
Springfield, MA 01103
413-787-6437
TTY: 413-787-6154
✉: moci@springfieldcityhall.com
www.springfieldcityhall.com

City Offices

Boston Consumer Affairs and Licensing
One City Hall Square, Room 817
Boston, MA 02201-2039
617-635-3834
✉: MOCAL@cityofboston.gov
www.cityofboston.gov/
consumeraffairs

Cambridge Consumers Council
831 Massachusetts Ave., 1st Floor
Cambridge, MA 02139
617-349-6150
TTY: 617-349-6112
✉: consumer@cambridgema.gov
www.cambridgema.gov/
consumercouncil

Newton Consumer Affairs
Newton City Hall
1000 Commonwealth Ave.
Newton Centre, MA 02459
617-796-1292
TTY: 617-796-1089
www.newtonma.gov

Revere Consumer Affairs Office
281 Broadway
Revere, MA 02151
781-286-8114
www.revere.org

Michigan

State Offices

Michigan Office of the Attorney General
Consumer Protection Division
PO Box 30213
Lansing, MI 48909-7713
517-373-1140
Toll free: 1-877-765-8388
www.michigan.gov/ag

Michigan Department of Agriculture and Rural Development
Weights & Measures
PO Box 30017
Lansing, MI 48909
Toll free: 1-800-292-3939
www.michigan.gov/wminfo

Minnesota

State Offices

Minnesota Office of the Attorney General
Consumer Services Division
1400 Bremer Tower
445 Minnesota St.
St. Paul, MN 55101
651-296-3353
Toll free: 1-800-657-3787
TTY: 1-800-366-4812
www.ag.state.mn.us

City Offices

Minneapolis Department of Regulatory Services
Business Licenses & Consumer Services
350 S. 5th St., Room 1C
Minneapolis, MN 55415
612-673-2080
TTY: 612-673-2157
✉: minneapolis311@minneapolismn.
gov
www.ci.minneapolis.mn.us/
licensing

Mississippi

State Offices

Mississippi Department of Agriculture and Commerce
Bureau of Regulatory Services
Consumer Protection
PO Box 1609
Jackson, MS 39215
601-359-1148
www.mdac.state.ms.us

Mississippi Office of the Attorney General
Consumer Protection Division
PO Box 22947
Jackson, MS 39225-2947
601-359-4230
Toll free: 1-800-281-4418
www.ago.state.ms.us

Mississippi Office of the Attorney General - Biloxi
Consumer Protection Division
1141 Bayview Ave., Suite 402
Biloxi, MS 39530
228-386-4400
Toll free: 1-877-667-5599
www.ago.state.ms.us

Missouri

State Offices

Missouri Office of the Attorney General
Consumer Protection Unit
PO Box 899
Jefferson City, MO 65102
573-751-3321
Toll free: 1-800-392-8222 (Consumer Protection Hotline)
✉: consumer.help@ago.mo.gov
www.ago.mo.gov

Regional Offices

Missouri Office of the Attorney General - Cape Girardeau
Consumer Protection Division
2860 Kage Rd.
Cape Girardeau, MO 63701
573-290-5679
Toll free: 1-800-392-8222 (Consumer Protection Hotline)
✉: consumer.help@ago.mo.gov
www.ago.mo.gov

Missouri Office of the Attorney General - Kansas City
Consumer Protection Division
Fletcher Daniels State Office Building
615 E. 13th St., Suite 401
Kansas City, MO 64106
816-889-5000
Toll free: 1-800-392-8222 (Consumer Protection Hotline)
✉: consumer.help@ago.mo.gov
www.ago.mo.gov

Missouri Office of the Attorney General - Springfield
Consumer Protection Division
Springfield State Office Building
149 Park Central Sq., Suite 1017
Springfield, MO 65806
417-895-6567
Toll free: 1-800-392-8222 (Consumer Protection Hotline)
✉: consumer.help@ago.mo.gov
www.ago.mo.gov

Missouri Office of the Attorney General - St Louis
Consumer Protection Division
Old Post Office Building
815 Olive St., Suite 200
St. Louis, MO 63101
314-340-6816
Toll free: 1-800-392-8222 (Consumer Protection Hotline)
✉: consumer.help@ago.mo.gov
www.ago.mo.gov

Montana

State Offices

Montana Department of Justice
Office of Consumer Protection
PO Box 200151
Helena, MT 59620-0151
406-444-4500
Toll free: 1-800-481-6896
✉: contactocp@mt.gov
www.doj.mt.gov/consumer

Nebraska

State Offices

Nebraska Office of the Attorney General
Consumer Protection Division
2115 State Capitol
Lincoln, NE 68509
402-471-2682
Toll free: 1-800-727-6432
Toll free: 1-888-850-7555 (in Spanish)
✉: ago.consumer@nebraska.gov
www.ago.ne.gov

Nevada

State Offices

Nevada Department of Business and Industry
Fight Fraud Task Force
555 E. Washington Ave., Suite 4900
Las Vegas, NV 89101
702-486-2750
www.fightfraud.nv.gov

Nevada Office of the Attorney General - Carson City
100 North Carson Street
Carson City, NV 89701
775-684-1100
702-486-3132 (Consumer Hotline)
www.ag.nv.gov

Nevada Office of the Attorney General - Reno
5420 Kietzke Lane, Suite 202
Reno, NV 89511
775-688-1818
702-486-3132 (Consumer Hotline)
www.ag.gov

New Hampshire

State Offices

New Hampshire Office of the Attorney General
Consumer Protection and Antitrust Bureau
33 Capitol St.
Concord, NH 03301
603-271-3641
Toll free: 1-888-468-4454 (Consumer Protection Hotline)
TTY: 1-800-735-2964
✉: doj-cpb@doj.nh.gov
www.doj.nh.gov/consumer

New Jersey

State Offices

Department of Law and Public Safety
Division of Consumer Affairs
124 Halsey St.
Newark, NJ 07102
973-504-6200
Toll free: 1-800-242-5846
TTY: 973-504-6588
✉: askconsumeraffairs@lps.state.nj.us
www.njconsumeraffairs.gov

County Offices

Bergen County Office of Consumer Protection
One Bergen County Plaza, 3rd Floor
Hackensack, NJ 07601-7076
201-336-6400
www.co.bergen.nj.us

Burlington County Office of Consumer Affairs/Weights & Measures
PO Box 6000
Mount Holly, NJ 08060
609-265-5098 (Weights & Measures)
609-265-5054 (Consumer Affairs)
✉: consumer@co.burlington.nj.us
www.co.burlington.nj.us

Cape May County Consumer Affairs
Four Moore Rd., DN 310/302
Cape May Court House, NJ 08210
609-886-2903
✉: consumer@co.cape-may.nj.us
www.capemaycountygov.net

Cumberland County Department of Consumer Affairs
788 E. Commerce St.
Bridgeton, NJ 08302
856-453-2203
www.co.cumberland.nj.us

Essex County Division of Consumer Services
50 S. Clinton St., Suite 3201
East Orange, NJ 07018
973-395-8350
www.essex-countynj.org

Gloucester County Office of Consumer Affairs and Weights & Measures
254 County House Rd.
Clarksboro, NJ 08020
856-384-6855
www.gloucestercountynj.gov/depts/c/cpwm

Hudson County Division of Consumer Affairs
583 Newark Ave., 1st Floor
Jersey City, NJ 07306
201-795-6295
✉: hcdca@hcnj.us
www.hudsoncountynj.org

Mercer County Office of Consumer Affairs
640 S. Broad St.
PO Box 8068
Trenton, NJ 08650-0068
609-989-6671
www.mercercounty.org

Middlesex County Division of Consumer Affairs and Weights & Measures
711 Jersey Ave.
New Brunswick, NJ 08901
732-745-3875
✉: consumer@co.middlesex.nj.us
www.co.middlesex.nj.us/
Government/Departments/PSH/
Pages/Office_Inspections.aspx

Monmouth County Department of Consumer Affairs
Hall of Records Annex
One E. Main St.
Freehold, NJ 07728-1255
732-431-7900
✉: consumeraffairs@co.monmouth.
nj.us
www.visitmonmouth.com

Ocean County Department of Consumer Affairs
1027 Hooper Ave., Bldg. 2
Toms River, NJ 08754-2191
732-929-2105
✉: OceanCountyConsumerAffairs@
co.ocean.nj.us
www.co.ocean.nj.us

Passaic County Department of Consumer Protection and Weights & Measures
Department of Law
1310 Route 23 N
Wayne, NJ 07470
973-305-5881 (Consumer Protection)
973-305-5750 (Weights Measures)
www.passaiccountynj.org

Union County Department of Public Safety
Division of Consumer Affairs
300 North Ave., E
Westfield, NJ 07090
908-654-9840
www.ucnj.org

City Offices

Nutley Consumer Affairs
Department of Public Affairs
149 Chestnut St.
Nutley, NJ 07110
973-284-4976
www.nutleynj.org

Secaucus Department of Consumer Affairs
Municipal Government Center
1203 Patterson Plank Rd.
Secaucus, NJ 07094
201-330-2008
www.njconsumeraffairs.gov/ocp/
countyoff.htm

New Mexico

State Offices

New Mexico Office of the Attorney General
Consumer Protection Division
PO Drawer 1508
Santa Fe, NM 87504-1508
505-827-6009 (Santa Fe)
505-222-9100 (Albuquerque)
575-526-2280(Las Cruces)
Toll free: 1-800-678-1508
www.nmag.gov

New York

State Offices

New York Department of State
Division of Consumer Protection
Consumer Assistance Unit
99 Washington Ave.
Albany, NY 12231-0001
518-474-8583
Toll free: 1-800-697-1220
www.dos.ny.gov/
consumerprotection

Office of the Attorney General - Albany
Consumer Frauds Bureau
State Capitol
Albany, NY 12224-0341
518-474-5481
Toll free: 1-800-771-7755
TTY: 1-800-788-9898
www.ag.ny.gov

Office of the Attorney General - New York City
Consumer Frauds Bureau
120 Broadway, 3rd Floor
New York, NY 10271-0332
212-416-8300
Toll free: 1-800-771-7755
TTY: 1-800-788-9898
www.ag.ny.gov

Regional Offices

Binghamton Regional Office of the Attorney General
State Office Building, 17th Floor
44 Hawley St.
Binghamton, NY 13901
607-721-8771
Toll free: 1-800-771-7755
TTY: 1-800-788-9898
www.ag.ny.gov

Brooklyn Regional Office of the Attorney General
55 Hanson Place, Suite 1080
Brooklyn, NY 11217
718-722-3949
Toll free: 1-800-771-7755
TTY: 1-800-788-9898
www.ag.ny.gov

Buffalo Regional Office of the Attorney General
Main Place Tower, Suite 300A
350 Main St.
Buffalo, NY 14202
716-853-8404
Toll free: 1-800-771-7755
TTY: 1-800-788-9898
www.ag.ny.gov

Harlem Regional Office of the Attorney General
163 W. 125th St., Suite 1324
New York, NY 10027
212-961-4475
Toll free: 1-800-771-7755
TTY: 1-800-788-9898
www.ag.ny.gov

Nassau Regional Office of the Attorney General
200 Old Country Rd., Suite 240
Mineola, NY 11501
516-248-3301
Toll free: 1-800-771-7755
TTY: 1-800-788-9898
www.ag.ny.gov

Plattsburgh Regional Office of the Attorney General
43 Durkee St., Suite 700
Plattsburgh, NY 12901
518-562-3282
Toll free: 1-800-771-7755
TTY: 1-800-788-9898
www.ag.ny.gov

Poughkeepsie Regional Office of the Attorney General
One Civic Center Plaza, Suite 401
Poughkeepsie, NY 12601-3157
845-485-3900
Toll free: 1-800-771-7755
TTY: 1-800-788-9898
www.ag.ny.gov

Rochester Regional Office of the Attorney General
144 Exchange Blvd., Suite 200
Rochester, NY 14614-2176
585-546-7430
Toll free: 1-800-771-7755
TTY: 1-800-788-9898
www.ag.ny.gov

Suffolk Regional Office of the Attorney General
300 Motor Pkwy., Suite 230
Hauppauge, NY 11788
631-231-2401
Toll free: 1-800-771-7755
TTY: 1-800-788-9898
www.ag.ny.gov

Syracuse Regional Office of the Attorney General
615 Erie Blvd. W, Suite 104
Syracuse, NY 13204
315-448-4848
Toll free: 1-800-771-7755
TTY: 1-800-788-9898
www.ag.ny.gov

Utica Regional Office of the Attorney General
207 Genesee St., Room 508
Utica, NY 13501
315-793-2225
Toll free: 1-800-771-7755
TTY: 1-800-788-9898
www.ag.ny.gov

Watertown Regional Office of the Attorney General
Dulles State Office Building
317 Washington St.
Watertown, NY 13601
315-785-2444
Toll free: 1-800-771-7755
TTY: 1-800-788-9898
www.ag.ny.gov

Westchester Regional Office of the Attorney General
44 S. Broadway
White Plains, NY 10601-5008
914-422-8794
Toll free: 1-800-771-7755
TTY: 1-800-788-9898
www.ag.ny.gov

County Offices

Rockland County Office of Consumer Protection
18 New Hempstead Rd.
New City, NY 10956
845-708-7600
www.rocklandgov.com

Albany County Office of Consumer Affairs
112 State St., Room 630
Albany, NY 12207
518-447-7581
✉: consumer_complaints@albanycounty.com
www.albanycounty.com

Nassau County Office of Consumer Affairs
240 Old County Rd.
Mineola, NY 11501
516-571-2600
www.nassaucountyny.gov

Orange County Department of Consumer Affairs
4 Glenmere Cove Rd.
Goshen, NY 10924
845-360-6700
www.co.orange.ny.us

Putnam County Department of Consumer Affairs
110 Old Route 6, Bldg. 3
Carmel, NY 10512
845-808-1617
✉: PutnamConsumerAffairs@putnamcountyny.gov
www.putnamcountyny.com

Schenectady County Department of Consumer Affairs/Bureau of Weights & Measures
64 Kellar Ave.
Schenectady, NY 12306
518-356-7473 (Consumer Affairs)
518-356-6795 (Weights & Measures)
www.schenectadycounty.com

Ulster County Consumer Fraud Bureau
275 Wall St.
Kingston, NY 12401
845-340-3280
www.ulstercountyny.gov/district-attorney/fraud-unit

Westchester County Department of Consumer Protection
148 Martine Ave., Room 407
White Plains, NY 10601
914-995-2155
✉: conpro@westchestergov.com
consumer.westchestergov.com

City Offices

Town of Colonie Attorney
Consumer Protection Board
Memorial Town Hall
534 Loudon Rd.
Newtonville, NY 12128
518-783-2790
www.colonie.org

Mt. Vernon Office of Consumer Affairs
City Hall
One Roosevelt Square
Mount Vernon, NY 10550
914-665-2433
www.cmvny.com

New York City Department of Consumer Affairs
42 Broadway, 9th Floor
New York, NY 10004
212-639-9675
TTY: 212-504-4115
www.nyc.gov/consumers

Yonkers Consumer Protection Bureau
87 Nepperhan Ave., Room 212
Yonkers, NY 10701
914-377-3000 (Helpline)
www.yonkersny.gov

North Carolina

State Offices

North Carolina Department of Agriculture and Consumer Services
1001 Mail Service Center
Raleigh, NC 27699-1001
919-707-3000
www.ncagr.gov

North Carolina Office of the Attorney General
Consumer Protection Division
9001 Mail Service Center
Raleigh, NC 27699-9001
919-716-6000
919-716-0058 (in Spanish)
Toll free: 1-877-566-7226
www.ncdoj.gov

North Dakota

State Offices

North Dakota Office of the Attorney General
Consumer Protection and Antitrust Division
Gateway Professional Center
1050 E. Interstate Ave., Suite 200
Bismarck, ND 58503-5574
701-328-3404
Toll free: 1-800-472-2600
TTY: 1-800-366-6888
✉: ndag@nd.gov
www.ag.nd.gov

Ohio

State Offices

Ohio Office of the Attorney General
Consumer Protection Section
30 E. Broad St., 14th Floor
Columbus, OH 43215-3400
614-466-4986
Toll free: 1-800-282-0515
www.ohioattorneygeneral.gov

County Offices

Cuyahoga County Department of Consumer Affairs
2079 E. 9th St.
Cleveland, OH 44115
216-443-7035
www.fiscalofficer.
cuyahogacounty.us/en-US/
ConsumerAffairs.aspx

Summit County Office of Consumer Affairs
175 S. Main St., Suite 209
Akron, OH 44308
330-643-2879
✉: consumeraffairs@summitoh.net
consumeraffairs.summitoh.net

Oklahoma

State Offices

Oklahoma Office of the Attorney General
Public Protection Unit
313 N.E. 21st St.
Oklahoma City, OK 73105
405-521-3921 (Oklahoma City)
918-581-2885 (Tulsa)
www.ok.gov/oag

Oklahoma Department of Consumer Credit
3613 N.W. 56th St., Suite 240
Oklahoma City, OK 73112-4512
405-521-3653
Toll free: 1-800-448-4904 (Consumer Hotline)
www.ok.gov/okdocc

Oregon

State Offices

Oregon Department of Justice
Financial Fraud/Consumer Protection Section
1162 Court St., NE
Salem, OR 97301-4096
503-378-4320 (Salem)
503-229-5576 (Portland)
Toll free: 1-877-877-9392
TTY: 1-800-735-2900
✉: help@oregonconsumer.gov
www.doj.state.or.us

Pennsylvania

State Offices

Pennsylvania Office of the Attorney General
Bureau of Consumer Protection
Strawberry Square, 16th Floor
Harrisburg, PA 17120
717-787-3391
Toll free: 1-800-441-2555
Toll free: 1-888-520-6680 (Home Improvement)
www.attorneygeneral.gov

Regional Offices

Erie Regional Office of the Attorney General
Bureau of Consumer Protection
1001 State St., 10th Floor
Erie, PA 16501
814-871-4371
www.attorneygeneral.gov

Philadelphia Regional Office of the Attorney General
Bureau of Consumer Protection
21 S. 12th St., 2nd Floor
Philadelphia, PA 19107
215-560-2414
www.attorneygeneral.gov

Pittsburgh Regional Office of the Attorney General
Bureau of Consumer Protection
Manor Complex, 6th Floor
564 Forbes Ave.
Pittsburgh, PA 15219
412-565-5135
www.attorneygeneral.gov

Scranton Regional Office of the Attorney General
Bureau of Consumer Protection
417 Lackawanna Ave.
Scranton, PA 18503
570-963-4913
www.attorneygeneral.gov

State College Regional Office of the Attorney General
Bureau of Consumer Protection
444 E. College Ave., Suite 440
State College, PA 16801
814-863-3900
www.attorneygeneral.gov

County Offices

Bucks County Department of Consumer Protection
1260 Almshouse Rd., 1st Floor
Doylestown, PA 18901
215-348-6060
✉: consumerprotection@co.bucks.pa.us
www.buckscounty.org

Delaware County Department of Consumer Affairs
Government Center Building
201 W. Front St.
Media, PA 19063
610-891-4865
✉: delcoca@co.delaware.pa.us
www.co.delaware.pa.us/consumeraffairs

Puerto Rico

State Offices

Puerto Rico Department of Consumer Affairs
Ave. Jose De Diego, Pda. 22
Centro Gubernamental Minillas
Edificio Torre Norte, Piso 8
San Juan, PR 00940
787-722-7555
www.daco.gobierno.pr

Rhode Island

State Offices

Rhode Island Office of the Attorney General
Consumer Protection Unit
150 S. Main St.
Providence, RI 02903
401-274-4400
✉: contactus@riag.ri.gov
www.riag.state.ri.us

South Carolina

State Offices

South Carolina Department of Consumer Affairs
PO Box 5757
Columbia, SC 29250
803-734-4200
Toll free: 1-800-922-1594
www.consumer.sc.gov

South Carolina Office of the Attorney General
PO Box 11549
Columbia, SC 29211
803-734-3970
www.scag.gov

South Dakota

State Offices

South Dakota Office of the Attorney General
Division of Consumer Protection
1302 E. Hwy. 14, Suite 3
Pierre, SD 57501-8503
605-773-4400
Toll free: 1-800-300-1986
TTY: 605-773-6585
✉: consumerhelp@state.sd.us
www.atg.sd.gov

Tennessee

State Offices

Tennessee Department of Commerce and Insurance
Division of Consumer Affairs
500 James Robertson Pkwy., 12th Floor
Nashville, TN 37243-0600
615-741-4737
Toll free: 1-800-342-8385
✉: consumer.affairs@tn.gov
www.tn.gov/consumer

Tennessee Office of the Attorney General
Consumer Advocate and Protection Division
PO Box 20207
Nashville, TN 37202-0207
615-741-1671
www.tn.gov/attorneygeneral

Texas

State Offices

Texas Office of the Attorney General
Consumer Protection Division
PO Box 12548
Austin, TX 78711-2548
512-463-2185
Toll free: 1-800-621-0508
www.texasattorneygeneral.gov

Regional Offices

Dallas Regional Office of the Attorney General
Consumer Protection Division
1412 Main St., Suite 810
Dallas, TX 75202
214-969-5310
Toll free: 1-800-621-0508
www.texasattorneygeneral.gov

El Paso Regional Office of the Attorney General
Consumer Protection Division
401 E. Franklin Ave., Suite 530
El Paso, TX 79901
915-834-5800
Toll free: 1-800-621-0508
www.texasattorneygeneral.gov

Houston Regional Office of the Attorney General
Consumer Protection Division
808 Travis St., Suite 1520
Houston, TX 77002-1702
713-223-5886
Toll free: 1-800-621-0508
www.texasattorneygeneral.gov

McAllen Regional Office of the Attorney General
Consumer Protection Division
3201 N. McColl Rd., Suite B
McAllen, TX 78501-1685
956-682-4547
Toll free: 1-800-621-0508
www.texasattorneygeneral.gov

San Antonio Regional Office of the Attorney General
Consumer Protection Division
115 E. Travis St., Suite 925
San Antonio, TX 78205-1605
210-225-4191
Toll free: 1-800-621-0508
www.texasattorneygeneral.gov

County Offices

Harris County District Attorney's Office
Consumer Fraud
1201 Franklin St., Suite 600
Houston, TX 77002-1923
713-755-5836
app.dao.hctx.net

Utah

State Offices

Utah Department of Commerce
Division of Consumer Protection
160 E. 300 S, 2nd Floor
PO Box 146704
Salt Lake City, UT 84114-6704
801-530-6601
Toll free: 1-800-721-7233
✉: consumerprotection@utah.gov
www.consumerprotection.utah.gov

Utah Office of the Attorney General
PO Box 142320
Salt Lake City, UT 84114-2320
Toll free: 1-800-244-4636
✉: uag@utah.gov
www.attorneygeneral.utah.gov

Vermont

State Offices

Vermont Agency of Agriculture, Food, and Markets
Food Safety and Consumer Protection
116 State St.
Montpelier, VT 05620
802-828-2426
✉: AGR.ConsumerProtection@state.vt.us
www.agriculture.vermont.gov

Vermont Office of the Attorney General
Consumer Assistance Program
146 University Pl.
Burlington, VT 05405
802-656-3183
Toll free: 1-800-649-2424
✉: consumer@uvm.edu
www.atg.state.vt.us

Virgin Islands

State Offices

Virgin Islands Department of Licensing and Consumer Affairs
Golden Rock Shopping Center
3000 Estate Golden Rock, Suite 9
St. Croix, VI 00820
340-773-2226
www.dlca.vi.gov

Virgin Islands Department of Licensing and Consumer Affairs
Property and Procurement Bldg.
8201 Sub Base, Suite 1
St. Thomas, VI 00802
340-774-3130
www.dlca.vi.gov

Virginia

State Offices

Virginia Office of the Attorney General
Consumer Protection Section
900 E. Main St.
Richmond, VA 23219
804-786-2042
Toll free: 1-800-552-9963
TTY: 1-800-828-1120
www.oag.state.va.us

Regional Offices

Office of the Attorney General - Northern Virginia
10555 Main St., Suite 350
Fairfax, VA 22030
703-277-3540
www.oag.state.va.us

Office of the Attorney General - Southwest Region
204 Abingdon Pl.
Abingdon, VA 24211
276-628-2759
www.oag.state.va.us

Office of the Attorney General - Western Region
3033 Peters Creek Rd.
Roanoke, VA 24019
540-562-3570
www.oag.state.va.us

County Offices

Fairfax County Department of Cable Communications and Consumer Services
12000 Government Center Pkwy., Suite 433
Fairfax, VA 22035
703-222-8435
✉: consumer@fairfaxcounty.gov
www.fairfaxcounty.gov/consumer

Washington

State Offices

Washington Office of the Attorney General
Consumer Protection Division
PO Box 40100
1125 Washington St., SE
Olympia, WA 98504-0100
206-464-6684
Toll free: 1-800-551-4636
TTY: 1-800-833-6388
www.atg.wa.gov

Regional Offices

Bellingham Regional Office of the Attorney General
Consumer Protection Division
103 E. Holly St., Suite 310
Bellingham, WA 98225
360-676-2037
Toll free: 1-800-551-4636
TTY: 1-800-833-6388
www.atg.wa.gov

Kennewick Regional Office of the Attorney General
Consumer Protection Division
8127 W. Klamath Ct.
Bldg. 6, Suite A
Kennewick, WA 99336-2607
509-734-7285
Toll free: 1-800-551-4636
TTY: 1-800-833-6388
www.atg.wa.gov

Seattle Regional Office of the Attorney General
Consumer Protection Division
800 5th Ave., Suite 2000
Seattle, WA 98104
206-464-7744
Toll free: 1-800-551-4636
TTY: 1-800-833-6388
www.atg.wa.gov

Spokane Regional Office of the Attorney General
Consumer Protection Division
1116 W. Riverside Ave.
Spokane, WA 99201-1194
509-456-3123
Toll free: 1-800-551-4636
TTY: 1-800-833-6388
www.atg.wa.gov

Tacoma Regional Office of the Attorney General
Consumer Protection Division
1250 Pacific Ave., Suite 105
Tacoma, WA 98402
253-593-5243
Toll free: 1-800-551-4636
TTY: 1-800-833-6388
www.atg.wa.gov

Vancouver Regional Office of the Attorney General
Consumer Protection Division
1220 Main St., Suite 510
Vancouver, WA 98660
360-759-2100
Toll free: 1-800-551-4636
TTY: 1-800-833-6388
www.atg.wa.gov

West Virginia

State Offices

West Virginia Office of the Attorney General
Consumer Protection Division
PO Box 1789
Charleston, WV 25326-1789
304-558-8986
Toll free: 1-800-368-8808
✉: consumer@wvago.gov
www.wvago.gov

Wisconsin

State Offices

Wisconsin Department of Agriculture, Trade and Consumer Protection
Bureau of Consumer Protection
PO Box 8911
2811 Agriculture Dr.
Madison, WI 53708-8911
608-224-5012
Toll free: 1-800-422-7128
TTY: 608-224-5058
✉: datcphotline@wisconsin.gov
datcp.wi.gov

Wisconsin Department of Justice
Consumer Protection and Antitrust Unit
PO Box 7857
Madison, WI 53707-7857
608-266-1221
www.doj.state.wi.us

Wyoming

State Offices

Wyoming Office of the Attorney General
Consumer Protection Unit
123 State Capitol
200 W. 24th St.
Cheyenne, WY 82002
307-777-5833
Toll free: 1-800-438-5799
TTY: 307-777-5351
✉: AG.Consumer@wyo.gov
ag.wyo.gov/cpu

Contact Your Local Banking Authority

The officials listed below regulate and supervise state-chartered banks. Many of them handle or refer problems and complaints about other types of financial institutions as well. Some also answer general questions about banking and consumer credit. If you are dealing with a federally-chartered bank, check Federal Agencies on page 89. Also see the chart in the Banking section on page 8.

Note: Toll free phone numbers may be restricted to use only within the state listed.

Alabama

State Banking Department
Consumer Affairs
PO Box 4600
Montgomery, AL 36103-4600
334-353-5705
Toll free: 1-866-465-2279
www.banking.alabama.gov

Alaska

Department of Commerce, Community and Economic Development
Division of Banking and Securities
PO Box 110807
Juneau, AK 99811-0807
907-465-2521
Toll free: 1-888-925-2521
TTY: 907-465-5437
✉: dbsc@commerce.state.ak.us
www.commerce.alaska.gov

Arizona

Department of Financial Institutions
Consumer Affairs
2910 N. 44th St., Suite 310
Phoenix, AZ 85018
602-771-2800
Toll free: 1-800-544-0708
✉: consumeraffairs@azdfi.gov
www.azdfi.gov

Arkansas

State Bank Department
400 Hardin Rd., Suite 100
Little Rock, AR 72211
501-324-9019
✉: asbd@banking.state.ar.us
banking.arkansas.gov

California

Department of Business Oversight
Consumer Services
1515 K St., Suite 200
Sacramento, CA 95814
916-327-7585
Toll free: 1-866-275-2677
www.dbo.ca.gov

Colorado

Department of Regulatory Agencies
Division of Banking
1560 Broadway, Suite 975
Denver, CO 80202
303-894-7575
✉: DORA_BankingWebsite@state.co.us
www.dora.state.co.us/banking

Connecticut

Department of Banking
Government Relations and Consumer Affairs
260 Constitution Plaza
Hartford, CT 06103-1800
860-240-8180
Toll free: 1-800-831-7225
Toll free: 1-877-472-8313 (Foreclosure Assistance)
www.ct.gov/dob

Delaware

Office of the State Bank Commissioner
Attn: Compliance
555 E. Loockerman St., Suite 210
Dover, DE 19901
302-739-4235
www.banking.delaware.gov

District Of Columbia

Department of Insurance, Securities and Banking
Attn: Consumer Services Section
810 1st St., NE, Suite 701
Washington, DC 20002
202-727-8000
✉: disb.complaints@dc.gov
www.disb.dc.gov

Florida

Office of Financial Regulation
Division of Financial Institutions
Consumer Assistance Group
200 E. Gaines St.
Tallahassee, FL 32399-0371
850-487-9687
www.flofr.com

Georgia

Department of Banking and Finance
2990 Brandywine Rd., Suite 200
Atlanta, GA 30341-5565
770-986-1633
Toll free: 1-888-986-1633
www.dbf.georgia.gov

Hawaii

Department of Commerce and Consumer Affairs
Division of Financial Institutions
PO Box 2054
Honolulu, HI 96805
808-586-2820 (Honolulu)
808-274-3141 (Kauai)
808-984-2400 (Maui)
808-974-4000 (Hawaii)
Toll free: 1-800-468-4644
✉: dfi@dcca.hawaii.gov
www.cca.hawaii.gov/dfi

Idaho

Department of Finance
Financial Institutions Bureau
PO Box 83720
Boise, ID 83720-0031
208-332-8000
Toll free: 1-888-346-3378
✉: finance@finance.idaho.gov
www.finance.idaho.gov

Illinois

Department of Financial and Professional Regulation
Division of Banking
320 W. Washington St.
Springfield, IL 62786
217-782-3000
Toll free: 1-800-532-8785
TTY: 217-524-6644
www.idfpr.com

Indiana

Department of Financial Institutions
30 S. Meridian St., Suite 300
Indianapolis, IN 46204
317-232-3955
Toll free: 1-800-382-4880
www.in.gov/dfi

Iowa

Division of Banking
200 E. Grand Ave., Suite 300
Des Moines, IA 50309-1827
515-281-4014
✉: IDOBcomplaints@idob.state.ia.us
www.idob.state.ia.us

Kansas

Office of the State Bank Commissioner
700 S.W. Jackson St., Suite 300
Topeka, KS 66603
785-296-2266
✉: complaints@osbckansas.org
www.osbckansas.org

Kentucky

Department of Financial Institutions
1025 Capitol Center Dr., Suite 200
Frankfort, KY 40601
502-573-3390
Toll free: 1-800-223-2579
✉: kfi.complaints@ky.gov
www.kfi.ky.gov/Pages/default.
aspx

Louisiana

Office of Financial Institutions
PO Box 94095
Baton Rouge, LA 70804-9095
225-925-4660
Toll free: 1-888-525-9414
✉: complaints@ofi.la.gov
www.ofi.state.la.us

Maine

Bureau of Financial Institutions
Consumer Outreach Program
36 State House Station
Augusta, ME 04333-0036
207-624-8570
Toll free: 1-800-965-5235
www.maine.gov/pfr/
financialinstitutions

Maryland

Department of Labor, Licensing and Regulation
Commissioner of Financial Regulation
500 N. Calvert St., Suite 402
Baltimore, MD 21202
410-230-6077 (Consumer Services)
Toll free: 1-888-784-0136
✉: CFRComplaints@dllr.state.md.us
www.dllr.state.md.us/finance

Massachusetts

Office of Consumer Affairs and Business Regulation
Division of Banks
Consumer Assistance Unit
1000 Washington St., 10th Floor
Boston, MA 02118-6400
617-956-1500
Toll free: 1-800-495-2265
TTY: 617-956-1577
www.mass.gov/ocabr

Michigan

Department of Insurance and Financial Services
PO Box 30220
Lansing, MI 48909-7720
517-373-0220
Toll free: 1-877-999-6442
✉: difs-info@michigan.gov
www.michigan.gov/difs

Minnesota

Department of Commerce
Financial Institutions Division
85 7th Pl. E, Suite 500
St. Paul, MN 55101
651-539-1700
Toll free: 1-800-657-3602
✉: consumer.protection@state.mn.us
www.mn.gov/commerce

Mississippi

Department of Banking and Consumer Finance
901 Woolfolk Building, Suite A
501 N. West St.
Jackson, MS 39201
601-359-1031
Toll free: 1-800-844-2499
www.dbcf.state.ms.us

Missouri

Division of Finance
PO Box 716
Jefferson City, MO 65102
573-751-3242
✉: finance@dof.mo.gov
www.finance.mo.gov

Montana

Division of Banking and Financial Institutions
PO Box 200546
Helena, MT 59620
406-841-2920
TTY: 406-841-2974
www.banking.mt.gov

Nebraska

Department of Banking and Finance
Financial Institutions Division
PO Box 95006
Lincoln, NE 68509-5006
402-471-2171
Toll free: 1-877-471-3445
www.ndbf.ne.gov

Nevada

Department of Business and Industry
Division of Financial Institutions
2785 E. Desert Inn Rd., Suite 180
Las Vegas, NV 89121
702-486-4120
✉: fidmaster@ifd.state.nv.us
www.fid.state.nv.us

New Hampshire

State Banking Department
53 Regional Dr., Suite 200
Concord, NH 03301
603-271-3561
Toll free: 1-800-437-5991
TTY: 1-800-735-2964
✉: nhbd@banking.state.nh.us
www.nh.gov/banking

New Jersey

Department of Banking and Insurance
Consumer Inquiry and Response Center
PO Box 471
Trenton, NJ 08625-0471
609-292-7272
Toll free: 1-800-446-7467
www.state.nj.us/dobi

New Mexico

Regulation and Licensing Department
Financial Institutions Division
PO Box 25101
Santa Fe, NM 87505
505-476-4885
www.rld.state.nm.us/
financialinstitutions

New York

State Banking Authorities Department of Financial Services
Consumer Assistance Unit
1 State St.
New York, NY 10004-1511
212-480-6400
Toll free: 1-800-342-3736
www.dfs.ny.gov

North Carolina

Commissioner of Banks
4309 Mail Service Center
Raleigh, NC 27699-4309
Toll free: 1-888-384-3811
www.nccob.org

North Dakota

Department of Financial Institutions
2000 Schafer St., Suite G
Bismarck, ND 58501-1204
701-328-9933
TTY: 1-800-366-6888
✉: dfi@nd.gov
www.nd.gov/dfi

Ohio

Department of Commerce
Division of Financial Institutions
77 S. High St., 21st Floor
Columbus, OH 43215-6120
614-728-8400
Toll free: 1-866-278-0003
✉: web.dfi@com.ohio.gov
www.com.ohio.gov/fiin

Oklahoma

State Banking Department
2900 N. Lincoln Blvd.
Oklahoma City, OK 73105
405-521-2782
www.ok.gov/banking

Oregon

Department of Consumer and Business Services
Division of Finance and Corporate Securities
PO Box 14480
Salem, OR 97309-0405
503-378-4140
Toll free: 1-866-814-9710
✉: dcbs.dfcsmail@state.or.us
www.dfcs.oregon.gov

Pennsylvania

Department of Banking and Securities
Consumer Services
17 N. Second St., Suite 1300
Harrisburg, PA 17101-2290
717-787-1854
Toll free: 1-800-722-2657
TTY: 1-800-679-5070
www.banking.state.pa.us

Puerto Rico

Office of the Commissioner of Financial Institutions
PO Box 11855
San Juan, PR 00910-3855
787-723-3131
www.ocif.gobierno.pr

Rhode Island

Department of Business Regulation
Division of Banking
1511 Pontiac Ave.
Bldg. 68-2
Cranston, RI 02920
401-462-9500
www.dbr.state.ri.us

South Carolina

Office of the Commissioner of Banking
State Board of Financial Institutions
1205 Pendleton St., Suite 305
Columbia, SC 29201
803-734-2001
www.banking.sc.gov

South Dakota

Department of Labor and Regulation
Division of Banking
1601 N. Harrison Ave., Suite 1
Pierre, SD 57501
605-773-3421
✉: banking@state.sd.us
dlr.sd.gov/banking

Tennessee

Department of Financial Institutions
Consumer Resources Division
400 Deaderick St., 6th Floor
Nashville, TN 37243
615-253-2023
Toll free: 1-800-778-4215
✉: TDFI.ConsumerResources@tn.gov
www.tennessee.gov/tdfi

Texas

Department of Banking
Consumer Assistance Activities
2601 N. Lamar Blvd.
Austin, TX 78705
512-475-1300
Toll free: 1-877-276-5554 (Consumer Hotline)
✉: consumer.complaints@dob.texas.gov
www.dob.texas.gov

Utah

Department of Financial Institutions
PO Box 146800
Salt Lake City, UT 84114-6800
801-538-8830
www.dfi.utah.gov

Vermont

Department of Financial Regulation
Banking Division
89 Main St.
Montpelier, VT 05620-3101
802-828-3301
Toll free: 1-888-568-4547
✉: dfr.bnkconsumer@state.vt.us
www.dfr.vermont.gov

Virgin Islands

Office of the Lieutenant Governor
Division of Banking and Insurance
1131 King St., Suite 101
Christiansted, VI 00820
340-773-6459
ltg.gov.vi

Virginia

State Corporation Commission
Bureau of Financial Institutions
PO Box 640
Richmond, VA 23218-0640
804-371-9657
Toll free: 1-800-552-7945
TTY: 804-371-9206
✉: bfiquestions@scc.virginia.gov
www.scc.virginia.gov

Washington

Department of Financial Institutions
Division of Consumer Services
PO Box 41200
Olympia, WA 98504-1200
360-902-8700
Toll free: 1-877-746-4334
TTY: 360-664-8126
www.dfi.wa.gov

West Virginia

Division of Financial Institutions
900 Pennsylvania Ave.
Suite 306
Charleston, WV 25302
304-558-2294
www.dfi.wv.gov

Wisconsin

Department of Financial Institutions
Bureau of Consumer Affairs
PO Box 8041
Madison, WI 53708-8041
608-264-7969
TTY: 608-266-8818
www.wdfi.org

Wyoming

Department of Audit
Division of Banking
122 W. 25th St.
Herschler Building, 3rd Floor, East
Cheyenne, WY 82002
307-777-7797
✉: wyomingbankingdivision@wyo.gov
audit.wyo.gov

Contact Your Local Insurance Regulator

The offices listed below enforce laws and regulations for each type of insurance. Many of these offices can also provide you with information to help you make informed insurance-buying decisions. See the Insurance section in Part I of this *Handbook* for advice (p. 29).

If you have a question or complaint about your insurance company's policies, contact the company before you contact your state insurance regulator.

Note: Toll free phone numbers may be restricted to use only within the state listed.

Alabama

Department of Insurance
PO Box 303351
Montgomery, AL 36130-3351
334-241-4141 (Consumer Services)
✉: ConsumerServices@insurance.
alabama.gov
www.aldoi.gov

Alaska

Department of Commerce, Community and Economic Development
Division of Insurance
Robert B. Atwood Building
550 W. 7th Ave., Suite 1560
Anchorage, AK 99501-3567
907-269-7900
Toll free: 1-800-467-8725
TTY: 907-465-5437
✉: insurance@alaska.gov
www.commerce.alaska.gov/dnn/
ins

Arizona

Department of Insurance
Consumer Affairs Division
2910 N. 44th St., Suite 210
Phoenix, AZ 85018-7269
602-364-2499
602-364-2977 (in Spanish)
Toll free: 1-800-325-2548
✉: consumers@azinsurance.gov
www.azinsurance.gov

Arkansas

Insurance Department
Consumer Services Division
1200 W. 3rd St.
Little Rock, AR 72201-1904
501-371-2640
Toll free: 1-800-852-5494
✉: insurance.consumers@arkansas.
gov
www.insurance.arkansas.gov

California

Department of Insurance
Consumer Services Division
300 S. Spring St., South Tower
Los Angeles, CA 90013
213-897-8921
Toll free: 1-800-927-4357
TTY: 1-800-482-4833
www.insurance.ca.gov

Department of Managed Health Care, California HMO Help Center
980 9th St., Suite 500
Sacramento, CA 95814-2725
Toll free: 1-888-466-2219
TTY: 1-877-688-9891
www.hmohelp.ca.gov

Colorado

Department of Regulatory Agencies
Division of Insurance
1560 Broadway, Suite 850
Denver, CO 80202
303-894-7490
Toll free: 1-800-930-3745
✉: insurance@dora.state.co.us
www.dora.state.co.us/Insurance

Connecticut

Insurance Department
Consumer Affairs Division
PO Box 816
Hartford, CT 06142-0816
860-297-3900
Toll free: 1-800-203-3447
✉: cid.ca@ct.gov
www.ct.gov/cid

Delaware

Department of Insurance
841 Silver Lake Blvd.
Dover, DE 19904
302-674-7310
Toll free: 1-800-282-8611
✉: consumer@state.de.us
www.delawareinsurance.gov

District Of Columbia

Department of Insurance, Securities and Banking
Attn: Consumer Services Division
810 First St., NE, Suite 701
Washington, DC 20002
202-727-8000
✉: disb.complaints@dc.gov
www.disb.dc.gov

Florida

Office of Insurance Regulation
200 E. Gaines St.
Tallahassee, FL 32399
850-413-3140
Toll free: 1-877-693-5236
www.floir.com

Georgia

Insurance and Safety Fire Commissioner
Two Martin Luther King, Jr., Dr.
West Tower, Suite 716
Atlanta, GA 30334
404-656-2070
Toll free: 1-800-656-2298
✉: consumer@oci.ga.gov
www.oci.ga.gov

Hawaii

Department of Commerce and Consumer Affairs
Insurance Division
PO Box 3614
Honolulu, HI 96811
808-586-2790
Toll free: 1-800-468-4644 (Lanai and Molokai)
✉: insurance@dcca.hawaii.gov
www.hawaii.gov/dcca/ins

Idaho

Department of Insurance
Consumer's Bureau
700 W. State St.
Boise, ID 83720-0043
208-334-4319
Toll free: 1-800-721-3272
✉: consumeraffairs@doi.idaho.gov
www.doi.idaho.gov

Illinois

Department of Insurance
320 W. Washington St.
Springfield, IL 62767-0001
217-782-4515
Toll free: 1-877-527-9431 (Health
Insurance)
Toll free: 1-866-445-5364 (Consumer
Assistance Hotline)
TTY: 1-866-323-5321
✉: doi.infodesk@illinois.gov
www.insurance.illinois.gov

Indiana

Department of Insurance
Consumer Services Division
311 W. Washington St., Suite 300
Indianapolis, IN 46204-2787
317-232-2395
Toll free: 1-800-622-4461
✉: consumerservices@idoi.in.gov
www.in.gov/idoi

Iowa

Division of Insurance
Market Regulation Bureau
601 Locust St., 4th Floor
Des Moines, IA 50309-3738
515-281-6348
Toll free: 1-877-955-1212
www.iid.state.ia.us

Kansas

Insurance Department
Consumer Assistance Division
420 S.W. 9th St.
Topeka, KS 66612
785-296-7829
Toll free: 1-800-432-2484
TTY: 1-877-235-3151
✉: webcomplaints@ksinsurance.org
www.ksinsurance.org

Kentucky

Department of Insurance
Consumer Protection Division
PO Box 517
Frankfort, KY 40602-0517
502-564-6034
Toll free: 1-800-595-6053
TTY: 1-800-648-6056
✉: doi.info@ky.gov
insurance.ky.gov

Louisiana

Department of Insurance
Office of Consumer Advocacy
PO Box 94214
Baton Rouge, LA 70804-9214
225-342-5900
Toll free: 1-800-259-5300
✉: consumeradvocacy@ldi.la.gov
www.ldi.state.la.us

Maine

Bureau of Insurance
34 State House Station
Augusta, ME 04333
207-624-8475
Toll free: 1-800-300-5000
✉: Insurance.PFR@maine.gov
www.maine.gov/pfr/insurance

Maryland

Insurance Administration
Consumer Division
200 St. Paul Pl., Suite 2700
Baltimore, MD 21202
410-468-2000
Toll free: 1-800-492-6116
TTY: 1-800-735-2258
www.mdinsurance.state.md.us

Massachusetts

**Office of Consumer Affairs &
Business Regulation**
Division of Insurance
1000 Washington St., Suite 810
Boston, MA 02118-6200
617-521-7794
Toll free: 1-877-563-4467
TTY: 1-800-720-3480
www.mass.gov/doi

Michigan

**Department of Insurance and
Financial Services**
PO Box 30220
Lansing, MI 48909-7720
517-373-0220
Toll free: 1-877-999-6442
✉: difs-ins-info@michigan.gov
www.michigan.gov/difs

Minnesota

Department of Commerce
Insurance Division
85 7th Pl. E, Suite 500
St. Paul, MN 55101
651-539-1600
Toll free: 1-800-657-3602
✉: consumer.protection@state.mn.us
www.insurance.mn.gov

Mississippi

Department of Insurance
PO Box 79
Jackson, MS 39205-0079
601-359-3569
Toll free: 1-800-562-2957
✉: consumer@mid.ms.gov
www.mid.ms.gov

Missouri

**Department of Insurance, Financial,
and Professional Registration**
Consumer Affairs Division
PO Box 690
Jefferson City, MO 65102-0690
Toll free: 1-800-726-7390
TTY: 573-526-4536
✉: consumeraffairs@insurance.
mo.gov
www.insurance.mo.gov

Montana

**Commissioner of Securities and
Insurance**
Insurance Division
840 Helena Ave.
Helena, MT 59601
406-444-2040
Toll free: 1-800-332-6148
TTY: 406-444-3246
www.csi.mt.gov/consumers

Nebraska

Department of Insurance
PO Box 82089
Lincoln, NE 68501-2089
402-471-2201
Toll free: 1-877-564-7323
TTY: 1-800-833-7352
✉: DOI.ConsumerAffairs@nebraska.gov
www.doi.ne.gov

Nevada

Department of Business and Industry
Division of Insurance
Consumer Services Section
2501 E. Sahara Ave., Suite 302
Las Vegas, NV 89104
702-486-4009
Toll free: 1-888-872-3234
www.doi.nv.gov

Department of Business and Industry
Division of Insurance
Consumer Services Section
1818 E. College Pkwy., Suite 103
Carson City, NV 89706
775-687-0700
Toll free: 1-888-872-3234
✉: cscc@doi.state.nv.us
www.doi.nv.gov

New Hampshire

Insurance Department
Consumer Services Division
21 S. Fruit St., Suite 14
Concord, NH 03301
603-271-2261
Toll free: 1-800-852-3416
TTY: 1-800-735-2964
✉: consumerservices@ins.nh.gov
www.nh.gov/insurance

New Jersey

Department of Banking and Insurance
Consumer Center
153 Halsey St.
Newark, NJ 07102
973-648-4713
Toll free: 1-800-446-7467
www.state.nj.us/dobi

Department of Banking and Insurance
Consumer Inquiries and Complaints
PO Box 471
Trenton, NJ 08625-0471
609-292-7272
Toll free: 1-800-446-7467
www.state.nj.us/dobi

New Mexico

Superintendent of Insurance
Consumer Assistance Bureau
PO Box 1689
Santa Fe, NM 87504-1689
505-827-4601
Toll free: 1-855-427-5674
✉: consumer@state.nm.us
www.osi.state.nm.us

New York

Department of Financial Services
Insurance Department
Consumer Assistance Unit
One Commerce Plaza
Albany, NY 12257
212-480-6400
Toll free: 1-800-342-3736
www.dfs.ny.gov

Insurance Department
Insurance Division
Consumer Assistance Unit
25 Beaver St.
New York, NY 10004
212-480-6400
Toll free: 1-800-342-3736
www.dfs.ny.gov

North Carolina

Department of Insurance
Consumer Services
1201 Mail Service Center
Raleigh, NC 27699-1201
919-807-6750
Toll free: 1-800-546-5664
www.ncdoi.com

North Dakota

Insurance Department
600 E. Boulevard Ave.
Bismarck, ND 58505-0320
701-328-2440
Toll free: 1-800-247-0560
TTY: 1-800-366-6888
✉: insurance@nd.gov
www.nd.gov/ndins

Ohio

Department of Insurance
Consumer Services
50 W. Town St., 3rd Floor, Suite 300
Columbus, OH 43215
614-644-2673
Toll free: 1-800-686-1526
Toll free: 1-800-686-1527 (Fraud Hotline)
TTY: 614-644-3745
www.insurance.ohio.gov

Oklahoma

Insurance Department
Consumer Assistance Division
Five Corporate Plaza
3625 N.W. 56th St., Suite 100
Oklahoma City, OK 73112
405-521-2991
Toll free: 1-800-522-0071
www.ok.gov/oid

Oregon

Consumer and Business Services
Insurance Division
PO Box 14480
Salem, OR 97309-0405
503-947-7984
Toll free: 1-888-877-4894
✉: cp.ins@state.or.us
www.insurance.oregon.gov

Pennsylvania

Insurance Department
Consumer Services
1209 Strawberry Square
Harrisburg, PA 17120
717-787-2317
Toll free: 1-877-881-6388
TTY: 717-783-3898
www.insurance.pa.gov

Puerto Rico

Office of the Commissioner of Insurance
B5 Calle Tabonuco, Suite 216
PMB 356
Guaynabo, PR 00968-3029
787-304-8686
www.ocs.gobierno.pr

STATE INSURANCE REGULATORS

Rhode Island

Department of Business Regulation
Insurance Division
1511 Pontiac Ave.
Bldg. 69-2
Cranston, RI 02920
401-462-9520
✉: InsuranceInquiry@dbr.ri.gov
www.dbr.state.ri.us

South Carolina

Department of Insurance
Consumer Services
PO Box 100105
Columbia, SC 29202-3105
803-737-6180
Toll free: 1-800-768-3467
✉: consumers@doi.sc.gov
www.doi.sc.gov

South Dakota

Department of Labor and Regulation
Division of Insurance
445 E. Capitol Ave.
Pierre, SD 57501
605-773-3563
✉: insurance@state.sd.us
www.dlr.sd.gov/insurance

Tennessee

Department of Commerce and Insurance
Consumer Insurance Services
500 James Robertson Pkwy.
Nashville, TN 37243
615-741-2218
Toll free: 1-800-342-4029
✉: CIS.complaints@tn.gov
www.tn.gov/commerce

Texas

Department of Insurance
Consumer Protection (111-1A)
PO Box 149091
Austin, TX 78714-9091
512-463-6169
Toll free: 1-800-252-3439
TTY: 512 322-4238
✉: consumerprotection@tdi.texas.gov
www.tdi.texas.gov

Utah

Insurance Department
Consumer Service
State Office Building, Suite 3110
450 N. State St.
Salt Lake City, UT 84114-6901
801-538-3800
Toll free: 1-800-439-3805
TTY: 801-538-3826
www.insurance.utah.gov

Vermont

Department of Financial Regulation
Insurance Consumer Services
89 Main St.
Montpelier, VT 05620-3101
802-828-3301
Toll free: 1-800-964-1784
✉: dfr.insuranceinfo@state.vt.us
www.dfr.vermont.gov

Virgin Islands

Division of Banking and Insurance
5049 Kongens Gade
Charlotte Amalie, VI 00802
340-774-7166
ltg.gov.vi

Virginia

State Corporation Commission
Bureau of Insurance
PO Box 1157
Richmond, VA 23218-1157
804-371-9741
Toll free: 1-877-310-6560
TTY: 804-371-9206
✉: bureauofinsurance@scc.virginia.gov
www.scc.virginia.gov

Washington

Office of the Insurance Commissioner
Consumer Protection
PO Box 40256
Olympia, WA 98504-0256
360-725-7080
Toll free: 1-800-562-6900
TTY: 360-586-0241
www.insurance.wa.gov

West Virginia

Offices of the Insurance Commissioner
Consumer Service Division
PO Box 50540
Charleston, WV 25305-0540
304-558-3386
Toll free: 1-888-879-9842
TTY: 1-800-435-7381
✉: consumer.service@wvinsurance.gov
www.wvinsurance.gov

Wisconsin

Office of the Commissioner of Insurance
PO Box 7873
Madison, WI 53707-7873
608-266-3585
Toll free: 1-800-236-8517
✉: ocicomplaints@wisconsin.gov
www.oci.wi.gov

Wyoming

Department of Insurance
Consumer Affairs Section
106 E. 6th Ave.
Cheyenne, WY 82001
307-777-7402
Toll free: 1-800-438-5768
doi.wyo.gov

Contact Your Local Securities Administrator

State securities regulators protect the investing public. Each state has its own laws and regulations for securities brokers and securities, including stocks, mutual funds, commodities, real estate, and more. The agencies listed below enforce these laws and regulations. They also license securities professionals, register securities, and investigate consumer complaints. While these agencies do not provide investment advice, many of them offer educational resources so investors can make informed investment decisions.

Contact the company involved if you have a question or complaint about an investment. If you are not satisfied with the response you get, contact your state securities administrator.

Note: Toll free phone numbers may be restricted to use only within the state listed.

Alabama

Securities Commission
PO Box 304700
Montgomery, AL 36130-4700
334-242-2984
Toll free: 1-800-222-1253
✉: asc@asc.alabama.gov
www.asc.state.al.us

Alaska

Department of Commerce, Community, and Economic Development
Division of Banking and Securities
PO Box 110807
Juneau, AK 99811-0807
907-465-2521
Toll free: 1-888-925-2521
TTY: 907-465-5437
✉: dbsc@alaska.gov
www.commerce.alaska.gov/dnn/dbs

Arizona

Arizona Corporation Commission
Securities Division
1300 W. Washington St., 3rd Floor
Phoenix, AZ 85007
602-542-4242
Toll free: 1-866-837-4399
✉: info@azinvestor.gov
www.azinvestor.gov

Arkansas

Securities Department
Heritage West Building, Suite 300
201 E. Markham St.
Little Rock, AR 72201-1692
501-324-9260
Toll free: 1-800-981-4429
✉: info@securities.arkansas.gov
www.securities.arkansas.gov

California

Department of Business Oversight
Consumer Services
1515 K St., Suite 200
Sacramento, CA 95814
Toll free: 1-866-275-2677
www.dbo.ca.gov

Colorado

Department of Regulatory Agencies
Division of Securities
1560 Broadway, Suite 900
Denver, CO 80202
303-894-2320
TTY: 1-800-659-2656
✉: dora_securitieswebsite@state.co.us
dora.colorado.gov/dos

Connecticut

Department of Banking
Securities and Business Investments Division
260 Constitution Plaza
Hartford, CT 06103-1800
860-240-8230
Toll free: 1-800-831-7225
www.ct.gov/dob

Delaware

Division of Securities
Carvel State Office Building, 5th Floor
820 N. French St.
Wilmington, DE 19801
302-577-8424
TTY: 302-577-5783
✉: Investor.Protection@state.de.us
www.investorresourcecenter.org

District Of Columbia

Department of Insurance, Securities and Banking
Consumer Protection Advocate
810 1st St., NE, Suite 701
Washington, DC 20002
202-727-8000
✉: disb.complaints@dc.gov
disb.dc.gov

Florida

Office of Financial Regulation
Division of Securities
200 E. Gaines St.
Tallahassee, FL 32399
850-487-9687
www.flofr.com

Georgia

Secretary of State
Division of Securities and Business Regulation
237 Coliseum Dr.
Macon, GA 31217-3858
478-207-2440
www.sos.ga.gov/securities

Hawaii

Department of Commerce and Consumer Affairs
Business Registration Division
Securities Enforcement Branch
PO Box 40
Honolulu, HI 96810
808-586-2744
Toll free: 1-877-447-2267
✉: seb@dcca.hawaii.gov
www.hawaii.gov/dcca/sec

Idaho

Department of Finance
Securities Bureau
PO Box 83720
Boise, ID 83720-0031
208-332-8000
Toll free: 1-888-346-3378
✉: finance@finance.idaho.gov
www.finance.idaho.gov

Illinois

Secretary of State
Securities Department
Jefferson Terrace
300 W. Jefferson St., Suite 300A
Springfield, IL 62702
217-782-2256
www.cyberdriveillinois.com/
departments/securities/home.html

Indiana

Secretary of State
Securities Division
302 W. Washington St., Room E111
Indianapolis, IN 46204
317-232-6681
Toll free: 1-800-223-8791
www.in.gov/sos/securities

Iowa

Securities Bureau
601 Locust St., 4th Floor
Des Moines, IA 50309-3738
515-281-5705
Toll free: 1-877-955-1212
✉: iowasec@iid.iowa.gov
www.iid.state.ia.us/securities

Kansas

Office of the Securities Commissioner
109 S.W. 9th St.
Suite 600
Topeka, KS 66612-1215
785-296-3307
Toll free: 1-800-232-9580
www.ksc.ks.gov

Kentucky

Department of Financial Institutions
Securities Division
1025 Capitol Center Dr., Suite 200
Frankfort, KY 40601
502-573-3390
Toll free: 1-800-223-2579
✉: kfi@ky.gov
www.kfi.ky.gov

Louisiana

Office of Financial Institutions
Securities Division
PO Box 94095
Baton Rouge, LA 70804-9095
225-925-4512
Toll free: 1-877-516-3653
✉: ofila@ofi.louisiana.gov
www.ofi.state.la.us

Maine

Department of Professional and Financial Regulation
Office of Securities
121 State House Station
Augusta, ME 04333
207-624-8551
Toll free: 1-877-624-8551
www.maine.gov/pfr/securities

Maryland

Office of the Attorney General
Securities Division
200 Saint Paul Pl.
Baltimore, MD 21202
410-576-6360
Toll free: 1-888-743-0023
TTY: 410-576-6372
✉: securities@oag.state.md.us
www.oag.state.md.us/securities

Massachusetts

Secretary of the Commonwealth
Securities Division
One Ashburton Pl., 17th Floor
McCormack Building
Boston, MA 02108
617-727-3548
Toll free: 1-800-269-5428
TTY: 617-878-3889
✉: securities@sec.state.ma.us
www.sec.state.ma.us/sct/sctidx.htm

Michigan

Department of Licensing and Regulatory Affairs
Securities Division
PO Box 30018
Lansing, MI 48909
517-241-6345
✉: bcs-sec-info@michigan.gov
www.michigan.gov/securities

Minnesota

Department of Commerce
Securities Unit
85 7th Pl. E, Suite 500
St. Paul, MN 55101-2198
651-539-1638
✉: securities.commerce@state.mn.us
www.mn.gov/commerce

Mississippi

Secretary of State
Securities Division
PO Box 136
Jackson, MS 39205-0136
601-359-1334
www.sos.ms.gov

Missouri

Office of the Secretary of State
Securities Division
600 W. Main St.
Jefferson City, MO 65101-1276
573-751-4136
Toll free: 1-800-721-7996
✉: securities@sos.mo.gov
www.sos.mo.gov

Montana

Commissioner of Securities and Insurance
Securities Department
840 Helena Ave.
Helena, MT 59601
406-444-2040
Toll free: 1-800-332-6148
www.csi.mt.gov/consumers

Nebraska

Department of Banking and Finance
Bureau of Securities
PO Box 95006
Lincoln, NE 68509-5006
402-471-3445
Toll free: 1-877-471-3445
www.ndbf.ne.gov

Nevada

Office of the Secretary of State
Securities Division
555 E. Washington Ave., Suite 5200
Las Vegas, NV 89101
702-486-2440
✉: nvsec@sos.nv.gov
www.nvsos.gov

New Hampshire

Secretary of State
Bureau of Securities Regulation
107 N. Main St., #204
Concord, NH 03301
603-271-1463
Toll free: 1-800-994-4200
✉: securities@sos.nh.gov
sos.nh.gov/sec_reg.aspx

New Jersey

Department of Law and Public Safety
Bureau of Securities
PO Box 47029
Newark, NJ 07101
973-504-3600
Toll free: 1-866-446-8378
✉: Askbureauofsecurities@dca.lps.state.nj.us
www.njsecurities.gov

New Mexico

Regulation and Licensing Department
Securities Division
2550 Cerrillos Rd., 3rd Floor
Santa Fe, NM 87505
505-476-4580
Toll free: 1-800-704-5533
www.rld.state.nm.us/securities

New York

Office of the Attorney General
Investor Protection Bureau
120 Broadway, 23rd Floor
New York, NY 10271
212-416-8222
www.ag.ny.gov

North Carolina

Secretary of State
Securities Division
PO Box 29622
Raleigh, NC 27626-0622
919-733-3924
Toll free: 1-800-688-4507
✉: secdiv@sosnc.com
www.secretary.state.nc.us/sec

North Dakota

Securities Department
State Capitol, 5th Floor
600 E. Boulevard Ave.
Bismarck, ND 58505-0510
701-328-2910
Toll free: 1-800-297-5124
✉: ndsecurities@nd.gov
www.nd.gov/securities

Ohio

Department of Commerce
Division of Securities
77 S. High St.
22nd Floor
Columbus, OH 43215-6131
614-644-7381
Toll free: 1-877-683-7841 (Investor Protection Hotline)
✉: securitiesgeneral.questions@com.state.oh.us
www.com.ohio.gov/secu

Oklahoma

Department of Securities
First National Center
120 N. Robinson Ave., Suite 860
Oklahoma City, OK 73102
405-280-7700
www.securities.ok.gov

Oregon

Department of Consumer and Business Services
Division of Finance and Corporate Securities
PO Box 14480
Salem, OR 97309-0405
503-378-4140
Toll free: 1-866-814-9710
TTY: 503-378-4100
✉: dcbs.dfcsmail@state.or.us
www.dfcs.oregon.gov

Pennsylvania

Securities Commission
17 N. 2nd St., Suite 1300
Harrisburg, PA 17101
717-787-1854
Toll free: 1-800-722-2657
www.psc.state.pa.us

Puerto Rico

Office of the Commissioner of Financial Institutions
Securities Division
PO Box 11855
San Juan, PR 00910-3855
787-723-3131
✉: valores@ocif.gobierno.pr
www.ocif.gobierno.pr

Rhode Island

Department of Business Regulation
Securities Division
1511 Pontiac Ave.
Cranston, RI 02920
401-462-9527
✉: securitiesinquiry@dbr.ri.gov
www.dbr.state.ri.us

South Carolina

Office of the Attorney General
Securities Division
PO Box 11549
Columbia, SC 29211-1549
803-734-9916
www.scag.gov/scsecurities

South Dakota

Department of Labor and Regulation
Division of Securities
445 E. Capitol Ave.
Pierre, SD 57501-3185
605-773-4823
www.dlr.sd.gov/securities

Tennessee

Department of Commerce and Insurance
Securities Division
500 James Robertson Pkwy.
Nashville, TN 37243-0575
615-741-2947
Toll free: 1-800-863-9117
✉: Securities.1@tn.gov
www.tn.gov/securities

Texas

State Securities Board
PO Box 13167
Austin, TX 78711-3167
512-305-8300
www.ssb.state.tx.us

Utah

Department of Commerce
Division of Securities
PO Box 146760
Salt Lake City, UT 84114-6760
801-530-6600
Toll free: 1-800-721-7233
✉: securities@utah.gov
www.securities.utah.gov

Vermont

Department of Financial Regulation
Securities Division
89 Main St.
Montpelier, VT 05620-3101
802-828-3301
✉: dfr.securitiesinfo@state.vt.us
www.dfr.vermont.gov

Virginia

State Corporation Commission
Division of Securities and Retail
Franchising
PO Box 1197
Richmond, VA 23218
804-371-9051
Toll free: 1-800-552-7945
TTY: 804-371-9206
✉: srf_general@scc.virginia.gov
www.scc.virginia.gov/srf

Washington

Department of Financial Institutions
Division of Securities
PO Box 41200
Olympia, WA 98504-1200
360-902-8760
Toll free: 1-877-746-4334
TTY: 360-664-8126
www.dfi.wa.gov

West Virginia

State Auditor's Office
Securities Commission
1900 Kanawha Blvd., E
Building 1, Room W-100
Charleston, WV 25305
304-558-2251
✉: securities@wvsao.gov
www.wvsao.gov/
securitiescommission

Wisconsin

Department of Financial Institutions
Division of Securities
PO Box 1768
Madison, WI 53701-1768
608-266-1064
www.wdfi.org

Wyoming

Office of the Secretary of State
Compliance Division
State Capitol Building
200 W. 24th St.
Cheyenne, WY 82002-0020
307-777-7370
✉: investing@wyo.gov
soswy.state.wy.us

Contact Your Local Utilities Commission

State utilities commissions regulate services and rates for gas, electricity, and telephones in your state. In some states, the utility commissions regulate other services such as water, transportation, and the moving of household goods. Rates for utilities and services provided between states are regulated by the federal government.

Many utilities commissions handle consumer complaints. Sometimes, if they receive a number of complaints about the same utility matter, they will conduct investigations.

Note: Toll free phone numbers may be restricted to use only within the state listed.

Alabama

Public Service Commission
Consumer Services
PO Box 304260
Montgomery, AL 36130
334-242-5218
Toll free: 1-800-392-8050
www.psc.state.al.us

Alaska

Regulatory Commission
Consumer Protection and Information Section
701 W. 8th Ave., Suite 300
Anchorage, AK 99501-3469
907-276-6222
Toll free: 1-800-390-2782
TTY: 907-276-4533
✉: cp.mail@alaska.gov
rca.alaska.gov

Arizona

Corporation Commission
Utilities Division
Consumer Services
1200 W. Washington St.
Phoenix, AZ 85007
602-542-4251
Toll free: 1-800-222-7000
www.azcc.gov

Arkansas

Public Service Commission
Consumer Services Division
PO Box 400
Little Rock, AR 72203-0400
501-682-1718
Toll free: 1-800-482-1164
TTY: 1-800-682-2698
www.arkansas.gov/psc

California

Public Utilities Commission
Consumer Affairs Branch
505 Van Ness Ave.
San Francisco, CA 94102
415-703-2782
Toll free: 1-800-649-7570
TTY: 1-866-836-7825
www.cpuc.ca.gov

Colorado

Public Utilities Commission
Consumer Protection Division
1560 Broadway, Suite 250
Denver, CO 80202
303-894-2070
Toll free: 1-800-456-0858
✉: dora_puc_complaints@state.co.us
www.dora.state.co.us/puc

Connecticut

Department of Energy and Environmental Protection
Public Utilities Regulatory Authority
Consumer Services Unit
10 Franklin Square
New Britain, CT 06051
860-827-2622
Toll free: 1-800-382-4586
TTY: 860-827-2837
✉: pura.information@ct.gov
www.ct.gov/pura

Delaware

Public Service Commission
Cannon Building, Suite 100
861 Silver Lake Blvd.
Dover, DE 19904
302-736-7500
Toll free: 1-800-282-8574
www.depsc.delaware.gov

District Of Columbia

Public Service Commission
Office of Consumer Services
1333 H St., NW, Suite 200, West Tower
Washington, DC 20005
202-626-5120
www.dcpsc.org

Florida

Public Service Commission
2540 Shumard Oak Blvd.
Tallahassee, FL 32399-0850
850-413-6100
Toll free: 1-800-342-3552
TTY: 1-800-955-8771
✉: contact@psc.state.fl.us
www.floridapsc.com

Georgia

Public Service Commission
Consumer Affairs Division
244 Washington St., SW
Atlanta, GA 30334
404-656-4501
Toll free: 1-800-282-5813
✉: gapsc@psc.state.ga.us
www.psc.state.ga.us

Hawaii

Public Utilities Commission
465 S. King St., Room 103
Honolulu, HI 96813
808-586-2020
✉: Hawaii.puc@hawaii.gov
www.puc.hawaii.gov

Idaho

Public Utilities Commission
Consumer Assistance Section
PO Box 83720
Boise, ID 83720-0074
208-334-0369
Toll free: 1-800-432-0369
www.puc.idaho.gov

Illinois

Commerce Commission
Consumer Affairs
527 E. Capitol Ave.
Springfield, IL 62701
217-782-2024
Toll free: 1-800-524-0795
TTY: 1-800-858-9277
www.icc.illinois.gov

Utility Regulatory Commission
Consumer Assistance Section
101 W. Washington St., Suite 1500E
Indianapolis, IN 46204
317-232-2712
Toll free: 1-800-851-4268
TTY: 317-232-8556
www.IN.gov/iurc

Utilities Board
Customer Service Group
1375 E. Court Ave., Room 69
Des Moines, IA 50319-0069
515-725-7321
Toll free: 1-877-565-4450
✉: customer@iub.iowa.gov
www.state.ia.us/iub

Corporation Commission
Office of Public Affairs and Consumer
Protection
1500 S.W. Arrowhead Rd.
Topeka, KS 66604-4027
785-271-3140
Toll free: 1-800-662-0027
TTY: 1-800-766-3777
✉: public.affairs@kcc.ks.gov
www.kcc.state.ks.us

Public Service Commission
Consumer Services
PO Box 615
Frankfort, KY 40602-0615
502-564-3940
Toll free: 1-800-772-4636
TTY: 1-800-648-6056
✉: psc.consumer.inquiry@ky.gov
www.psc.state.ky.us

Public Service Commission
PO Box 91154
Baton Rouge, LA 70821-9154
225-342-4404
Toll free: 1-800-256-2397
www.lpsc.org

Public Utilities Commission
Consumer Assistance Division
18 State House Station
Augusta, ME 04333-0018
207-287-3831
Toll free: 1-800-452-4699
TTY: 1-800-437-1220
✉: maine.puc@maine.gov
www.maine.gov/mpuc

Public Service Commission
6 Saint Paul St., 16th Floor
Baltimore, MD 21202-6806
410-767-8000
Toll free: 1-800-492-0474
TTY: 1-800-201-7165
www.psc.state.md.us

Department of Public Utilities
Consumer Division
One South Station, Suite 2
Boston, MA 02110
617-737-2836
Toll free: 1-877-886-5066
✉: DPUConsumer.Complaints@state.
ma.us
www.mass.gov/dpu

Public Service Commission
4300 W. Saginaw Hwy.
PO Box 30221
Lansing, MI 48909
517-241-6180
Toll free: 1-800-292-9555
✉: mpsc_commissioners@michigan.
gov
www.michigan.gov/mpsc

Public Utilities Commission
Consumer Affairs Office
121 7th Pl. E, Suite 350
St. Paul, MN 55101-2147
651-296-0406
Toll free: 1-800-657-3782
✉: consumer.puc@state.mn.us
www.mn.gov/puc

Public Service Commission
P.O. Box 1174
Jackson, MS 39215
601-961-5430 (Central District)
601-961-5450 (Northern District)
601-961-5440 (Southern District)
Toll free: 1-800-356-6430 (Central
District)
Toll free: 1-800-356-6428 (Northern
District)
Toll free: 1-800-356-6429 (Southern
District)
www.psc.state.ms.us

Public Service Commission
Consumer Services Department
200 Madison St.
PO Box 360
Jefferson City, MO 65102-0360
Toll free: 1-800-392-4211
TTY: 1-866-735-2460
✉: pscinfo@psc.mo.gov
www.psc.mo.gov

Public Service Commission
PO Box 202601
Helena, MT 59620-2601
406-444-6150
Toll free: 1-800-646-6150
TTY: 406-444-4212
www.psc.mt.gov

Public Service Commission
1200 N St., Suite 300
Lincoln, NE 68508
402-471-3101
Toll free: 1-800-526-0017
TTY: 402-471-0213
www.psc.state.ne.us

**Public Utilities Commission -
Northern NV**
Consumer Complaint Resolution
Division
1150 E. William St.
Carson City, NV 89701-3109
775-684-6100
puc.nv.gov

Public Utilities Commission - Southern NV
Consumer Complaint Resolution Division
9075 W. Diablo Dr., Suite 250
Las Vegas, NV 89148
702-486-2600
puc.nv.gov

New Hampshire

Public Utilities Commission
Consumer Affairs Division
21 S. Fruit St., Suite 10
Concord, NH 03301-2429
603-271-2431
Toll free: 1-800-852-3793
TTY: 1-800-735-2964
✉: puc@puc.nh.gov
www.puc.state.nh.us

New Jersey

Board of Public Utilities
Division of Customer Assistance
44 S. Clinton Ave.
Trenton, NJ 08625
609-341-9188
Toll free: 1-800-624-0241
Toll free: 1-800-624-0331 (Cable complaint)
www.bpu.state.nj.us

New Mexico

Public Regulation Commission
Consumer Relations Division
1120 Paseo de Peralta
PO Box 1269
Santa Fe, NM 87504
505-827-4592
Toll free: 1-888-427-5772
✉: crd.complaints@state.nm.us
www.nmprc.state.nm.us

New York

Public Service Commission
Office of Consumer Services
3 Empire State Plaza
Albany, NY 12223-1350
Toll free: 1-800-342-3377
Toll free: 1-800-342-3355 (Termination)
TTY: 1-800-662-1220
www.askpsc.com

North Carolina

Utilities Commission
Consumer Services
4325 Mail Service Center
Raleigh, NC 27699-4325
919-733-9277
Toll free: 1-866-380-9816
✉: consumer.services@psncuc.nc.gov
www.ncuc.net

North Dakota

Public Service Commission
600 E. Boulevard Ave., Dept. 408
Bismarck, ND 58505-0480
701-328-2400
Toll free: 1-877-245-6685
TTY: 1-800-366-6888
✉: ndpsc@nd.gov
www.psc.nd.gov

Ohio

Public Utilities Commission
180 E. Broad St.
Columbus, OH 43215
614-466-3292
Toll free: 1-800-686-7826
www.puco.ohio.gov

Consumers' Counsel
10 W. Broad St., Suite 1800
Columbus, OH 43215-3485
614-466-8574
Toll free: 1-877-742-5622
✉: occ@occ.ohio.gov
www.occ.ohio.gov

Oklahoma

Corporation Commission
Consumer Services Division
PO Box 52000
Oklahoma City, OK 73152-2000
405-522-2331
Toll free: 1-800-522-8154
www.occeweb.com

Oregon

Public Utility Commission
Consumer Services Division
PO Box 1088
Salem, OR 97308-1088
503-378-6600
Toll free: 1-800-522-2404
✉: puc.consumer@state.or.us
www.puc.state.or.us

Pennsylvania

Pennsylvania Office of Consumer Advocate
Office of the Attorney General
555 Walnut St.
5th Floor, Forum Place
Harrisburg, PA 17101-1923
717-783-5048
Toll free: 1-800-684-6560
✉: consumer@paoca.org
www.oca.state.pa.us

Public Utility Commission
Bureau of Consumer Services
PO Box 3265
Harrisburg, PA 17105-3265
www.puc.state.pa.us

Puerto Rico

Public Service Commission
PO Box 190870
San Juan, PR 00918
787-756-1919
www.csp.gobierno.pr

Rhode Island

Public Utilities Commission
Consumer Section
89 Jefferson Blvd.
Warwick, RI 02888
401-780-9700
✉: consumer.section@ripuc.org
www.ripuc.org

South Carolina

Office of Regulatory Staff
Consumer Services Division
1401 Main St., Suite 900
Columbia, SC 29201
803-737-5230
Toll free: 1-800-922-1531
TTY: 1-800-334-2217
www.regulatorystaff.sc.gov

South Dakota

Public Utilities Commission
Consumer Affairs
500 E. Capitol Ave.
Pierre, SD 57501-5070
605-773-3201
Toll free: 1-800-332-1782
✉: PUCConsumerInfo@state.sd.us
www.puc.sd.gov

Tennessee

Regulatory Authority
Consumer Services Division
502 Deaderick St., 4th Floor
Nashville, TN 37243
615-741-2904
Toll free: 1-800-342-8359
TTY: 1-888-276-0677
www.state.tn.us/tra

Texas

Public Utility Commission
Customer Protection
PO Box 13326
Austin, TX 78711-3326
512-936-7120
Toll free: 1-888-782-8477
TTY: 1-800-735-2988
✉: customer@puc.texas.gov
www.puc.texas.gov

Utah

Public Service Commission
Division of Public Utilities
PO Box 146751
Salt Lake City, UT 84114-6751
801-530-7622
Toll free: 1-800-874-0904
✉: psc@utah.gov
www.psc.utah.gov

Vermont

Public Service Board
Consumer Affairs and Public
Information Division
112 State St., 4th Floor
Montpelier, VT 05620-2601
802-828-2332
TTY: 1-800-253-0191
✉: consumer@state.vt.us
www.psb.vermont.gov

Virginia

State Corporation Commission
Division of Energy Regulation
PO Box 1197
Richmond, VA 23218
804-371-9611
Toll free: 1-800-552-7945
TTY: 804-371-9206
✉: EnergyReg@scc.virginia.gov
www.scc.virginia.gov

Washington

**Utilities and Transportation
Commission**
Consumer Protection
1300 S. Evergreen Park Dr., SW
Olympia, WA 98504-7250
360-664-1120
Toll free: 1-888-333-9882
TTY: 360-586-8203
✉: consumer@utc.wa.gov
www.utc.wa.gov

West Virginia

Consumer Advocate Division
723 Kanawha Blvd., E
Union Building, Suite 700
Charleston, WV 25301
304-558-0526
www.cad.state.wv.us

Public Service Commission
Customer Assistance
PO Box 812
201 Brooks St.
Charleston, WV 25323
Toll free: 1-800-642-8544
www.psc.state.wv.us

Wisconsin

Public Service Commission
Consumer Affairs
PO Box 7854
Madison, WI 53707-7854
608-266-2001
Toll free: 1-800-225-7729
TTY: 608-267-1479
www.psc.wi.gov

Wyoming

Public Service Commission
2515 Warren Ave., Suite 300
Cheyenne, WY 82002
307-777-7427
Toll free: 1-888-570-9905
✉: wpsc_complaints@wyo.gov
psc.state.wy.us

Contact Trade & Professional Organizations

Companies that manufacture similar products or offer similar services often belong to an industry association. These associations help resolve problems between their member companies and consumers. Most also provide consumer information through publications and websites.

America's Health Insurance Plans (AHIP)

601 Pennsylvania Ave., NW
South Bldg., Suite 500
Washington, DC 20004
202-778-3200
✉: ahip@ahip.org
www.ahip.org
America's Health Insurance Plans (AHIP) is the national association that represents the health insurance industry. Member companies offer health insurance through employer-sponsored coverage, individual insurance policies, and public programs such as Medicare and Medicaid.

American Arbitration Association (AAA)

1633 Broadway, 10th Floor
New York, NY 10019
Toll free: 1-800-778-7879
www.adr.org
AAA is a not-for-profit public service organization committed to the resolution of disputes through arbitration, mediation, conciliation and other voluntary procedures.

American Bankers Association (ABA)

1120 Connecticut Ave., NW
Washington, DC 20036
Toll free: 1-800-226-5377
www.aba.com
ABA represents the concerns of banks and their employees. The ABA's Community Engagement Foundation offers personal finance resources to help consumers understand their financial choices and responsibilities.

American Cleaning Institute (ACI)

1331 L St., NW, Suite 650
Washington, DC 20005
202-347-2900
✉: info@cleaninginstitute.org
www.cleaninginstitute.org
ACI is the consumer source for free and low cost educational materials, designed to help people make safe choices for cleaning products.

American Council of Life Insurers (ACLI)

101 Constitution Ave., NW, Suite 700
Washington, DC 20001-2133
202-624-2000
✉: contact@acli.com
www.acli.com
ACLI is a trade association of over 300 insurance companies that provide life insurance, pensions and annuities, long-term care, and disability income insurance.

American Financial Services Association Education Foundation (AFSAEF) ♦

919 18th St., NW Suite 300
Washington, DC 20006-5517
202-466-8611
✉: info@afsaef.org
www.afsaef.org
The AFSAEF educates consumers on personal finance concepts, to help them realize the benefits of responsible money management and understand the credit process. Their MoneySKILL® program educates young adults on basic money management, such as income, expenses, assets, liabilities, and risk management.

American Institute of Certified Public Accountants (AICPA)

220 Leigh Farm Rd.
Durham, NC 27707
919-402-4500
Toll free: 1-888-777-7077 (Ethics Hotline)
www.aicpa.org
www.360financialliteracy.org
AICPA works to ensure that the public remains confident in the integrity, competence and professionalism of CPAs.

American Moving and Storage Association (AMSA)

1611 Duke St.
Alexandria, VA 22314
703-683-7410
Toll free: 1-888-849-2672
✉: info@moving.org
www.moving.org
The AMSA is the trade association for the professional moving and storage industry. They also offer moving related information to the public on its consumer website, including a Mover Referral Service. It also sponsors a dispute settlement program to help consumers resolve loss and damage claims on interstate moves.

Association of Credit Counseling Professionals (ACCPros)

369 Falmouth Rd.
Falmouth, ME 04105
Toll free: 1-866-278-1567
✉: info@accpros.org
www.accpros.org
ACCPros is a trade association that represents the credit counseling industry. They set standards for ethical and professional behavior, while also providing a database to find a credit counselor in your area.

Association of Independent Consumer Credit Counseling Agencies (AICCCA)

10332 Main St.
Fairfax, VA 22030
Toll free: 1-866-703-8787
✉: assoc@aiccca.org
www.aiccca.org
AICCCA represents not-for-profit credit counseling companies. AICCCA sets industry standards for member companies and provides information directly to consumers.

Cellular Telecommunications and Internet Association (CTIA)
1400 16th St., NW, Suite 600
Washington, DC 20036
202-785-0081
www.ctia.org
www.gowirelessgogreen.org
CTIA is the trade association for the wireless telecommunications industry. They also provide consumer resources for choosing wireless devices and services.

Certified Financial Planner Board of Standards
1425 K St., NW, Suite 800
Washington, DC 20005
202-379-2200
Toll free: 1-800-487-1497
✉: mail@cfpboard.org
www.cfp.net
letsmakeaplan.org
The CFP Board works to ensure that the public benefits from competent financial planning. The CFP Board certifies financial planners who meet its requirements by granting use of their trademarks.

Commission on the Accreditation of Rehabilitation Facilities (CARF)
6951 E. Southpoint Rd.
Tucson, AZ 85756
Toll free: 1-888-281-6531
www.carf.org
CARF is an independent accrediting body of rehabilitation, addiction, substance abuse, and retirement living services. The organization provides an online search tool to find services that match your rehabilitiation needs, as well as links to consumer resources.

Consumer Electronics Association (CEA)
1919 S. Eads St.
Arlington, VA 22202
703-907-7600
Toll free: 1-866-858-1555
✉: cea@Ce.org
www.ce.org
CEA represents corporations that design, develop, manufacture, and distribute consumer electronics. They offer free buying guides and tips to consumers.

Direct Marketing Association (DMA)
1615 L St., NW
Washington, DC 20036
212-768-7277 ext. 1888
✉: consumer@the-dma.org
www.DMAchoice.org
The DMA is the trade association for organizations involved in direct marketing via direct mail, catalogs, the Internet, telemarketing, magazines, newspaper and TV ads. DMA's consumer website offers consumers options (free of charge) to manage their physical and electronic mail.

Direct Selling Education Foundation (DSEF) ♦
1667 K St., NW, Suite 1100
Washington, DC 20006
202-452-8866
✉: info@dsef.org
www.dsef.org
DSEF partners with consumer advocates, educators and students, public policy officials, and the small business and entrepreneurship communities. They deliver programs to educate the public on the ways that direct selling empowers individuals, supports communities and strengthens the economy.

Financial Industry Regulatory Authority (FINRA) ♦
1735 K St., NW
Washington, DC 20006
301-590-6500 (Call Center)
Toll free: 1-800-289-9999 (BrokerCheck Hotline)
www.finra.org
FINRA is the largest independent regulator for all U.S. securities firms. The organization operates the largest dispute resolution forum for disputes between investors and securities firms. Consumers may check the background of individual investment professionals and firms using the BrokerCheck tool on the FINRA website.

Financial Planning Association (FPA)
7535 E. Hampden Ave., Suite 600
Denver, CO 80231
Toll free: 1-800-322-4237
✉: info@onefpa.org
www.plannersearch.org
The Financial Planning Association is a trade organization for financial planners. FPA helps consumers by ensuring that planners adhere to a code of ethics as well as providing guides, brochures, and financial worksheets for consumers.

Insurance Information Institute (III)
110 William St.
New York, NY 10038
212-346-5500
www.iii.org
The III is a nonprofit communications organization supported by the property and casualty insurance industry that works to improve public understanding of insurance.

International Association of Movers (IAM)
5904 Richmond Hwy., Suite 404
Alexandria, VA 22303
703-317-9950
✉: info@iamovers.org
www.iamovers.org
IAM is a global association of movers and forwarders committed to providing customers with the highest level of service available. IAM offers consumer tips for moving, domestically or internationally, on their website.

International Cemetery, Cremation and Funeral Association (ICCFA)
107 Carpenter Dr., Suite 100
Sterling, VA 20164
Toll free: 1-800-645-7700
✉: hq@iccfa.com
www.iccfa.com

ICCFA is a trade association for the cemetery, funeral service, cremation and memorialization profession. The ICCFA assists consumers directly through information resources and a dispute resolution service.

LeadingAge ♦
2519 Connecticut Ave., NW
Washington, DC 20008
202-783-2242
✉: info@leadingage.org
www.leadingage.org
LeadingAge represents not-for-profit nursing homes, continuing care retirement communities, assisted living and senior housing facilities, and community service organizations. Consumers may search LeadingAge's online database for providers and facilities that fit their needs.

Money Management International (MMI)
14141 Southwest Fwy., Suite 1000
Sugar Land, TX 77478-3494
Toll free: 1-866-889-9347
www.moneymanagement.org
MMI is a nonprofit operator of credit counseling agencies. They offer credit counseling, debt management, and education services.

National Association of Attorneys General (NAAG)
2030 M St., NW, 8th Floor
Washington, DC 20036
202-326-6000
✉: feedback@naag.org
www.naag.org
This organization facilitates communication and collaboration among attorneys general, who are responsible for enforcing civil laws in their respective states.

National Association of Home Builders (NAHB)
1201 15th St., NW
Washington, DC 20005
202-266-8200
Toll free: 1-800-368-5242
www.nahb.org
NAHB represents the housing and the building industry. This organization provides information for consumers interested in buying, financing, building or remodeling their home. The NAHB website features a searchable directory of builders.

National Association of Insurance Commissioners (NAIC)
1100 Walnut St., Suite 1500
Kansas City, MO 64106-2197
816-842-3600
Toll free: 1-866-470-6242
✉: webpost@naic.org
www.naic.org
www.InsureUonline.org
NAIC is a national organization of insurance regulators. The organization helps insurance regulators facilitate the fair and equitable treatment of consumers.

National Foundation for Credit Counseling (NFCC)
2000 M St., NW, Suite 505
Washington, DC 20036
Toll free: 1-800-388-2227
www.nfcc.org

The NFCC promotes financially responsible habits and makes it possible for its members to deliver financial education and counseling services. Contact NFCC to locate an affiliated financial counseling agency in your area.

National Funeral Directors Association (NFDA)
13625 Bishops Dr.
Brookfield, WI 53005-6607
262-789-1880
Toll free: 1-800-228-6332
✉: nfda@nfda.org
www.nfda.org
NFDA is the trade association for funeral service providers. NFDA's Funeral Service Help Line helps consumers make informed decisions about funeral services, and address concerns about funeral service experiences.

National Futures Association (NFA) ♦
300 S. Riverside Plaza, Suite 1800
Chicago, IL 60606-6615
312-781-1410
Toll free: 1-800-621-3570
✉: information@nfa.futures.org
www.nfa.futures.org
NFA is the industrywide self-regulatory organization for the U.S. futures industry. NFA provides innovative and efficient regulatory programs and services that safeguard the integrity of the derivatives markets. Contact the NFA's Information Center for your futures related questions.

National Institute for Automotive Service Excellence (ASE)
101 Blue Seal Dr., SE, Suite 101
Leesburg, VA 20175
703-669-6600
Toll free: 1-877-346-9327
✉: asehelp@ase.com
www.ase.com
ASE is an independent organization that works to improve the quality of automotive service and repair through the voluntary testing and certification of automotive repair professionals.

North American Securities Administrators Association, Inc. (NASAA)
750 1st St, NE, Suite 1140
Washington, DC 20002
202-737-0900
www.nasaa.org
NASAA is the voice of the 50 state securities agencies responsible for grass-roots investor protection, investor education, and efficient capital formation.

Society of Consumer Affairs Professionals (SOCAP)
625 N. Washington St., Suite 304
Alexandria, VA 22314
www.socap.org
SOCAP provides training, conferences and publications to encourage and promote effective communication and understanding among business, government and consumers. SOCAP does not investigate individual consumer complaints against companies.

This alphabetical index will help you find the right organization to contact for information or for assistance with your complaint. First, look for the specific topic, for example, Cars. Under this topic there will be one or more contacts, followed by the *Handbook* page number(s). Sometimes you will be directed to "See" another entry for information and a list of contacts. "See also" references direct you to other topics that might be related to your problem and may help you locate the right contact. For company names see the alphabetical listings under "Corporate Consumer Contacts" (p. 68), and "Automotive Manufacturers" (p. 61)

Federal Communications Commission
contact information, 98
lost or stolen cell phones, 43
phone bills, 43
slamming and cramming, 42
Federal Deposit Insurance Corporation
Consumer Response Center, 98
contact information, 98
Division of Depositor and Consumer Protection, 98
financial privacy and, 39
regulatory authority, 8
Federal Emergency Management Agency, 94
Federal Housing Administration
contact information, 94
mortgage loans, 26
refinancing, 28
Federal Maritime Commission, 98
Federal Motor Carrier Safety Administration, 96
Federal Relay Services, 57
Federal Reserve Consumer Help, 98
Federal Reserve System
contact information, 98
mortgage refinancing, 28
regulatory authority, 8
Federal Student Aid Information Center, 90
Federal student loan, 19
Federal Trade Commission
Bureau of Consumer Protection, 98
contact information, 98
fraud reporting, 56
fraudulent employment opportunity advertisements,
20
Funeral Rule, 52
identity theft reports, 38
medical identity theft reporting, 25
shopping from home requirements, 4
Telemarketing Sales Calls, 45-46
3-Day Cooling-Off Rule, 4
Federal Student Loans, 18, 19
college closed, 18
Federal Work-Study Program, 18
Federation of State Medical Boards, 23
FedsHireVets, 58
Fee-for-service health insurance, 31
FEMA. See Federal Emergency Management Agency
FEMA Disaster Assistance, 94
FHA. See Federal Housing Administration
Financial aid. See Student financial aid
Financial brokers and advisors, 35
Financial Industry Regulatory Authority
contact information, 132
dispute resolution programs, 35
investment information, 35
Financial Planning Association, 132
Financial privacy, 39
FINRA. See Financial Industry Regulatory Authority
Firewalls, 38
Fish and Wildlife Service, 95
Fixed-rate mortgages, 26, 28
Fleet and Family Support Programs, 58
Fleet Vehicle Sales, 98
Flexible funding, 36
Flood insurance, 32
Fluctuating value, 35
Flying. See Air travel
FMCSA. See Federal Motor Carrier Safety
Administration
Food. See also Nutrition
farmers' markets, 21

healthy choices, 20
organic, 21
recalls, 3
resources, 21
safety issues, 20
saving money on groceries, 21
Supplemental Nutrition Assistance Program, 21
Food and Drug Administration
contact information, 92
food and nutrition information, 21
prescription drug information, 24
recall information website, 3
reporting safety hazards to, 56
Food and Nutrition Services, 89
Food Information Hotline, 21
Food Safety and Inspection Services, 3, 21
Forbearance, 19
Foreclosure, 27
Fragmented file, 37
Fraud. See also Identity theft
affinity fraud, 36
employment agencies, 19
employment opportunity advertisements, 20
foreclosure rescue, 27
health insurance, 24
home improvement contractors, 28
identifying, 2
insurance, 30
military personnel, 59
pension, 59
postal related, 56
reporting, 56
scholarships, 18
timeshare resale, 48
tips for avoiding, 2
veterans, 59
virtual currencies, 35
Free Application for Federal Student Aid, 18
Free-range animals, 21
FRS. See Federal Relay Service
FSAIC. See Federal Student Aid Information Center
FSAs. See Flexible spending accounts
FTC. See Federal Trade Commission
Fuel economy, 9
Funeral Consumers Alliance, 101
Funeral Rule, 51
Funeral Service Consumer Assistance Program, 52
Funerals. 51
prepaying, 52

G
Garnishment, 19
General Services Administration
contact information, 98
Federal Citizen Information Center, 56, 98
Fleet Vehicle Sales, 98
GobiernoUSA.gov, 57, 98
Kids.gov, 98
Publications.USA.gov, 57, 98
Surplus Federal Property Sales, 98
telephone relay service, 57
USA.gov 57, 98
Gift card, 7
Gold investments, 36
Government agencies. See also specific agencies
directory of federal agencies, 89-99
directory of state and local agencies, 102-114
federal job announcements, 19
GPS,
car privacy, 10
pay as you go car insurance, 30

privacy, 38
Grants, education, 18
Grass-fed animals, 21
Grey charges, 4
Grocery buying tips, 21
Group health insurance, 31
GSA. See General Services Administration

H
Hackers,
virtual currencies, 35
Wi-Fi, 41
HARP. See Home Affordable Refinance Program
Health Care
advance medical directives, 25
Affordable Care Act 23
complaints concerning, 23
Do Not Resuscitate orders, 25
doctor selection, 22
durable power of attorney, 25
elder care, 23
filing complaints, 23
health care facility selection, 23
Healthcare.gov, 31, 92
information resources, 22
insurance, 31
insurance scams, 24
medical credit cards, 23
medical identity theft, 25
medical privacy, 39
Medicare prescription drug coverage, 24
patient portals, 23
prescription drugs,24
reporting safety hazards, 56
Health care facilities selection, 23
Health care professionals selection, 22
Health insurance. See also Long-term care insurance;
Medicaid; Medicare
Affordable Care Act, 23
catastrophic, 33
group policies, 31
Healthcare.gov, 31, 92
international plans, 33
questions to ask about, 31
types of plans, 31
Health Insurance Marketplace, 31, 92
Health Insurance Portability and Accountability Act, 39
Health Maintenance Organizations, 31
Health records privacy, 39
Health Resources and Services Administration, 91
HealthCare.gov, 31, 92
HealthFinder.gov, 22
HealthIT.gov, 23
Hearing loss. See Deaf or hard of hearing persons
HHS. See U.S. Department of Health and Human
Services
HHS-TIPS fraud hotline, 91
Higher education. See Colleges and universities;
Student financial aid
HIPAA. See Health Insurance Portability and
Accountability Act
HMOs. See Health Maintenance Organizations
Home Affordable Refinance Program, 28
Home equity loans, 17
Home improvement contractors, 28
Home inspections, 26
Home shopping. See Shopping from home
Homeowners association fees, 26
Homeowner's insurance, 31
actual cash value, 32

www.ingramcontent.com/pod-product-compliance
Lightning Source LLC
Chambersburg PA
CBHW081150180526
45170CB00006B/2010